Professor Alice Roberts is an academic, author and broadcaster – specialising in anatomy and biological anthropology. She has presented over a hundred television programmes, on biology, archaeology and history, including landmark BBC series such as *The Incredible Human Journey, Origins of Us* and *Digging for Britain*. She also presents *Britain's Most Historic Towns* on Channel 4. She wrote and presented the Royal Institution Christmas Lectures in 2018.

Alice has written ten popular science books, including *The Incredible Human Journey, The Incredible Unlikeliness of Being*, and *Tamed: Ten Species That Changed Our World*. In *Ancestors* and *Buried*, she continues to explore the intersection between archaeology and genetics.

Alice has been Professor of Public Engagement with Science at the University of Birmingham since 2012. In 2020, she received the Royal Anthropological Institute's Public Anthropology Award, and the Royal Society's David Attenborough Prize for Public Engagement.

Praise for *Buried*

'*Buried* is a tender, fascinating act of listening – of listening to the tales the dead have to tell us about the landscapes we share with them, the histories we have constructed around them, and the futures we imagine for ourselves. Lucid and illuminating, Alice Roberts here opens new perspectives on to first-millennium Britain, from the appearance of churchyards in the sixth century, to Romano-British "decapitation" burial practices. I learned so much from this book, and hearing my description of Alice's excavations and investigations, my nine-year-old confirmed absolutely his ambition to become an aDNA (ancient DNA) scientist when he grows up.' **Robert Macfarlane**

Also by Alice Roberts

Ancestors

Anatomical Oddities

BURIED

An alternative history of the first
millennium in Britain

PROFESSOR
ALICE ROBERTS

**SIMON &
SCHUSTER**

London · New York · Sydney · Toronto · New Delhi

First published in Great Britain by Simon & Schuster UK Ltd, 2022
This edition published in Great Britain by Simon & Schuster UK Ltd, 2023

1 3 5 7 9 10 8 6 4 2

Simon & Schuster UK Ltd
1st Floor
222 Gray's Inn Road
London WC1X 8HB

www.simonandschuster.co.uk
www.simonandschuster.com.au
www.simonandschuster.co.in

Simon & Schuster Australia, Sydney
Simon & Schuster India, New Delhi

A CIP catalogue record for this book is available from the British Library

Paperback ISBN: 978-1-3985-1005-0
eBook ISBN: 978-1-3985-1004-3

Typeset in Perpetua by M Rules
Printed and Bound in the UK using 100% Renewable
Electricity at CPI Group (UK) Ltd

In memoriam
Kate Edwards

CONTENTS

A BLESSING AND A CURSE

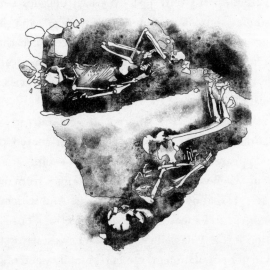

There's a lot you can tell from a skeleton. As a biological anthropologist, I've specialised in drawing out information from old bones. It's not always easy, and how much I can reliably infer depends on the state of preservation of the human remains. But I might be able to determine the biological sex of an individual, give a good idea of their age at death, and also offer some details about some of the illnesses and injuries they suffered during their lives.

In the last decade, the information I can extract by careful, visual analysis of bones and teeth, helped by the judicious use of X-rays, has been vastly extended by a range of different biochemical techniques. It's now possible to analyse the chemical composition of bones and teeth and draw inferences about where a person lived and what their diet was like. But we're also experiencing a revolution in archaeology, driven by ancient DNA (aDNA). Archaeogeneticists are now able to extract DNA from ancient bones and sequence entire genomes. It's only just over two decades since the first – single – human genome was sequenced, and the pace of change in genetic technology has been breathtaking. Sequencing is now faster by several orders of magnitude, and we have the ability to compile whole DNA libraries drawn from both the living and the dead.

On an individual basis, an ancient genome can provide information about the sex of a person, and even provide clues to appearance. But the revelations become even more interesting when we start to compare genomes from different individuals, revealing family connections. And wider studies of relatedness and ancestry can help us to track changes at a population level. Amassed genomic data are starting to shed light on major population movements, mobility and migration in the past. It's an exciting time, but when new technologies burst onto the scene like this, they can also be disruptive. Scholarly feathers are ruffled, and sometimes the claws come out. The potential for huge advances in understanding is there – but it's also important not to rush to conclusions or to be seduced by sensational headlines about breakthroughs. We can be excited and cautious at the same time.

In prehistory, that great swathe of time before the written word, archaeology is the *only* way that we can hope to learn anything about our ancestors. We look at the physical traces of their culture, and at the remains of individuals themselves, usually reduced to just their bones and teeth – but with precious DNA locked away inside those hard tissues, and now amenable to analysis.

Once we move into the realm of history, we have some documentary evidence to look at. The written history of Britain begins with occasional classical references to an island off the coast of continental northwest Europe, going back to the middle of the first millennium BCE – Before the Common Era. (I use BCE/CE rather than BC/AD – it's the academic standard and is religiously neutral, as well as having been in use since the seventeenth century, so it's not a new thing.) By the first century BCE, Britain is drawing the attention of the expanding Roman Empire, with Julius Caesar visiting in a not-particularly-friendly sort of way in 55 and 54, and Claudius following up with a full-on invasion in 43 CE. For almost four centuries after that, we have the luxury of quite a lot of written information about life in Roman Britain. I say 'luxury', but that history is both a blessing and a curse. First of all, it's very biased – it was necessarily produced by literate individuals, who were elite Romanophiles. Most of the classical authors who wrote about Roman Britain didn't even live here, such as the senators Tacitus and Dio Cassius. And they focused on military history, giving us a very skewed view. There are some written records from Roman Britain itself, but these are quite specialised and narrow in what they reveal. They include stone inscriptions, which once again give us a biased, military view – as most are associated with the army. But since the 1950s, archaeologists have added to the corpus of writing from Roman Britain, finding ephemeral pieces of text that have, quite astonishingly, survived the test of time – in the form of ink on thin wooden sheets, and scratched impressions of writing on the wooden casings of wax tablets. Again, these are often linked to military communities, but they do offer us different insights into life – for Roman officials and army personnel – in Britain. There are also some wax tablet finds from London which relate to legal and mercantile matters. Another set of written inscriptions comes in the form of curses or *defixiones*, on small lead sheets, deposited in springs and shrines. More often than not, the curse is asking a particular god to punish a thief – with ill health, insomnia, infertility or even death. There are also makers' marks on pottery, leather and silver, and scratched names on objects, too. And of course, there is writing on coins. Although writing turns up in a lot of places, those are mostly cities and military settings, and it's thought that less than 5 per cent of the population of Roman Britain was literate.

All this documentary evidence is alluring, and there's something wonderful about suddenly knowing the names of groups of people and individuals. Before the Romans arrive, we didn't know that the people who lived in what is now Dorset called themselves the Durotriges, that people in Norfolk were the Iceni, or that modern Kent was inhabited by the Cantiaci. We didn't know the specific names of any British kings and queens. And suddenly we meet Cunobelinus, Caratacus, Verica, Togidubnus, Boudica, Prasutagus and the rest.

But all that history is also a curse. It suggests interpretations to us before we even start to look at the archaeological evidence. The archaeological discovery of a bit of burned sediment, some pottery and a Claudian coin in London might be interpreted as evidence of military occupation – because we know the history of the Claudian invasion. But this isn't how archaeology should work. It shouldn't be a footnote to history or merely an illustration of what we think we already know.

It's an entirely different source of evidence, and should enable us to ask much wider questions about what life was like in the past, and to *test* the historical interpretations, not to prove them. Of course, archaeology and history – and now archaeogenetics too – should come together in the final analysis, to tell the story of the past – but these disciplines should be treated with equal respect and given equal weight. Archaeology also offers us the potential to understand society in a much more comprehensive way – as we find the traces of ordinary lives, and people whose stories were never written down.

In the post-Roman period in Britain, contemporary written records all but disappear. Literacy is still there, but it's harder to find traces of it. We get some glimpses from high-status sites, including monasteries. This is the period which used to be referred to as the 'Dark Ages', which is now seen as a pejorative term, suggesting that Britain descended into 'darkness', into a period of ignorance and barbarism, when the Roman army pulled out in the fifth century. But even if the term is problematic, there's no denying that the historical record for the fifth to eighth centuries is patchy at best. The few sources we possess have ended up carrying undue weight, introducing even more bias into our reconstructions of the past. Archaeology is crucially important to understanding what was really happening in those shadowy centuries after Roman rule in Britain ended. And burials have important tales to tell.

Looking at the first millennium of the Common Era, burial archaeology can provide us with precious glimpses of individuals, their culture and beliefs. We can see how funerary practices change over time, as different influences arrive or wane. And archaeogenomics now holds out the promise of finding out just how important migration was – how much people were moving around at different times, and where they were coming from. History becomes very personal – as we learn about people who lived in this land all those centuries before us. Their lives were different to ours in so many ways, but there are also moments of striking similarity, when you can suddenly grasp a thread of familiarity and empathy that stretches back through time, and is part of a wider story about what it means, what it *feels like*, to be human.

This is not a comprehensive survey of British archaeology in the first millennium CE. It is a personal selection of stories, including some individuals whose bones I know very well, but I hope it captures some of the diversity of lives, cultures and beliefs in Britain over those centuries. I'm writing this at an exciting time, when aDNA is transforming, or at the very least challenging, some of our long-held assumptions about what Roman Britain was really like, and about what was actually happening during those historically dark post-Roman centuries.

There's also something here about belonging; being part of a landscape that has been inhabited for a very long time. Bones and burials tell the stories of those generations who have gone before, with aDNA unlocking new secrets all the time, and new archaeological discoveries providing fresh insights. Funerary ritual and burial itself represent attempts to under-stand mortality, to make sense of loss, to fix the departed in memory, and to tie them – and us – to a landscape.

A landscape in which we are just the latest inhabitants.

1.

WATER AND WINE

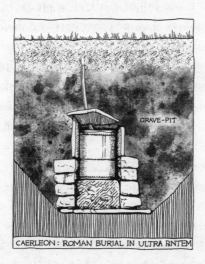

CAERLEON: ROMAN BURIAL IN ULTRA RNTEM

I sat in the dissection room on a Wednesday afternoon. It was very quiet – the students always had a sports afternoon on Wednesdays. The specimens from the morning's teaching session had all been put away: the bones in their cupboards, small dissections in buckets, large ones in huge steel tanks. A couple of the demonstrators were working away, dissecting cadavers laid on long, steel tables. The sickly sweet smell of formalin hung in the air.

At the other end of the long room, I pulled a spare table out, applied the brakes to the wheels, and lifted a tall stool down from one of the neat stacks that the students had left them in. I carried a box over to the table, then went to find a couple of large white trays and a pair of forceps. I spent a bit of time choosing a perfect pair for the job, with narrow tips – and not bent out of shape, as so many were in the towers of small crates in the prep room.

Back at the table, I opened my notebook and lifted the lid off the large box. It was full of small, clear plastic bags, carefully laid out with sheets of tissue paper between them. I took one of the bags, pulled its seal open, and very, very gently, emptied out its contents onto the plastic tray. A pile of fragments, the largest of them 2 centimetres across. They sounded like pieces of porcelain, chinking as they tipped out and I moved them around on the tray. But they were bone. Human bone.

In the year 43 CE, the Roman Empire was no longer content with simply trading with the inhabitants of a large island lying off the northwest coast of Europe. Those islanders had control of precious resources – grain, cattle, gold, silver and iron – and had also assisted with uprisings in northern Gaul a century before. Aside from that, Claudius was just two years into his emperorship. He could do with a military victory to strengthen his position in Rome.

The Atrebates of southern England – whose territory broadly coincided with modern-day Hampshire and Sussex – had been friendly with the Roman Empire for some time. One deposed leader had even sought military assistance from Rome in the year 7 CE. His appeal to Emperor Augustus at that time fell on deaf ears. Augustus was too busy to get embroiled in such tussles for scraps of power on a remote island at the distant edge of the Empire. Around the same time, the Greek historian Strabo was writing his *Geography*. In it, he described how some of the British chieftains had pledged allegiance to Rome, and were happily paying duties on exports and imports between Britain and Gaul, managing 'to make the whole of the island virtually Roman property'.

But in 43 CE, the Atrebates were back asking Rome for help – this time, wanting some military support to sort out their troublesome neighbours, the Catuvellauni. That lot, led by Caratacus, had seized much of the territory of the Atrebates, and their king, Verica (as he appeared on his own coins) or Berikos (as Dio Cassius calls him), now appealed to Claudius for help getting his kingdom back.

It was perfect timing for Claudius – he could respond to this request for assistance and make everything a lot simpler by bringing Britain under Imperial rule. He sent four legions, supported by an equivalent number of auxiliaries – some forty thousand soldiers in all. The Romans were essentially invited into southeast Britain, but then they met with opposition from factions not yet amenable to their rule. The Romans were by now pretty good at this sort of thing. You don't create and maintain an empire without some strategic prowess. The invasion was led by Aulus Plautius, who pushed in as far as the Thames, before waiting for his emperor, Claudius, to come – and symbolically lead the Roman forces to victory at Colchester.

What we don't know is what happened to Verica. Perhaps he was reinstated as king of the Atrebates. By the time history catches up with what was happening in this southern part of Britain, Togidubnus is the king there. He may have been Verica's son, or some other relative.

Despite the fact that Togidubnus looms large in just about

any modern account of Roman Britain, his name only appears twice in the historical and archaeological record. There is a single documentary source – Tacitus's biography of Agricola, in which he writes, 'Certain municipalities were given to Togidubnus (who stayed loyal over time) according to the successful tradition of using kings as agents of servitude.' And the other mention is written in stone, an inscription carved into a great slab of Purbeck marble discovered in Chichester, during building work in 1723. It's effectively a dedication plaque, and though it has suffered the ravages of time, it appears to say something like:

> The guild of artisans provide this temple to Neptune and Minerva for the protection of the Divine House on the authority of Tiberius Claudius Togidubnus, great king of Britain . . .

What do we learn from this? Chichester might have been Togidubnus's capital. Togidubnus may have spent his childhood in Rome, as any good client king-in-waiting should do – being instructed in Roman ways just like the princes of the British Empire's colonies being trained at Eton. His loyalty to Rome was enshrined in those extra names, Tiberius and Claudius – the first two names of the emperor (which might even suggest it was Claudius himself who granted Roman citizenship to the Briton). Did Togidubnus arrive back in Britain on the deck of one of the ships of the Claudian invasion fleet?

The granting of *civitates* – states or municipalities – to Togidubnus perhaps suggests that his territory was not only restored but enlarged, within the newly created Roman province. But some scholars have argued that it simply relates to the original territory that Togidubnus could claim some hereditary right to rule – and that Tacitus is being cynical or condescending: Rome deigns to gift Togidubnus's own kingdom back to him.

He may have ruled that region from a base in Chichester, and perhaps that base was the palace at Fishbourne – the largest Roman palace anyone's ever found north of the Alps, larger even than Buckingham Palace. Silchester is another important administrative capital – which may have come under his control as well. But then, everything now was under the Empire, ultimately. And when Togidubnus dies, those *civitates* are just absorbed into the wider province of Britannia. Old kings were useful intermediaries for a time, then forgotten.

The name of Togidubnus's kingdom was, according to a map of Roman roads in Britain, 'Regno'. Some have interpreted this simply as a version of *regnum*, 'kingdom' – a kingdom existing with Roman support, part of the Imperial system. Others suggest it is an old Celtic name, meaning 'proud'. Historians argue about this distinction – perhaps because it seems relevant to whether some sort of 'British' identity was maintained while 'British' kings invited Roman troops into the land of their fathers. But for ordinary people, I wonder if they would have even noticed the difference. Roman goods had been coming into the region for a century or more; the locals could export their livestock, grain and metal to the continent. The rulers changed from time to time. The tariffs changed. The economy might falter – then recover. Whether officially in or out of the Empire, in or out of the wider European economic union, life in Britain – would go on.

The effect on ordinary life in southeast England – of becoming more closely affiliated with the economic hub in

Rome – might not have made much of a difference to most people. There would have been economic gains for some – perhaps trade across the Channel became even easier. But further away from that point of contact with the continent, the Empire would surely have been seen very differently. A foreign power that was flexing its muscles now, on British soil. A way of life that might entice you in with nice things – pretty pottery, wine and olive oil. But then there would come a sword, and a threat. Render unto Caesar those taxes that you suddenly now owe him.

Perhaps you accept it, with a shrug of your shoulders. But perhaps the tariffs are too much, and you resist. Well, that's certainly how the people of south Wales reacted. The Silures – the people who had grown out of the land, seeded in the valleys, united by ties of kinship across the Brecon Beacons – were not going to take Roman expansionism lying down.

The Romans reacted in a way that was completely typical of a colonising superpower – they weren't about to give up either. After some thirty years of military campaigning against the Silurian freedom fighters, the Roman army finally crushed the resistance in southeast Wales. And then they built a fortress, to maintain a permanent military presence there. A presence which very definitely said, *Hey, you Silurian barbarians – resistance is futile.* They built this fortress on the Usk, close to an existing Iron Age stronghold. A Roman roadmap dating to the second century, the Antonine Itinerary, labels it 'Iscae leg. ii Augusta' – the fort of the Second Augustan Legion on the Usk. William Camden's *Britannia*, published in 1586, records that the original local name of the fortress was 'Kaer Lheion on Wysk' – the Fortress of the Legion on the Usk. Geoffrey of Monmouth, writing his *History of the Kings of Britain* in the twelfth century, says that an ancient British king, Belinus, founded a city even earlier than that – in the fourth century BCE – called Kaerusc, and that the Romans then renamed it the 'City of Legions'. It's kept that name, even though the legion left long ago: Caerleon. The legionary fortress lay on a road called the Julia Strata – and that must have been named after Sextus Julius Frontinus, the governor of Britain, who originally led the forces into south Wales to subjugate those recalcitrant Silures.

The Second Augustan Legion had moved around a bit before they settled at Caerleon. They'd fought in the Cantabrian Wars as Rome extended its empire into Spain in the first century BCE, and then in Germany, in the early first century CE, after which they were stationed at Argentoratum, now Strasbourg. After dealing with an insurgency in Gaul, they became one of the four legions involved in the invasion of Britain in 43 CE. Marching westwards through southern England, under the leadership of Vespasian, they brought Dorset and Devon – the territories of the Durotriges and Dumnonii – under Roman control. They are said to have been stationed at another Isca for a while – Isca Dumnoniorum. So there was a River Isca in Devon and another in south Wales. It seems that the Celtic root of the name simply means 'water' – just as *uisge* still means 'water' in Gaelic (as in *uisge beatha*, 'water of life' – whisky). Whereas the Isca in the Brecons became the Usk, the Devonian Isca became the Exe. From the fort of Isca Dumnoniorum, at present-day Exeter, the legion moved northwards to Glevum, Gloucester, for a while. And then in the seventies of the first century, they were dispatched to south Wales, to sort out the Silures and build their fortress on the Usk.

Caerleon would become one of three permanent legionary fortresses in Roman-occupied Britain – the other two being Chester and York. It would be the primary base for the Second Augustan Legion for almost two centuries – though during that time, detachments would be sent up to Hadrian's Wall and over to Londinium. And then, in the early third century, most of the legion moved up to Scotland, as the emperor Septimius Severus launched another attempt to bring the Caledonians under the yoke of Rome. In 210 it seemed he'd been successful, as the northern tribes agreed to some sort of peace treaty. But just a year later, in 211, they were rebelling again, and Severus was dying of gout in Eboracum, York. And then we lose sight of the Second Augustan Legion, until a document dating to the early fifth century mentions them having been stationed at Richborough, in Kent, the fort at Caerleon having long since been abandoned.

The peak for Roman Caerleon really was the second century, when there were over five thousand soldiers garrisoned in the fortress, which contained a massive barracks, a huge bath-house, a hospital, latrines, training grounds and workshops. Outside the fortress walls, a civilian town grew up. And there was even an amphitheatre.

Once the legion left, the place began to fall apart – but a much-diminished population continued to live amongst the ruins, keeping their cattle in the bath-house of the old fortress. (History doesn't record whether the cows preferred the steamy *caldarium* or the chilly *frigidarium*.) The amphitheatre became grown over, and the circle of grassy mounds was linked in legend to King Arthur – as his round table, no less. Geoffrey of Monmouth, in his (somewhat fanciful and not terribly reliable) *History of the Kings of Britain*, describes how Arthur chooses the City of Legions 'upon the River Usk, near the Severn Sea' as the venue for his coronation. It was a city, he wrote, whose 'magnificent royal palaces, with lofty gilded roofs, made it even rival the grandeur of Rome'. That 'history', penned centuries later, doesn't quite fit with the picture of post-Roman Caerleon that the archaeological record provides us with, where people lived in shacks amongst the crumbling barracks and cattle cooled their hooves in the ruined bath-house. Into the medieval period and beyond, Caerleon remained small – occupying just a fraction of the original footprint of the fortress. And although the grassy banks of 'King Arthur's Round Table' provided a convenient source of dressed stone, ready for use in much less ambitious building projects in the town, much of Roman Caerleon lay undisturbed, underground, forgotten.

In 1908, antiquarians from Liverpool became interested in the circular earthwork on the edge of Caerleon. Interested enough to dig it. A tithe map from 1840 suggests that they should have known what to expect – the circular feature was labelled 'amphitheatre'. But apparently they weren't sure whether it was just an earth structure or would contain stone when they started; perhaps the locals had forgotten where much of the building stone in the town had actually come from. Very quickly, they found that the banks concealed two massive, concentric elliptical walls. The outer walls were 2 metres thick and supported with regular buttresses. The 11-metre gap between the inner and outer walls was filled with earth – presumably to create a raised platform for timber seating around the central arena, which was floored in cobbles covered with a deep layer of sand. The structure was so well preserved that the decision was taken to leave it uncovered – and it's still the best, most complete example of a Roman amphitheatre in Britain today. It's well worth a visit.

In the year following those initial excavations, there were plans to extend the nearby churchyard into an adjacent field, and the Liverpool Antiquarian Society teamed up with the Monmouthshire Antiquarian Society to excavate, before the church began to fill up the field with bodies. The antiquarians uncovered the hefty base of a watch tower, together with well-built latrines and a haul of small finds including brooches – and coins of Vespasian and Domitian. Vespasian – following military successes in Britain, and then in Judaea – had become emperor in 69 CE, with his eldest son, Titus, succeeding him in 79. Just two years later, when Titus died of a fever, Vespasian's younger son, Domitian, succeeded him, and would reign for fifteen years. The coins, then, were from a time when the fortress at Isca had just been founded.

Further excavations, on the amphitheatre, were carried out in the winter of 1926 into 1927, after the *Daily Mail* raised funds, with additional financial support coming in from – quite bizarrely – American fans of King Arthur. There's a wonderful sepia-tinted photograph of the excavation team: twenty-three men, one small boy and – in the centre, holding a book – one woman. She is the 'trowelblazing' Tessa Wheeler – the wife of Dr (later Sir) Mortimer Wheeler, but an accomplished archaeologist in her own right. Over her career, she worked with Mortimer on many excavations, including Segontium – the Roman fort at Caernarfon – and later, Verulamium (St Albans) and Maiden Castle in Dorset. But Caerleon was her own project, and the summary monograph on the amphitheatre, published in 1928, bears just her name.

Shortly after those excavations at Caerleon itself, some building work was happening on the southern side of the river, in the village still known at that point as Ultra Pontem ('Over the Bridge'), turning up more evidence from Roman times. A cesspit was being dug for some new bungalows, and nearly a metre down, the workmen came across a stone slab. It turned out to be part of a small stone-lined chamber or cist. Inside it was a rectangular lead canister. The workmen downed tools and Mortimer Wheeler was called in to inspect the find. Having recorded everything in situ, Wheeler dug the canister out and took it to Caerleon Museum.

A piece of red samian-ware pottery recovered from the earth just above the canister in its cist suggested an early second-century date. And when the canister itself was opened, it was found to be full of fragments of cremated bone. The anatomist Arthur Keith, curator at the Hunterian Museum of the Royal College of Surgeons, inspected the fragmentary remains. His verdict:

'Amongst the contents of the urn I can trace parts of only one individual, apparently a man – so I judge from the largeness of the fragments; and, as the sutures of the skull are partly closed, at least over 35 years of age. The cremation was imperfectly done, the bones being less reduced than usual.'

There was another odd feature in this cremation burial. The canister had a lead pipe sticking out of the top of it. 'The upper end of the pipe', Wheeler wrote, 'was found at a depth of about a foot beneath the present surface, but to this depth the soil was merely surface-mould, and there is no doubt that the pipe originally reached the open air.'

Only one other vaguely similar burial had ever been discovered in Britain – a lead coffin in Colchester, with a lead pipe sticking out of it. But across the rest of the Roman world, there were several other examples known to Mortimer Wheeler – from western France to Italy and Sicily – some with lead pipes, others with earthenware pipes. And the second-century Greek geographer and travel writer Pausanius recorded a ritual in central Greece that seemed to provide an explanation for this very particular style of burial: a ceremony where blood from sacrifices was offered to the dead, poured 'through a hole into the grave'.

So is this the significance of the Caerleon pipe burial? It's a very particular type of grave which allows the dead to be sealed away – yet still open to be provided with sustenance from time to time. 'These facts', wrote the folklorist Sir James Frazer, discussing such burial rites in typically expansive terms, 'bring vividly before us the belief of the Greeks and Romans that the souls of the dead still lived and retained their bodily appetites in the tomb.' Whatever the friends and relatives of the deceased were pouring down that pipe – blood, or wine, perhaps – this was clearly a funerary rite which didn't stop with the cremation of the body, or the burial of the cremated remains. It was done with the expectation that the bereaved would continue communing with the dead. You could visit the cemetery where old Grandpa Pontus was buried, have a picnic, chat about family memories and the old country, and share some of your wine with him, down the tube. As archaeologist Miles Russell told me, some tombstones from the first and second century show this communion quite explicitly – with the deceased person lying on a couch, as in life, inviting visitors to dine with them.

I mentioned the pipe burial to my friend Natasha, who grew up in Siberia. She told me about a tradition in Russia where families gathered in graveyards each year, on a 'Parents' Day', to eat a meal and drink. She said that as a child, she'd been told it was important to eat some of the food, and that the adults were drinking alcohol as well. And then a portion of food was left on the grave. Her recollections prompted me to find out more. It seems that this was a ritual which persisted right through the Soviet era, even while the churches themselves were closed or even destroyed – and it was carried out by people who were still privately Christian, but also by atheists. It also turns out that similar traditions of feasting and toasting at the graveside exist in countries following the Greek Orthodox Christian tradition, with the death marked on specific days and then months after the passing of the deceased, and then again, on the anniversary of the day of death. The similarities between the Russian and Greek Orthodox traditions are not so surprising – both these branches of Christianity grew out of the Eastern Roman or Byzantine Empire. But it's the antiquity of these customs that's quite astonishing. One Greek anthropologist has written, 'We see here the astonishing obstinacy of ritual, of the whole system of deeply rooted gestures, reproduced even when they are no longer understood.' Although the Orthodox Church officially frowns upon it, offerings of food and drink are still left on Russian graves at various times through the year, including Easter. A small table may even be set up, with cake, decorated eggs, apples and biscuits placed on it – perhaps a shot glass of vodka too. Alternatively, vodka may be poured onto the grave.

The tending of graves, the repeated offerings of food and drink at the graveside – all this helps to create a connection with a homeland or *rodina*. It seems to suggest a belief in the continued presence of the soul of the deceased – although the 'obstinacy of ritual' means that such a belief is no longer necessary or implicit once a tradition is established. Indeed, the practice as it exists within the Russian Orthodox tradition is so ancient that it seems to pre-date Christianity.

The existence of Roman funerary banquets is well attested in the literature, with the first feast, the *silcernium*, taking place on the day of the funeral itself. Wine seems to have been an important part of various Roman funerary rituals. We can speculate about wine being poured into the pipe burial, but other graves contain more explicit evidence in the form of cups, bottles, flagons, even amphorae – the last being equivalent to being buried with two nebuchadnezzars (30 litres) of champagne. Funerals involved feasting, with the dead joining in; the bones of pigs, sheep and poultry provide evidence of meat being placed into graves.

Tacitus, writing at the end of the first century into the early second century CE, described another feast, the *cena novendialis* – a 'ninth-day meal' – eaten at the graveside, at the end of the nine days of full mourning. The meal included a libation, poured onto the grave. (And there were reports that hungry and destitute individuals sometimes helped themselves to the food offerings left in graveyards.) Romans would leave money in their wills to pay for all the food, wine, incense and roses which would be left as offerings on the grave. There are also plenty of representations of funeral feasts on Roman gravestones and on walls of larger tombs.

One man from Andematunnum (modern-day Langres, in eastern France), who died in the first or second century CE, left an extremely elaborate and comprehensive set of instructions in his will for rituals to be carried out at his shrine, after his death. Offerings were expected annually, on the first days of April, May, June, July, August and October. (He let his visitors off in winter.) But it seems that the birthday of the departed was also a common time for a visit, with more feasting and grave offerings being left. And there were a few official 'days of the dead' throughout the year: one in May, called Lemuria, when hungry, unremembered ghosts, *lemures*, were thought to roam around; Rosàlia in June, which seemed to be a wider 'rose festival' but included commemoration of the dead; and – in February – the Parentalia or *dies parentales*, a nine-day-long festival of the ancestors. The ritual Natasha remembered from her childhood had extremely deep roots.

She later sent me a link to a website describing Russian Parents' Day. The authors acknowledged that the tradition originated in pagan customs – which had become incorporated into the Orthodox calendar. No longer in February, it had become a truly moveable feast – celebrated after Easter. Nine days after Easter. So Parents' Day, or Radonitsa, the 'day of rejoicing', was also the *cena novendialis* for Christ himself, as well as harking back to the nine-day tradition of the original Parentalia. This was the main memorial day for the dead in the Orthodox calendar – but the website mentioned five other 'small parental days', on 5 March, 2 and 9 April, 18 June and 5 November. The website was full of photos with offerings of fruit, cakes and flowers beside graves, although the current recommendations from the church seemed to be that food shouldn't be left on graves – and that, while moderate consumption of alcohol was permitted, drinking to excess was not encouraged, and merriment was definitely to be avoided.

There's another Christian holiday which harks back to the old, pagan Roman festivals. Another moveable feast, it's celebrated fifty days after Easter: it is Pentecost, also known as Whitsun in the United Kingdom. But it has other names: Pasqua delle Rose in Italy, Pâques des Roses in France and Rusalii in Romania. In medieval texts, it's still referred to by its more ancient name: Rosalia. Old habits die hard.

So it seems there would have been plenty of opportunities through the year for relatives to visit the grave just outside Isca, to eat a meal at the graveside and pour a libation down the lead pipe. This little piece of Roman culture, so unusual and unfamiliar in Britain, was – as Mortimer Wheeler had known – a relatively common and widespread custom, across other parts of the Empire. And we can also see it as very much part of that even wider custom of eating meals at the graveside and leaving offerings of food and wine for the departed, a custom depicted on gravestones, written about in ancient texts and surviving right through to the present, despite all the fluctuations in religion and politics over the intervening centuries. And we do in fact have some evidence of funeral feasting from Britain – even before the Romans moved in. It's not as widespread, and of course, not contextualised by any written accounts, as it takes us back into prehistory. But it is there.

The dead of the Iron Age are largely missing from the British landscape – perhaps bodies were most often exposed, to be excarnated, as in modern Tibetan 'sky burials', or cremated remains were scattered. Inhumation cemeteries down in Dorset and up in Yorkshire are the exception rather than the rule. And there, the most eye-popping graves – some containing whole chariots, one even including ponies – also include evidence of funeral feasts, in the form of animal bones from joints of meat. One striking example from Yorkshire is a rack of ribs with the iron meat hook still embedded in it.

The very patchy burial record of Britain changes when the south comes under Roman rule. While the Romans initially had a reputation for being very tolerant of local religions – even combining British and Roman deities, as with 'Sulis Minerva', to whom the Roman temple in Bath was dedicated – Roman funerary ritual seems to have spread fairly quickly. The early military garrisons would of course bring their own, Romanised way of death with them – just as they followed a Romanised way of life. (They even put up gravestones for the first time, at least for those who could afford it, so we find out the names of dead people as well as learning from their bones.) These new practices seem to have quickly seeped out into the surrounding communities; certainly it has proved difficult to identify cemeteries that are exclusively military. By the end of the first century, cremation had become the major burial rite throughout Roman Britain – and would remain so until the third century, when inhumations started to become increasingly common, following a trend which started a century earlier, in Italy. But old funerary traditions from pre-Roman times would also persist – with round barrows still being constructed, particularly in the southeast, into which cremation burials were inserted.

In contrast, that pipe burial is a complete novelty in Britain – the idea of it is just so *Roman*. And its location is Roman too – outside the settlement, on one of the roads leading away from Caerleon. That positioning of cemeteries was something that was enshrined in Roman law, from the middle of the first millennium BCE. Table 10 of the Twelve Tables of foundational Roman law included the rule that corpses should not be burned or buried within a city. The reason behind this may have included concerns about the potential of pollution – but also the very practical need to keep land free for building. Cicero mentions another good reason for avoiding cremations inside the city walls: the fire hazard presented by towering funeral pyres. Cremations were the standard funeral rite across much of the Empire – so common as to be unremarkable. So it's only when things went badly wrong that we get reports popping up in the literature. Pliny the Elder describes the corpse of a certain M. Lepidus being catapulted off a raging inferno of a pyre. Another report describes a corpse gruesomely bursting – and putting out a pyre. Sometimes the survival of a body part was seen as a miracle which guaranteed its further preservation; when the Greek king Pyrrhus was cremated, his right big toe refused to burn – and was subsequently collected up and kept in a special (presumably quite small) shrine. There are lots of other mentions of corpses *semiustum* – half-burned – which was considered a most inauspicious way to go, an insult to the dead. According to Suetonius, the murdered corpse of Caligula was hurriedly placed on an emergency pyre, only half-burned and then buried in a very shallow grave – and then later exhumed and properly cremated by his sisters, when they returned from exile.

The poet Lucan includes a luridly imaginative account of an inadequate cremation in his long poem on the civil war between Pompey and Julius Caesar. Towards the end of the poem, Pompey is killed by one of his own traitorous soldiers when he lands on the coast of Egypt. His head is clumsily severed from its body and delivered to the king of Egypt as definitive proof of Pompey's demise. The young pharaoh has the head embalmed, presumably so that it could be displayed. Meanwhile, Pompey's headless body is left in the sea. One of his companions, Cordus, goes down to the beach under cover of darkness and drags the corpse out of the waves, finds some timber from a wrecked boat and steals a burning branch from another funeral pyre on the beach, to light the fire under Pompey's body. The pyre burns through the night, fed with melting fat from the corpse. But the body is left less than *semiustum*. In the morning, Cordus pulls out charred bones, still with sinews attached and oozing marrow, from the embers, before quenching them in the sea. Then he piles them into a very shallow grave, scrapes a bit of earth over them, and lays a stone on top, writing on it with a charred stick, 'Pompey lies here.'

While the state of Pompey's cremation seems regrettable – and a source of shame for Egypt, Lucan suggests – other half-burnings may have been carried out as an intentional insult to the deceased. Suetonius wrote that many people wanted the body of Tiberius, for instance, to be taken off and 'half-burned' in an amphitheatre. On the other hand, there seems to have been a worry that ghosts of the dead could linger until cremation rites were properly completed. Suetonius, again, describes the ghost of Caligula hanging around for a while in this way.

There seem to have been many different attitudes to death and the possibility of an afterlife across the Roman Empire – not surprisingly, considering the vast landscape it grew to envelop, and the centuries it lasted for. The writings of the Epicureans and Stoics present a very modern-sounding, humanist approach to death: it was the end of life, and that was that. In the first century CE, the Epicurean poet Lucretius wrote a long philosophical poem, *On the Nature of Things*, in which he reflects: 'Look back on the eternity that passed before we were born and consider how it counts as absolutely nothing to us. This is a mirror, held up for us by Nature, that shows how it will be after we are dead. Is there anything frightening in this sight? Anything depressing? Anything that is not more restful than the deepest of sleeps?' In the second century, the emperor Marcus Aurelius was typically Stoic in his view of death: 'A little while and you will be nobody nowhere, nor will anything which you now see exist, nor any of those now alive. Nature's law is that all things change and turn, and pass away, so that in due course, different things may be.'

The fact that there were these views, long before Christianity got going, makes you wonder how far back these sorts of ideas went. We tend to think that people were more superstitious the further back in time we go. Certainly, the pursuit and advancement of science has encouraged a perspective on the world as a natural place, where supernatural explanations are neither needed nor sought after by many. But even with much less understanding of the physical nature of the world than we enjoy today, and poorer knowledge of the relationship of humans to the rest of life on earth, some ancient philosophers were still coming up with these extremely practical and rational perspectives. Perhaps there have always been some people who prefer rational explanations and others who like to indulge in a little mysticism, placing faith in things that can never be tested, let alone proven. Certainly, we know from the literature that a diversity of views on life, death and whatever 'hereafter' you chose to believe in – if any – clearly existed in the Roman world before the hegemony of Christianity – which simply didn't tolerate any alternative views once it became the established religion of Rome. (Though I suspect diverse beliefs still persisted, even if they weren't shared or written down quite so freely.)

But what beliefs did the Caerleon pipe burial represent? The body of the dead person was thoroughly cremated, so we can presume there was no expectation of a bodily resurrection there. But somehow, the spirit of the departed was still associated with the pile of calcined bone fragments in the lead canister – so much so that this spirit of the cinders could continue to enjoy libations delivered down the pipe. Did the surviving relatives and friends *really* believe in such a lingering spirit? Or was the ritual simply 'what was done'? We have to admit to ourselves that, while the physical traces of a ritual may be all we have to go on when trying to reconstruct *belief* systems in the past, the link between ritual and belief is not – and probably never has been – as firm or as simple as we'd like to think.

Humans are creatures of imagination. We have huge brains and are great at problem-solving, and are even fairly good at rational enquiry. But we also *love* stories. In human evolutionary biology, we talk about the 'cognitive niche' – the idea that human intelligence has evolved as a unique survival tactic, underpinning our prodigious abilities to make tools, and to cooperate and learn from each other – allowing us to carve out our own ecological position. But as much as we inhabit that cognitive niche within an ecosystem, we *live in it*, in our heads. We create a whole world for ourselves in there. We tell ourselves stories all the time. Some of those stories are grounded in reality, in science. They are more like hypotheses, even theories. We test them against evidence, and chuck them out if they don't stand up to scrutiny. But others are simply fictions – and we *know it*. Those stories might be helpful in certain situations. Perhaps they provide us with comfort or solace when we're depressed, or wracked with

grief. Or perhaps they're just entertaining or somehow deli-
cious. We might accept that they're not in the least bit real or
true, while enjoying the flirtation with mystery and magic and
drama. Santa Claus, tooth fairies, life after death. We go along
with them because we like a good story – even if we know
it's not true. I know that some readers will nod along – until
I get to the life-after-death bit, and then you might baulk at
it. Can you bear to be brutally honest with yourself? There
is no evidence at all for such a phenomenon. So why do you
believe it? It could be tradition – it's what you were taught,
and just the way some people talk about death, and perhaps
you really think it's poetic and metaphorical but not *actually*
true. A comforting fiction. And that's OK. Or perhaps you
really *do* believe in it, deep down. I don't want to wrench that
away – just to gently point out that such a concept is not there
because you've any evidence for it, out in the world. Someone
has placed that idea in your head, however real it may seem.
(You may disagree with me, of course, but I think Lucretius
and Marcus Aurelius had it right.)

Having turned the lens on ourselves, we can go back to
that roadside cemetery just south of Isca, where a family is
gathered to pay respects at the grave. Is it a solemn affair, the
paterfamilias pouring a cup of blood or wine into his father's
grave, while the children are desperate for it all to be over? Or
is it more joyful – was *merriment* permitted? Someone raising
a glass, another cracking a joke, while yet another tells one
of those family stories that become richer with every telling,
binding the clan in that fabric of stories that tie us together.

Three quarters of a century after it was excavated, there I was, in the dissection room at the University of Bristol, reanalysing a sample of cremated remains labelled 'Bulmore Road, no. 31.78' – the Caerleon pipe burial.

Modern gas-fired crematoria tend to operate at around 1,000°C, reducing a corpse to a pile of calcined bone in just an hour – and that bone is then ground into a fine powder in a cremulator. (Modern relatives don't like to collect recognisable bone fragments.) Some cultures still use wood-fuelled funerary pyres, and osteoarchaeologist and cremation expert Jackie McKinley reports on modern pyres burning for three to eight hours – to reduce the body to *cineres* – 'cinders' or 'ashes'. (Really what's left is not ash at all, but fragments of baked bone.) But it may take much longer for the remains to cool down before they can safely be collected up. Roman cremations would have been similar, taking hours to complete. During all that time – according to the author Varro, writing in the first century BCE – the relatives would have stayed in attendance.

Pyres were built of stacked logs, alternating by right angles each layer, rather like those odd towers of chips you sometimes get in pretentious restaurants. The role of *ustor* is mentioned in Roman literature: literally a 'burner', this individual may have been a cremation funeral director – perhaps a professional pyre builder. All the stories of cremations gone wrong no doubt helped fuel a desire to enlist the services of such a knowledgeable and professional pyromaniac. How had the Isca *ustor* done?

The remains from the lead canister weighed in at 1.3 kilograms. I spread out the chinking bone fragments on the white trays. Many were simply too small to to be identifiable – it was impossible to work out *which* specific bone of the body they had belonged to. But there were plenty of larger fragments, many of which were more than a centimetre long. These I could identify more precisely. Some flat, smooth fragments were obviously from the skull; others were bits of long bone shafts. Painstakingly working my way through, picking out larger pieces with the tips of my forceps, turning them round and inspecting them, I separated the fragments into groups on the tray, scribbling down notes as I went.

There were more than forty pieces from the skull vault – the flat bones which form the dome of the brain case. The largest of these was 6 centimetres across. Some had clearly warped in the heat of the pyre. Those vault bones are made up of two layers of compact bone – the inner and outer 'tables', each a couple of millimetres thick – separated by a layer of lattice-like cancellous bone – the diploë. An odd-sounding word, this comes from the Greek *diplóē*, 'fold' – presumably because it is trapped between those two layers of solid bone. In life, the tiny gaps around the lattice are filled with red bone marrow, busy making red blood cells. I inspected these fragments particularly carefully, as they can hold clues to pathology. In anaemia, bone marrow throughout the body expands – in the skull too – in an attempt to pump out more blood cells. But the diploë in these fragments looked quite normal.

Some of the vault fragments had meandering suture lines running across them. The flat bones of the skull meet at these joints – interdigitating with each other just like interwoven fingers. The very narrow gap between one bone and its neighbour in these sutures is filled with fibrous tissue in life. When you're young, the skull can grow a little at these edges of bones. In older adults, the bones fuse together and the sutures close and disappear. They'd closed over on the internal surface of the fragments I was inspecting, while still being open and visible on the outer side. An enormous amount of work has gone into recording suture closure in skulls of known age at death, with the disappointing conclusion emerging that the timing of closure is so variable, it's not a very useful marker of age at all. There's the added complication that sutures can burst open at cremations. But with these half-closed sutures, I could at least be sure that this individual had reached adulthood.

There were eight or so more interestingly shaped cranial fragments – fragments of facial bones and skull base. One tiny piece looked like it had once helped to form the margin of the orbit, or eye socket. Another piece – identifiable as part of the petrous temporal bone, from the base of the skull – was blackened rather than white like most of the bone on the trays. There wasn't much evidence of the mandible, the lower jaw, apart from a fragment of the left condyle – the knobbly bit which forms the jaw joint. I found three roots of teeth – long and conical. I looked at their tips carefully to see if the root canal was visibly open – it wasn't. Closure of the apex of the root is the last stage of tooth development, occurring at different ages for the various permanent teeth in a mouth, with the first molars and incisors reaching this stage first, from around nine to twelve years of age. So this individual was very unlikely to have been younger than nine.

I found about twenty pieces of vertebrae, some big enough to pin down to specific regions in the spine. I picked out a piece of a cervical vertebra, from the neck, and a large chunk of lower thoracic vertebra, 46 millimetres at its widest. The bodies of vertebrae have rims of separate bone while they're still growing, but all the ring epiphyses I could see were well fused – that happens from around eighteen years of age. There were a few pieces of rib and four fragments identifiable as pelvis. Amongst a pile of long bone fragments, from the limbs, I could identify the complete head of a radius, a fragment of the ulnar head, and a piece of the head of a femur. There were around a hundred and sixty fragments from the shafts of long bones; for most of these, it was impossible to tell exactly which bone they were from. The longest one, 74 millimetres in length, looked like it might have once been part of a tibia. Several chunky fragments bore crescentic fracture lines – a sign that the body had been burned with flesh on it, rather than as bare bones. There were very few fragments that I could reliably determine to have come from hands or feet: just half a middle phalanx from one finger, three heads of metatarsals from the feet, and one fragment of the back of a heel bone or calcaneus.

Cremations are frustrating. After hours of picking over the remains, I had been able to either roughly or precisely identify only around a quarter of the fragments, by weight. I was left with almost a kilogram of very small, unidentifiable frag-ments – I could do no more. And yet, there was some useful information here – and certainly much more than I'd ever have been able to glean from a modern cremation, after the bone fragments are sent through the cremulator and ground down into that fine, heavy dust.

There wasn't enough to tell the sex of this individual – for that I would have needed some large, well-preserved fragments of pelvis or skull. But there were no duplicated fragments, so those 1.3 kilograms of cremated bone were likely to have just come from one individual. And that person was an adult – I

could be sure of that, based on those fused vertebral ring epiphyses and half-fused skull sutures. Perhaps that doesn't sound
like much, for all my effort. But across a whole cemetery,
those nuggets of information can add up to understanding
quite a bit about a population, and about approaches to burial
rites. I prepared reports on nineteen other Roman cremations
from Caerleon, found close to the pipe burial – but none as
remarkable in the style of their burial. These others were
mostly small samples compared with the pipe burial – ranging
from just 2 grams to 250 grams in weight. Some contained
animal bones, and no obvious identifiable fragments of human
bones. In each case, the bone was well burned, but whoever
collected up the remains hadn't been anywhere near as fastidious as the director of the pipe burial person's last rites.

There was one sample, however, which was even larger than
the pipe burial. It was labelled 94.47H/019, and was a hefty
2.2 kilograms' worth of bone fragments. There were also fifty-
five tooth roots – which is pushing it for just one mouth. I also
found two duplicated fragments of mandible, from around the
chin. This collection, then, represented the cremated remains
of at least two people. Dual cremation burials don't necessarily
mean the individuals died at the same time, of course – an
urn containing the cremated remains of one individual could
be kept unburied until the other bones come to join it. That
physical proximity in death might suggest close relations in
life – but that's untestable, unfortunately. Cremation thoroughly destroys DNA.

The pipe burial *ustor* had done a good job. Most of the bone
was pale, if not white – and had that 'porcelain' texture to
it. There were only a couple of less well-burned fragments,
like that blackened piece of petrous temporal bone, and only

a few extraneous objects – pieces of animal bone and a bit of charcoal. There were some small pieces of lead in the sample but these had presumably come from the canister, after excavation. The pipe burial stood out, not only because of the unusual style of the grave, but also because of the care that had been taken, both in achieving a complete cremation and in gathering up the shattered bone afterwards. Modern cremations typically yield between 1.0 and 3.6 kilograms of calcined bone for one adult. As Jackie McKinley has pointed out, cremation burials were always tokenistic in that they only preserved part of the body – and indeed usually only a portion of the cremated skeleton – but the pipe burial person had received unusual attention in this regard. Another indication of high status perhaps, in addition to the elaborate burial that followed.

The colour and texture of cremated bone provides a clue to the temperatures reached in a pyre. Bone is a biphasic tissue – combining the fibrous protein, collagen, and the hard mineral, apatite – a type of calcium phosphate. The mineral makes it immensely strong, but would be brittle on its own; the collagen makes it tough. It's an incredible material. And when it's finished doing its job in a living body and it's burned, different things happen to those protein and mineral components.

When a body starts to burn, moisture is driven off. Skin shrinks and splits; fat reduces and melts; muscles contract and harden, often pulling limbs into flexed positions. Bones will be protected by soft tissues for a while, but as the temperature rises, their colour changes. Experimental burning of bone in the laboratory reveals the stages of combustion. Unburned bone is white in colour. As bone reaches a temperature between 200 and 400°C it becomes brown and black – essentially charred – then blue and grey, as the carbon in the protein is oxidised. At 500–700°C, bone goes greyish white. Above 800°C, once the carbon has fully combusted, it becomes pure white again. Carbonate disappears completely above 1,000°C. And all the time, the crystal structure of the bone mineral is changing. Once the organic – protein – components begin to disappear, the apatite crystals come into direct contact with each other, and they merge and grow. It's this crystallinity which makes well-burned, calcined bone feel – and sound – like ceramic. Microscopically, tiny fractures which occur in bones at lower temperatures fuse – fully cremated bone is much harder and stronger than half-burned bone, which easily fragments.

Such lab experiments are great for understanding how bone changes as it's burned. But the changes depend not only on temperature, but on availability of oxygen – and crucially, the duration of burning. Experiments with timber pyres in outdoor settings suggest that temperatures in excess of 1,000°C can be achieved, and that a temperature of at least 600°C for a good few hours is what's required to cremate a body – but that would also vary with the specific fuel being used and the ambient temperature. The amount of wood needed to burn one body is phenomenal – the equivalent of 150 kilograms of pine. Then there's the weather – a light wind can fan the flames, a strong wind can collapse the pyre and blow it out. Heavy rain – and it's all over. There are so many variables. All we can say is that whoever arranged the cremation destined for the pipe burial – official *ustor* or not – knew what they were doing.

Some colour variation is normal in bone from pyre cremations. But most of the pipe burial bone fragments were white or light grey, suggesting a fairly uniform temperature had been reached. That blackened petrous temporal suggests perhaps that the body was laid supine on the pyre – but it's also a bone that's tucked away, deep under the skull. The fragmentation of the bones is likely to have happened incidentally as the remains were recovered from the burned-out pyre. Although cremated bones often look fairly complete and intact immediately after burning, they are crazed with fractures and very brittle, falling to pieces quite easily – even though those individual fragments are hard and strong; think of a smashed plate. The fragments of animal bone could potentially have been incidental – perhaps scooped up with the rest when the fire had burned out. But many of the other Caerleon cremations contained identifiable fragments of animal bone as well – suggesting that there could well have been a tradition of placing meat as an offering on the pyre. For the calcined remains scraped up and interred in the lead canister beside what would eventually become known as Bulmore Road, it was just the first of many feasts.

And here's a weird thing. I'm a humanist. Like Lucretius and Marcus Aurelius, I just don't buy the idea of life after death. But I feel a real connection with that person whose bones I spent so much time poring over, as though I was trying to retrieve each scrap of information from the burned-out pyre. The story takes over. In my imagination, I travel back in time, walk out of the fortress of Isca, sit by that grave, raise a glass – and pour it down the pipe.

2.

DEATH IN THE VILLA

Another set of bones. These ones are tiny, and fragile – but not cremated. The ends of them look blunt, truncated. I'm unpacking them out of an old cigar box in a store room in a museum.

I pick them up extremely carefully, and lay them out on a folded piece of tissue paper. I place the eggshell-thin pieces of skull bones at one end, and arrange the few vertebrae that have survived, like tiny buttons, in a vertical column under those skull pieces. There are quite a few little ribs, but no pelvic bones that I can make out. Although there's very little of the hands and feet, the long bones of the limbs are all here: the humerus, radius and ulna in each of the arms, and the femur, tibia and fibula in each leg.

These were the bones of a baby. A baby so tiny it must have died around the time of birth. Although I maintained my professional composure, laying out these bones, I felt a stab of grief for this child who had died so young, nearly 2,000 years ago. This was my first day back at work after having my first baby, a daughter, just five weeks before.

(Indeed, this is a sad and gruesome story, so you may feel like skipping this chapter. I'm putting this warning here as it's not necessarily something I would have wanted to read about while I was pregnant, for instance.)

In 2009, I'd taken the plunge and resigned from my lecturing role at Bristol University. I'd been there, in the Anatomy Department, for eleven years. But baroque departmental politics, an impenetrable glass ceiling and cuts to staffing levels that made the pips squeak eventually got the better of me. I felt crushed, disempowered and exhausted. I'd left a career in surgery to become a university lecturer, and I'd loved it. I had no regrets, but I couldn't stay in a job which was hollowing me out. I made the decision to take control of my life, and handed in my letter of resignation. And then, just as I came to the end of my month's notice, I discovered I was pregnant. I was elated – but a little worried about what the future would hold. But I was lucky. The writing was going well, and suddenly, there was an exciting new television project on the horizon: a series for BBC Two, looking at fresh archaeological discoveries across the UK. It already had a title, *Digging for Britain*. I'd been discussing this series with its creator, producer John Farren. At first it seemed like a vague possibility, but as it started to look more concrete, I knew I had something important to tell him.

His first reaction was that he imagined I wouldn't want to present the series after all. He hoped we'd get another chance to work together in the future. But I'd been talking to my old friend Miranda Krestovnikoff. We'd both presented a long-running series about British landscape, history and wildlife, called *Coast* – and I knew she'd kept filming not only while pregnant, but while she was looking after a small baby. She'd shown that it was possible, and she encouraged me to try it.

John Farren was amazing. When I suggested I'd like to try presenting this new series, bringing my baby with me, he was completely on board with the idea. My husband, Dave, would join me on the adventure, looking after the baby while I was off filming. I'd be able to hook up with them at lunchtime to breastfeed her. And so the three of us headed off to film the first series of *Digging for Britain* in the spring of 2010. The very first shoot was in Hambleden, Buckinghamshire – for a story about a new look at an archaeological site that had originally been excavated in 1912.

———

Yewden Lodge, in the Hambleden Valley, is an extremely grand house, with eight bedrooms, and its own swimming pool and tennis court. It was once home to the late composer and keyboard player Jon Lord, of Deep Purple and Whitesnake fame. But just 180 metres to the northwest, there had been an even more impressive building, around 2,000 years ago – one of the largest Roman villas in the Thames Valley.

Yewden Roman Villa was extensively excavated in 1912.

The associated remains cover a huge area, straddling Skirmett Road, reaching 550 metres to the west of the road and 150 to the east. There's nothing to see there now – just fields. But stone and pottery still turn up in the plough soil, and the buildings are visible from the air as crop marks, at certain times of the year. I visited the site with archaeologist Jill Eyers, who had reappraised the findings from the original excavation, and sifted through the physical archive – all the discoveries that had been boxed up and deposited in the museum. It was a beautiful day, in an idyllic setting. Red kites wheeled overhead, in a clear blue sky.

Villas were a New Thing in the parts of Britain that came under Roman control: country houses with their own farmland. Some were modest farmsteads, others palatial ranches – of which Yewden was a fine example. While villas themselves were a new Roman fashion, archaeological evidence shows that the farming that went on around them was much the same as it had been in the Iron Age. There may have been some changes in land ownership. Anyone either managing to hold onto land – accumulating more, or acquiring brand-new assets – clearly had the opportunity to become quite wealthy under the new regime. If you then wanted to use wealth to express a Romanised identity – what better way than to build a lavish villa? And over time, they got bigger and more splendid. As one scholar has put it, 'social elites were now competing with each other through this new form of personal status display in the countryside'. Keeping up with the Joneses, Roman-style.

The earliest British villas, in the first century CE, were large, and simple in plan. They were single-storey, with a series of rooms linked by a corridor or an open verandah, like a motel. By the second century, villas were becoming more complex, with extra wings added. And by the fourth century, it was common for larger villas to include a central courtyard or garden, either completely enclosed by buildings, or on three sides, with one side open. That open courtyard plan was the one followed at Yewden.

The courtyard was huge: 120 metres long and 70 metres wide. Three large buildings stood on the north, west and south sides. The buildings, and their function, seems to have evolved over time. The northern building looked like it had been residential to start with, and was then repurposed as a series of workshops, with flint or chalk floors. The southern building was thought by the original excavator, Alfred Heneage Cocks, to have been constructed as a barn or workshop, with the western end converted into living quarters in the fourth century (he was wrong – archaeologists now believe it was built as a house originally). A pot containing 294 bronze coins, pointing to a date around 320 CE, was buried in one of the rooms of this building. Other coins were dug up from the floor – the earliest being a pre-Roman, Iron Age coin, and the latest dating to the end of the fourth century.

Both the northern and the southern buildings – as well as two smaller buildings to the east – contained sunken 'ovens' or furnaces. They were perhaps for drying grain – or, more likely, malting barley. There were fourteen of these furnaces in total at the site – suggesting that some kind of cereal-processing was happening here on a fairly large, almost industrial scale. But one or two of the furnaces may have had other uses – pieces of bronze slag suggest that some metal-working was also taking place at the farmstead.

The building to the west of the courtyard is thought to

have been the main house, from the third century onwards. It would originally have been a simple but imposing rectangular building, with four large rooms inside. Later, wings were added at each end, and corridors front and back, linking the rooms. The interior walls were plastered and painted. Most of the floors were pounded chalk, but the corridors and one room had more hard-wearing, waterproof floors – tiled with terracotta tesserae. The southernmost room in this house boasted a hypocaust for underfloor heating, and it also had the latest design of window frame – complete with glass. Who lives in a villa like this? The owners were clearly extremely rich – and they'd enthusiastically embraced the idea of having a state-of-the-art home with Roman mod cons: underfloor heating, window glass and even, eventually, a tiled roof. But otherwise, the build looks very local – with traditional flint foundations, a wooden frame and wattle-and-daub infill. It's the epitome of high class, hybrid Romano-British-style.

Some of the most valuable evidence on archaeological digs emerges out of old rubbish pits, or middens. The detritus of the past holds all sorts of clues: bone fragments give away the types of meat being eaten; sherds of a particular pottery type reveal culinary secrets and may even be linked to a particular time period; broken or lost brooches, rings and pendants show changing fashions over time and help to provide dates. Yewden Roman Villa was particularly rich in this respect, with twenty-six pits for the archaeologists to explore. A particularly deep one contained more than just rubbish – four skeletons were recovered from its depths. The individuals were three adults: two young males and one female – and a child around six years old. This seems strange to us, but in fact it's not that unusual for Roman Britain. Multiple burials like this turn up occasionally, close to buildings, and may relate to outbreaks of disease. Their final resting place seemed odd, though, with building stone piled on top of them.

But those four skeletons weren't the only human remains. Alfred Cocks and his team started to find the skeletal remains of infants buried in some of the pits. More and more tiny bones appeared. Eventually they counted *ninety-seven* burials of babies. Five came from the same pit as the older individuals – and there could have been more in there. It was full of water, which Cocks doesn't seem to have been able or willing to pump out. He adopted an extremely unorthodox approach to excavation, writing, 'As the bones had to be felt for, under water, it was impossible to say much about the positions, except that they were all more or less in contact. The people, whether dead or alive, had evidently been thrown in without ceremony.' He seems to be making a bit of a leap in his interpretation here, given that he couldn't even see the burials as he excavated them. But Jill Eyers thought this 'pit' was probably a filled-in well. The older individuals were buried in it at some depth – more than 4 metres down; the infant burials were shallower. Most of the other infant remains were discovered in pits in the yard area, but a few were found inside the buildings, under the floors.

When Jill went through the site archive, she tracked down thirty-five of the infant burials excavated by Cocks's team. They'd been packed up into various little boxes, which were then packed into bigger boxes, and ended up on a shelf in the stores of the Buckinghamshire Museum.

And now I was looking at one of those little skeletons – burial 38 – laying out those tiny bones, on a table in the museum stores. I looked carefully at each one, to make sure it was indeed human, to identify it and place it on the correct side. But when I came to look at one of the femurs, I saw something which made me pause. We stopped filming for a moment while I grabbed a magnifying glass and inspected it even more closely. There were cut marks on it. I was sure of it. A series of fine, straight cuts on the bone, towards its upper end.

When you see something like this, the first question to ask yourself is whether such features really are cut marks – rather than perhaps the result of some natural process or breakage. But these looked convincing. The next question was: when were these marks made? Was this something that could have happened to the bones when they were excavated perhaps? Or, later, when they were looked at in a lab? The marks were far too narrow to have been made with a trowel, even a thin leaf-trowel. This was tricky. They hadn't been spotted before, and I was in the middle of making a television sequence about

Yewden Villa and the infant burials. I couldn't say too much at that point, but I did remark on the presence of the cuts. After we'd finished filming, I put the cut-marked femur in a separate, small plastic bag, on which I'd written all the details of the burial including its context number – the unique reference which ties any archaeological find to its precise 3D location in the excavation. I had also made some small puncture-holes in the plastic bag to prevent condensation, which could damage the delicate bone. That evening, I emailed Simon Mays, the human skeletal biologist for Historic England, letting him know what I thought I had found.

We kept in touch. Simon agreed that the marks did indeed look like incisions – and then he re-examined all the other infant burials from Yewden Roman Villa to see if there were any more examples. He identified some 'dubious' marks on other bones from the same burial, and in one other skeleton from the site. The finding was so unusual we decided to examine the potential cut marks in more detail using a high-resolution form of CT scanning. CT, computed tomography, is now a fairly standard form of medical imaging. It uses X-rays to build up a three-dimensional picture, which it then renders as sections or 'slices' through the body or body part. It's a fantastic diagnostic tool for doctors working with living patients, but it can also be used to examine human remains, from people who died long ago. My friend Kate Robson-Brown (who had been partly responsible for luring me from surgery into academia, and had also supervised my PhD) had recently acquired a micro-CT scanner for her lab in Archaeology. She'd focused its powerful beam on such diverse subjects as the inner architecture of Neanderthal vertebrae, the structure of ants' nests and a skull fracture in a homicide case. Now we used it to scrutinise the cross-section of those cutmarks on the Roman infant bones.

The resolution of micro-CT is quite mind-blowing. With the machine we were using, each pixel in the image could be as small as 17.55 micrometres. That's equivalent to 570 dots per centimetre, or about 1,450 dots per inch (dpi). With that kind of resolution, we'd be able to look at the profile of the cut in microscopic detail.

The femur from burial 38 had five potential cut marks on it, towards the top of the bone. They were only 3 to 4 millimetres long. Looking at the cross-sections through these cuts with micro-CT, we could see that the incisions were wider than they were deep – so we'd technically describe them as cuts rather than stabs. They were also symmetrical and V-shaped, with smooth sides, suggesting the use of a knife with a straight rather than a serrated edge – and probably made of metal. They were quite uniform, probably made by the same blade. We could also measure the depth of them – they were just 0.55 millimetres deep. There were crumbs of soil in the depths of the cuts – making it likely that the cuts were old, and had been present when the tiny body was buried, rather than having happened more recently.

Having satisfied ourselves that these *were* cut marks, the next question was of course *why* someone would have cut into the thigh of a baby. The length of the bones from burial 38 suggested that the infant had died late in gestation – around thirty-five to thirty-seven weeks. The normal length of a pregnancy is between thirty-eight and forty-one weeks, so this baby is likely to have been delivered a few weeks early. What we can't possibly know is whether the cuts were made before or after the infant died. We had to think of all the possibilities.

There is some evidence for skeletons being 'cleaned' or defleshed in Roman Britain – but there were no other marks on this skeleton. We felt that the location of the cut marks on the femur was an important clue; the position of these incisions, across the back of the upper femur, seemed odd.

There was another possibility that, in the end, we thought was more likely – and that was obstetric surgery. Rather than some strange ritual involving dismembering or defleshing a baby, what if those cut marks reflected a surgical operation carried out to remove a fetus in an intractably obstructed labour? If this is right, the intention was clearly not to save the baby's life – far from it – but it could have been life-saving for the mother.

The precise position of these cuts might suggest that attempts were being made to detach the legs in a breech presentation – where the fetus's hips enter the birth canal first. The surgeon could have been cutting up into the back of the thigh, trying to locate the hip joint. What we cannot tell is whether the fetus was already dead at that point.

A very ancient text – part of the collection attributed to Hippocrates, but in reality drawing together many, some even older, medical treatises – is entitled 'On the Cutting Apart of the Embryo'. This text, which is thought to date from the fourth or fifth century BCE, mentions several such procedures – as a way of dealing with an obstructed labour, where the fetus has become stuck in the birth canal. In one operation, where a fetus's arm has emerged before the head, the surgeon is directed to 'dissect the upper arm and strip its bone bare; bind a fish-skin around two fingers of the hand so that the flesh will not slip away, and after that make an incision all around the shoulder and separate it at the joint' before collapsing the chest of the fetus in order to draw it out. It sounds incredibly gruesome – but those ancient surgeons would have performed such operations hoping to save the mother's life.

Another Hippocratic treatise, called 'Superfetation' – which is actually about problems occurring during the delivery of twins – describes how to extract a dead fetus that has remained in the womb. A hand is inserted into the uterus, to cut apart the fetus, using a knife mounted on a finger-ring, and remove it, piece by piece.

As well as these surgical approaches to traumatic childbirth, there are plenty of references to abortion in the classical literature – revealing various different attitudes. Although the Hippocratic Oath was later considered to represent a professional ban on doctors performing abortions, there don't seem to have been any specific religious or legal injunctions against abortions in the fifth and fourth centuries BCE, although Aristotle stated that fetuses should only be aborted before they developed 'sensation and life' – without defining when that was. In the third and second centuries BCE, opinions diverged. Some philosophers considered that a fetus was part of the mother's body – and should only be considered as a human being once it was born and had taken its first breath. Others – following Aristotle – drew a distinction between the rights of the 'formed' and 'unformed' fetus. And then an inscription from Dionysus's Sanctuary in ancient Philadelphia (modern Turkey) takes a different view, banning anyone who practises or encourages contraception, abortion or infanticide from the temple precinct. References to abortion increase in the first century BCE through to the first century CE, but at the same time, public attitudes seem to become more negative. Ovid writes about an abortion in his book, *Amores*, and criticises the woman for this choice – but then tends towards forgiveness by the end of one poem. He also refers to the instruments involved, making this the first mention of surgical abortion in the literature.

The Greek physician Soranus of Ephesus, living and writing in the first century CE and into the second, describes a familiar controversy around the practice of abortion, with some doctors refusing to offer abortive treatments, 'citing the testimony of Hippocrates who says: "I will give to no-one an abortive"; moreover, because it is the specific task of medicine to guard and preserve what has been engendered by nature'. Others, he says, will prescribe abortives – but only for medical reasons, 'to prevent subsequent danger in parturition' – and not 'because of adultery or out of consideration for youthful beauty'. (He also says that it's preferable – safer – to prevent conception in the first place, rather than to destroy the fetus.) He recommends non-invasive techniques first, such as violent exercise, or riding in a carriage, as well as various ointments, baths and medicines – a meal of lupins, ox bile and absinth is suggested. Soranus is very wary of surgical intervention, writing, 'One must be on guard concerning treatments that are too powerful and of detaching the embryo with some sharp instrument, for there is a danger that the surrounding tissues may be injured.' But at the same time, that very reference to surgical abortion suggests it happened commonly enough to be worth commenting on – bearing in mind that only the social elite would have had access to doctors anyway.

By the third century CE, the attitude to abortion across the Roman Empire was changing, with early Christian writers condemning it as murder. But Roman law around this time seems to have been more concerned with the rights of the parents than with the rights of the unborn child. The focus could lie with the reproductive rights of the father – exiling a woman who aborted a baby after a divorce, for instance – or with the safety of abortifacient drugs for the mother. By the fourth and fifth centuries, with Christianity now the official religion of the Empire, abortion was forbidden. That stringent Christian attitude to abortion has of course continued right up to the present day, in the Catholic Church, the Eastern Orthodox Church and various evangelical branches. Outlawing abortion doesn't mean, of course, that it ceases – but it makes it harder, and presumably more dangerous, for women to access.

It seems that there are two likely explanations for that cut-marked infant femur from Yewden Roman Villa. There's little doubt that this late fetus or early neonate was subject to dismemberment, and this gruesome task may have been carried out as part of a very late abortion, or – perhaps more likely – obstetric surgery for an obstructed labour. What we can never know is whether the mother survived.

There is one other example of what appears to have been embryotomy in Roman Britain – in a full-term infant skeleton from a fourth-century cemetery at Poundbury Camp in Dorset. That skeleton bears many cut marks – including one on the proximal femur. The infant was buried in a small wooden coffin, the normal funerary custom for that time and place. The care taken to bury this tiny body suggests that this death was unexpected, perhaps associated with a traumatic delivery, rather than intentional – though it's impossible to know.

At Yewden, that one cut-marked femur, in one skeleton, with potential cut marks in one other, must also be placed in the context of the very large number of infant burials around the villa complex. The ninety-seven infant burials recorded at the excavations in 1912 seems an extraordinarily high number, and Cocks didn't even excavate the whole site. The high prevalence of infant burials around Romano-British settlements more generally has long been interpreted as evidence of widespread, regular infanticide – with the suggestion that neonates were not considered to be fully human, and so were not mourned – and often disposed of in pits as 'just another item of refuse'.

The idea that infanticide was widespread in the Roman Empire is inspired by historical references to the 'exposure' of infants – essentially, leaving them out to die. But historians have debated just how much this actually happened. So what does the documentary evidence *actually* say?

Greek mythology is certainly full of stories of infants – especially illegitimate offspring of gods – being abandoned at birth (but often surviving to have superhero careers of their own). There's only one legend about exposure from the Roman mythological canon, but it's an important one: the foundation myth of Rome itself. In some versions, Romulus and Remus are simply abandoned. In others, the king Amulius wants to ensure their demise – ordering them to be thrown into the River Tiber. The servants don't quite manage to complete the task, leaving the infants in the shallows at the river's edge. It's a great literary device, introducing jeopardy – and marking the protagonists out as special – survivors against the odds. It's a very common theme in origin stories of heroes, ancient and modern. Harry Potter is nearly slain as a baby by Voldemort. Peter Parker nearly dies from a radioactive spider bite. Tony Stark's heart is struck by shrapnel, before he is transformed into Iron Man. Romulus and Remus are nearly drowned. Subsequently being found and raised by a she-wolf only adds to the sense of drama and magic. But how much does the legend tell us about the reality of exposure and infanticide in ancient Rome? Using myths to reconstruct social mores in the ancient world is like depending on Marvel films to tell us all about modern morals and sensibilities. (I say this as a great fan of the Marvel Universe, which is a rich source of wonderful new myths. But we cannot deny that it is fantastical.)

Roman plays provide another source of evidence; the playwrights Plautus and Terence write about exposure of infants in their dramas, for instance. Some historians have suggested, though, that this could reflect more of a Greek obsession and influence, rather than a common Roman practice. But then, aside from fictional accounts, there are laws and contemporary reports that actually leave us in no doubt about the practice of infanticide and the circumstances under which it which it was condoned – or indeed required. The Twelve Tables of Roman law stipulated that babies born with deformities should be killed at birth. Livy, in his *History of Rome*, mentions an infant of indeterminate sex that was ordered to be drowned. Seneca adds his voice: 'Unnatural progeny we destroy; we drown even children who at birth are weakly and abnormal. Yet it is not anger, but reason that separates the harmful from the sound.'

This legal obligation to kill a deformed child is something which seems utterly abhorrent to us today. It sounds completely, utterly brutal, unashamedly eugenicist. But pause for a moment, and remember that the Romans had no access to antenatal testing, and would not know about birth defects – including any which could be severely life-limiting – until an infant was born.

We must also remind ourselves that our paediatric surgeons' ability to correct defects was unthinkable in Roman times. Indeed, it's unthinkable today in countries without widespread access to advanced healthcare. And even where we have the best neonatal care, there are still times when doctors know there is no remedy, and when parents are faced with that dreadful choice about limiting suffering when faced with inoperable, life-limiting abnormalities. For some Roman parents, without the option of transformative surgery, or indeed, without the material means to care for such a dependent child, neonaticide may have seemed like a humane choice.

Indeed, Soranus – the doctor who wrote about the ethics of abortion – provides us with another clue to attitudes towards infanticide. He recounts that barbarians would plunge newborns into cold water to see if they were worth keeping – a practice he clearly sees as abhorrent. And his careful consideration of the ethics around abortion suggests that Roman doctors did not in fact end the lives of infants lightly. (In one of those connections that tend to surface with increasing frequency over academic and medical careers, I searched for a paper on Soranus and up popped one by the late Peter Dunn – a pathologist who lived across the road from my childhood home, and gave me his half-skeleton to take to medical school with me in 1991.)

In the later, Christian Roman literature, the idea of exposure becomes explicitly abhorrent – a practice that only heathens would consider. As one classicist drily notes, those Christian authors 'speak of exposure as if it had been practised by every unconverted citizen of the Roman world'. In 374, the Christian emperor Valentinian introduced the death penalty for exposure of infants, in Rome. Maybe this was virtue-signalling – making an ancient, pagan practice illegal – or perhaps it suggests that exposure was common enough to require legislation to discourage it.

Surveying all these textual clues, some historians have concluded that infanticide was indeed frequent in the Roman world. But others have sounded a more cautious note – and have pointed out that exposure itself did not always lead to death. There may be something lost in translation here. The Latin word *expositio* is usually translated as 'exposure' – with the implication that an infant is abandoned outside, to the elements – but its original meaning is more like 'place beyond'. Could it be that infants were more often abandoned in the hope that someone else might actually adopt them?

Suetonius, writing in the later first century CE and into the second, provides us with the first specific report of an infant who was exposed – but then survives. That infant was Marcus Antonius Gnipho, who was born in Gaul, exposed (for reasons we are never told) but then found, growing up as a slave. Later freed, he made a name for himself as a scholar – finding employment as Julius Caesar's private tutor. In the same work, in which he recorded the lives of famous grammarians, Suetonius mentions Gaius Melissus – who was freeborn, but abandoned by his parents 'due to a disagreement', then raised as a slave. It seems that there may even have been regular places where babies could be left, making it more likely that they'd survive as a foundling, even if survival then meant a lifetime of slavery. The poet Juvenal provides us with an astonishing insight into a shady world where infants disappear – and reappear. He writes despairingly of upper-class women who 'lie on a golden bed, but eschew the duty of childbirth' – but then somehow fetch potential heirs from 'a muddy lakeside', perhaps a place where foundlings could be left in the hope that they'd be adopted.

Letters between Pliny and Trajan contain discussions about the status of freeborn infants, adopted and raised as slaves, in Bithynia (northern Turkey today). In 315 CE, the emperor Constantine I passed a law which is often seen as an act of Christian piety but which also has resonance with that very modern idea of a welfare state – providing funds for parents who were simply too poor to provide for their children. It proved too much of a drain on the state, however, and Constantine I later reversed it, allowing unwanted infants to be sold into slavery.

Giving up a newborn – with at least a chance of it being found and cared for – may have been more common in poor families and amongst slaves. Illegitimate children and those with obvious birth defects are thought to have been particularly at risk. In wealthier families, exposure may have been used to limit family size – to reduce the number of heirs and stop inheritance being too fragmented. Female babies, it has been suggested, may have been more likely to be rejected – though Roman demographics are too opaque to really test this hypothesis.

Some cases of abandonment may have led to lucky infants being rescued, but it would be obtuse to argue that infanticide didn't happen in the Roman world. Bringing our focus back to Yewden, we need to know whether that very high number of infant burials is beyond what we might expect from natural mortality. At this point, it's worth looking at the levels of infant mortality that exist today, at how things have changed relatively recently, and thinking about differences around the world as well. The very first month of life is the riskiest for a child. In 1990, 5 million babies died within twenty-eight days of being born, around the world. By 2019, that number had more than halved. That global progress is something to be welcomed and celebrated – but there are huge disparities between countries. In 2009, the mortality rate for newborns, expressed as the number of deaths per thousand live births, averaged 27/1,000 in low-income countries, dropping to 7/1,000 in high-income countries. The difference becomes more stark when you look at the countries at the very top and bottom of the range: 43/1,000 in Lesotho and 41/1,000 in Pakistan, but just 1/1,000 in Sweden and Norway. The main causes of death in newborns are pneumonia, birth defects and diarrhoea. Malnutrition is often a contributing factor, but women who have access to continuity of care from professional midwives are 16 per cent less likely to lose their babies than those who don't. These disparities show what a huge difference it makes if families have access to good healthcare, good nutrition and clean drinking water.

Reaching back into the Roman period, we have some text-based evidence to go on – but not much. Most of it comes from age at death recorded on tombstones – but of course this a biased sample, affected by age, social class, location, and variations in mortuary practices and commemoration. The majority of people in the Roman world lived in rural settings, and yet tombstones are much more common in urban environments. We know that tombstones underrepresent infants and children, the rural population, poor people and, indeed, women. One scholar has even pronounced tombstones to be 'useless for understanding Roman patterns of death'. There are other sources of textual information – biographies and death taxes – but these are also heavily biased. Then we have archaeological human remains, of course – but those are biased too. Very often, only part of a cemetery is excavated, giving us a skewed sample of a sample. People may have been buried at different locations in the cemetery depending on age and sex, family relationships, and wealth and status in society. But there's still potential for producing 'model life-tables' based on wide-ranging demographic evidence that we can pull together from modern and historical records, complemented with an epidemiological approach, looking at potential causes of death. The burden of disease in Roman Europe was probably quite similar to that just a few centuries ago, when typhoid, cholera, infections causing diarrhoea and dysentery, pneumonia and TB would have been fairly common, along with sporadic outbreaks of plague, measles and smallpox.

The results of such a model-based approach are rough estimates, of course, but give us some insights into what we might expect patterns of mortality to have looked like in Roman Britain – while remembering that there's considerable variability *within* countries today, and there would have been in the past, too. One researcher has argued that life expectancy at birth could have varied hugely in Roman Italy from around twenty years in some very unhealthy localities to around fifty in others. Cities were 'less healthy' than the countryside. Wealthy people – as today – had much higher life expectancy than those living in poverty.

Bearing in mind that there would have been considerable variation, the average life expectancy at birth in the Roman Empire has been calculated to have been around twenty-five years. This seems really low – but it's dragged right down by high rates of infant and child mortality. Infant mortality, in the first year of life, has been estimated to have been as high as 300–400 per 1,000 – meaning a third of babies wouldn't have made it to their first birthday. The implication of such a high rate of infant mortality is that only half of children would have survived to adulthood. Much of that mortality is concentrated around the time of birth, with an estimated 8 per cent or 80/1,000 perinatal mortality – which includes stillbirths and deaths of infants in their first month of life.

So, parents would have *expected* to lose children. And indeed, naming a new baby in Roman times was traditionally delayed until eight or nine days after birth – something that is seen as a cultural response to the high risk of losing a baby in the first week or so of its life. One twentieth-century classical scholar suggested that 'in a world in which such early deaths and burials were routine, so to speak, the intensity and duration of the emotional responses were unlike modern reactions', though he did then say, 'I confess that I know no way to measure or even to identify the differences.' More recently, a classicist and journalist wrote, very definitely, 'Ancients did not feel about babies as we do. About one in three died within a month, and about half by the age of five.'

It's an untestable hypothesis: that life was more fragile and death in infancy and childhood much more common – and so the depth or length of grief over each loss would be reduced. Other historians and archaeologists have criticised this 'demographic determinism'. Do human emotions correlate so neatly with population statistics? Does that delay in naming a child imply that parents withheld attachment, love and care until they were sure the infant was robust enough to live at least a little longer? As a parent, I can't quite believe it. Though I must confess, that's entirely subjective too – I have no way to measure the differences, either.

There are suggestions in the literature that some parents may indeed have suspended emotional attachment to infants. Cicero wrote, 'If a young child dies, the survivors ought to bear this loss with equanimity; if an infant dies in the cradle, one doesn't even complain.' The Roman lawyer Ulpian recorded that 'children younger than three are not formally mourned, but are mourned in marginal form; a child less than a year receives neither formal mourning nor marginal mourning'. How many parents would have agreed with Cicero? How many mourned, or rather, did not mourn, in the way that Ulpian describes? We simply don't know – but there is also plenty of evidence for grief and pity too. In the *Aeneid*, Virgil describes Aeneas's journey into the Underworld. Having just crossed the Styx, he hears

> *a loud crying of voices . . . the spirits*
> *of weeping infants, whom a dark day stole at the first*
> *threshold of this sweet life, those chosen to be torn*
> *from the breast, and drowned in bitter death.*

There are other expressions of tenderness, love and deep grief for lost infants, found in Roman epitaphs. And then there are criticisms of parents who are too public in their grief. Plutarch, in his letter of consolation to his wife, when they lost their two-year-old daughter, asks her to keep her emotion 'within bounds'; he writes, 'If I find any extravagance of distress in you, this will be more grievous to me than what has happened.' But he doesn't come across as completely cold and callous either. In fact, he writes with immense tenderness about their daughter, and wants to keep her memory alive. There's a particularly beautiful passage where he says, 'I do not see, my dear wife, why these things . . . after delighting us while she lived, should now distress and dismay us as we take thought of them. Rather I fear on the contrary that while we banish painful thoughts we may banish memory as well.' Still, he seems to approve of reports that his wife has exhibited utmost restraint in dealing with the bereavement and has behaved in a decorous manner, organising a simple, no-frills burial. Plutarch's particularly pleased that she's managed to avoid the 'never-sated passion for lamentation, a passion which incites us to transports of wailing and of beating the breast'.

The literature gives us astonishing insights, but also has us squinting through a very narrow lens. Most of that writing is from Italy, focusing on Rome itself – and we're only hearing from the social elite, and actually, mainly from aristocratic men – for whom restraint and self-control, a Roman 'stiff upper lip', seemed incredibly important. (There are still people like this today, of course.) We don't hear from Plutarch's wife herself; we're not hearing any voices from the poor – and certainly not from slaves, who accounted for perhaps a third of the population. And we're talking about human experience here, which by its nature, our nature, is diverse – there is no single, set response to the loss of a pregnancy or a baby today. And there's also a big difference between what any society may expect or condone in terms of behaviour, and how individuals deal with loss and grief privately. Read between the lines of Plutarch's letter, and there's a deeply compassionate man whose focus at that awful time of loss – despite that resolutely stiff upper lip – is his wife's state of mind. It's a protracted letter: a long embrace full of love, support and togetherness – just the two of them, in that moment of grief. And Cicero, for all his buttoned-up stoicism, was utterly devastated when he lost his daughter, who was in her thirties when she herself died in childbirth.

The archaeology of infant and child burials provides us with a counterpoint to the literature. Archaeology shows us behaviour as it actually happened, rather than, perhaps, what was expected. Although the number of burials at Yewden Roman Villa was exceptional, the practice of burying infants in such a setting is not: numerous infant remains have been discovered at Romano-British settlements, and in other parts of the Roman Empire.

The interpretation of such burials has often focused on the disposal of the bodies, assuming that there was little in the way of emotional attachment to those dead babies, as well as linking those burials to the practice of infanticide. The idea that infant burials around buildings could have been more about expedient disposal of a body, rather than a thoughtful funerary ritual, seems to be supported by an apparent absence of infants in formal cemeteries. And it's true that babies are rarely recorded on gravestones. Of 31,000 funerary inscriptions from Rome, for example, less than 0.4 per cent record the deaths of babies under a year old. Some infants do appear on other grave markers – shown in their mothers' arms. Perhaps these reflect deaths of women and their babies during childbirth. But the lack of memorials to infants does not, as one archaeologist puts it, mean those infants were not loved. And it turns out the grave markers underestimate the number of actual burials. A recent, careful study of Roman cemeteries in Italy found many where infants less than a year old were indeed dramatically underrepresented, accounting for only 2 per cent of burials. This could be a sampling problem – infants may appear to be underrepresented in a cemetery which is not excavated in its entirety, but also because of the fragile nature of small bones. In one cemetery, at Saxa Rubra-Grottarossa, the acidic soil meant that infant bones had completely disappeared – all the archaeologists found were small grave pits which they presumed must have contained tiny burials. But there were some Italian cemeteries where the proportion of babies was much higher – around 10 per cent. A cemetery at the port of Velia was extraordinary: infants made up almost a third of the burials – and this probably reflects actual mortality rates. Perhaps less careful standards of excavation in the past led to the assertion that Roman infants were not often buried – and therefore not considered fully 'human'. Perhaps vanishing bones like those at Saxa Rubra-Grottarossa have played into that perception. Infant bones may be missed on excavations – sometimes misidentified as animal bones, too. But this fastidious study of Italian cemeteries reveals a different picture: infants may be statistically underrepresented – but they are absolutely not absent. And neither do the burials speak of peremptory 'disposal' of bodies. Some infants are found buried with objects which emphatically resonate with loss: amulets, beads, cups and coins; even a terracotta doll and a feeding bottle have been found in those Italian babies' graves.

So it seems that infant burials, in the regular Roman out-of-town cemeteries, are not as rare as once thought – at least in Italy. On the other hand, some infants may be 'missing' from cemeteries because of a tradition, like that at Yewden, of burying infants elsewhere – in and around buildings. This practice is seen in Italy, in the later Roman period and then the post-Roman period. But it is even more common in Roman Britain, where in fact the majority of infant burials discovered have been from domestic settings – some under floors inside buildings, others close to walls, on the outside. Rather than demonstrating indifference towards loss of infants, this may simply reflect a more private funerary ritual for ones so young. As one archaeologist has written, these burials do not represent 'the random disposal of the unwanted or marginalised, but [are] the result of careful choices and decisions relating to concepts associated with the physical and spiritual worlds'. At sites like Yewden, the ages of the babies cover a range – from six-month fetuses to around six months of age from birth. The younger fetuses may represent stillbirths.

But this may not all be natural mortality. Simon Mays was the first to undertake a systematic assessment of infant burials in Roman Britain – and he found that the ages at death were very heavily concentrated around the time of birth. This suggested that more infants were dying as newborns than would be expected from natural mortality – supporting an inference of infanticide, or more precisely, neonaticide, contributing to the pattern. A team of other osteologists – Rebecca Gowland, Andrew Chamberlain and Rebecca Redfern – have applied different methods of estimating age at death from the length of long bones, and have argued that the spread of ages is actually much wider. If that's true, then we could be looking at burials of babies who died naturally, in the weeks and months after birth.

The choice of method makes a real difference when interpreting the infant burials from Yewden Roman Villa. Of the ninety-seven infant burials that Alfred Cocks recorded, around a third were boxed up and kept. But none of these remains had been inspected in any detail, until Jill came to reassess the site. Cocks didn't know the ages at death of those infants, but he nonetheless jumped to the conclusion that they were evidence of a nefarious, clandestine practice. He adds a Gothic twist in his report on the site: 'As nothing marked the position of these tiny graves, a second little corpse was sometimes deposited on one already in occupation of a spot, apparently showing that these interments took place secretly, after dark.'

When Simon Mays examined the skeletons in the archive, applying the traditional method of ageing yielded a high peak of mortality around the time of birth – with around 75 per cent of infants dying at thirty-eight to forty weeks of gestation. Simon has argued that this peak was indicative of infanticide – which would be expected to be carried out immediately after birth. This was the same pattern he'd seen at other Romano-British sites: a similar high peak around birth. The alternative method of ageing infant bones flattens the peak – then the spread of ages starts to look more natural – reflecting high perinatal mortality, in those most risky last weeks of pregnancy and first weeks of life. But Simon also applied his technique of ageing infant bones to a medieval burial ground and found a wider spread of ages, with a flatter peak – reflecting a more natural pattern of mortality. So whether or not his method tends to produce a higher peak around birth, there was still a difference in the Roman pattern compared with the medieval one. Simon is careful to say that he doesn't therefore think *all* the babies were victims of infanticide – but if a proportion were, that could explain the pattern.

It seems reasonable to accept that at least some of the babies buried at Yewden Roman Villa could have been victims of infanticide – enough to skew the age range, narrowing it to the weeks around the expected time of birth. However uncomfortable we feel about that interpretation, our discomfort shouldn't lead us to look for more palatable explanations. We can't help but see that practice as barbaric – and criminal. But we have to place it in context. This was a society with no effective or safe methods of birth control. Abortions happened, as attested in the medical literature, but would have been very risky for the mother – and presumably expensive. It is only very recently that women have had access to effective contraception – and to safe abortions. And even with those options available, the reality is that infanticide still happens today. In fact, infants less than twelve months old are more at risk of homicide in modern England and Wales *than any other age group*; their risk is around four times greater than it is for older children. A similar pattern exists in the US, Canada and Australia. We don't talk about it much, as a society, but when we do, it's with complete outrage – especially in the US, where sentences for mothers committing infanticide are much harsher, even where there's clear evidence of depression or psychosis.

In seven out of ten modern criminal infanticide cases, the perpetrator is a parent – and it is just as often the mother as the father that commits the crime. Of genetically unrelated offenders, stepfathers are the most common. The average age of those committing infanticide is young: 26 years. And the babies are most often killed by being shaken, suffocated or otherwise battered – the deaths are fatal outcomes of child abuse. Some happen by negligence; in a third of cases, the carers are intoxicated. It can be very hard to distinguish deaths caused intentionally from those happening accidentally, or from sudden infant death syndrome (SIDS). And it's been suggested that as many as one in ten cases of SIDS may actually be misdiagnosed homicides.

It was during the later Roman period that European society changed its mind about infanticide and exposure – those measures passed from being acceptable and legal in a limited way to being taboo and unlawful. Just as it prohibited abortions, the Church also outlawed infanticide. Christian countries have a history of dealing extremely harshly with women who were found to have committed this crime – often unmarried women who had hidden their pregnancies, then secretly given birth and quickly killed their babies. Although harsh penalties in the sixteenth and seventeenth centuries became more lenient in the eighteenth, the charge of 'newborn child murder' became recorded more frequently in British court records. The phenomenon was surely not new – but the heightened attention to it was. The law was rewritten in 1922 and again in 1938, with some leniency introduced for cases where the mother was found to be suffering from postpartum psychosis.

Infanticide – whether legal or illegal – may be a human universal. At least, it's been recorded in every society where people have looked for it. Demographic historians suspect that infanticide was much more common in Europe, historically, than has previously been acknowledged. A sex ratio at birth of more than 108 males for every 100 females suggests that female babies are being 'selected out' of the population. Studies have uncovered high rates of masculinity – unnaturally high sex ratios – in several historical populations: in seventeenth-century Cambridgeshire and Tuscany, and in the French population before 1800. It would have been easy for parents to disguise neonaticide as a stillbirth; it's still difficult for pathologists to tell the difference. But once you look at a population level, the clues are there. Historians can see patterns which cannot be explained by biological factors alone: suspiciously low rates of twins in baptism records; the ratio of male births to female births increasing in years of famine – particularly in poorer sections of society; high masculinity in rural populations (where boys are valuable as agricultural workers) compared with urban ones (where girls could work in the textile industry) – spotted in seventeenth-century Tuscany. There doesn't seem to be a universal bias against female offspring – instead the reproductive strategy varies according to environmental conditions. As anthropologist Sarah Blaffer Hrdy has written, 'humans, like other animals, use flexible rules to bias invest-ment towards sons in some cases, towards daughters in others. They evaluate contingencies like birth order, offspring quality, available assistance, inheritance prospects . . . There is nothing innate . . . in a preference of one sex over another.'

Given all this historical evidence for infanticide, and the fact that it still persists today, even in countries with access to contraception and abortion, it would be extraordinary if it had *not* happened in Roman Britain. Some cases of infanticide in Roman times would undoubtedly have been carried out by women suffering from postpartum psychosis, just as they are today. Some may have been acts of violence – child abuse taken to its fatal extreme – again, just as we see today in some tragic cases. But in a time before safe abortions, others could have been more rational choices, fulfilling that function of birth control. It's very hard not to be judgmental. But as Jill Eyers wrote in her conclusions about Yewden Roman Villa, 'the first emotion from a modern European society is one of horror – but is it the act of an uncaring society, or population control for a family who care very much for their existing children, and who would not be able to provide for more?'

For Jill, the evidence for infanticide at Yewden rests not on the large number of infant burials in and around the villa – as the area excavated was extensive, and the villa was in use for several centuries – but on that high peak of ages at death around the time of birth. DNA analysis suggests that there were equal numbers of males and females, so the reason for those infanticides doesn't seem to have been linked to reducing the numbers of female offspring.

Jill also tentatively suggested in her report the possibility that part of the villa may have been used as a brothel. River traffic along the Thames, running close to the villa, may have provided a source of customers, and a stream of unwanted pregnancies. Jill pointed out in her report that there were several objects depicting deities found at the site – and all of them were female. There was a small fragment of a pipe-clay figurine showing a woman in a wickerwork chair, nursing a baby – the classic image of a *Dea Nutrix* (nursing goddess). And another fragment of a female figurine – just the head, this time. On the basis of her hairstyle, with a middle parting, braided behind the ears, she could be a little Venus. Such pottery statuettes are well known in Britain and on the continent. They were mass-produced terracotta figurines, made of fine white pipe-clay and pressed into moulds, and ranging from 5 to 20 centimetres in height. They were manufactured in central Gaul, and almost a thousand have been discovered in Britain – most of them goddesses, with Venus being the most popular, but *Dea Nutrix* was also very common. They're thought to have been used in small household shrines. (Animal pipe-clay figurines may also have represented deities – horses for Epona, cockerels for Mercury. But then again, they may have been toys; several have been found within children's graves.) Jill also noted that there was a fragment of a Samian bowl from Yewden with an 'erotic group' pictured on it – though, as she notes, 'one erotic vessel does not make a brothel!'

Another Roman site – at Ashkelon in Palestine – has been interpreted in a similar way. There, the remains of over a hundred neonates were found in a sewer under a fourth-century bath-house. Again, infanticide was proposed as the most likely explanation for such a large number of infants, who all appeared to have died around the time of birth. And the discovery of fragments of oil lamps with erotic scenes on them led again to the suggestion that the bath-house may have been a brothel. (Although, it has to be said, Romans seem to have been generally very fond of erotica – paintings, sculptures, the lot – so the Ashkelon site may well have been an ordinary bath-house. Which is not to say nobody ever went there for sex!) This is all extremely conjectural, though, and using a site from the other side of the Empire as a comparison is stretching it a little – there must have been so much variation in beliefs, attitudes and practices across time and space.

In conversation with me at Yewden, Jill suggested another possibility – that the villa could have been known as a birth centre – somewhere that women knew there were people with experience in midwifery or obstetrics. The buried infants could represent a sort of hospital cemetery. Alternatively, the place could have been somewhere where women could be sent, or could seek help, to terminate pregnancies – or indeed to get rid of unwanted babies, once they were born. These are all possibilities – but there are no documentary sources to suggest any such places existed in Roman Britain. Even if they did, they would surely have been cloaked in secrecy given the increasingly negative attitudes to abortion – and infanticide – in the third and fourth centuries.

While it's interesting to speculate, in the end we may simply be looking at a pattern of high natural mortality together with some infanticides. That seems a reasonable conclusion – based not only on Simon's work on that statistical cluster of the ages of the infants around the time of birth, but also on the fact that, through history, infanticide has been a method of birth control – effectively a very late abortion. What seemed unusual at first sight, then, was simply the norm for the time.

But finally, there is a question remaining about the burials themselves. The large number catches our eye. Only sixteen have been dated, and seem to fall within a narrow date range from around 150 to 200 CE. But this is a small sample, and it's possible that all the infant burials may have been spread over the nearly three centuries that the villa was in use. And in fact, Simon Mays believes that Cocks's original tally of ninety-seven infant burials may also have been exaggerated – including some separated and redeposited bones in the count. But in the end, the number of burials – in an era of high infant mortality – is not so important. It really is that tight cluster of ages around birth that lends weight to an interpretation of infanticide, on top of natural infant mortality. And actually, we don't really need to adduce any additional explanation or invoke peculiar local circumstances to explain the picture at Hambleden. Infanticide in the Roman world was, as Simon has shown, a general and widespread practice.

What that doesn't tell us, though, is what the people who buried those infants were thinking or feeling. It's all too easy to jump to conclusions about how those deaths were understood at the time. Are we really looking at a clandestine activity – infants being interred, 'secretly, after dark', as Cocks put it? Or was burying babies in or close to a house just a perfectly normal tradition – a discrete funerary rite for the very young? Other Roman sites suggest this was the case. And it's not that unusual for infants to be buried in a different way to older children and adults. Historically, many church-yards have had special areas reserved for graves of children. In Ireland, *cilliní* were separate, secular burial sites used for stillborn and unbaptised infants. Looking again at infant burials in Roman Britain, Rebecca Gowland and her colleagues wrote that 'burial within the settlements . . . should not be seen as denigrating to these infants, but instead they were buried within their own social world, close to the people whom their short lives would have affected'.

A more careful reading of both the literature and the archaeological record shows that the stereotype of Romans as not only stoically indifferent to infant mortality, but also particularly callous and enthusiastic about infanticide compared with later Christian cultures – and indeed, modern-day Britain – doesn't really stack up any more. The picture is far more nuanced – and varied. We emerge with a different picture of the Romans. Perhaps we've enjoyed painting them as barbaric. Perhaps our interpretations have been clouded by a certain, lingering Christian horror of all things pagan.

I think we need to start recognising and expecting a diversity of human experience and practice in the past – and not to become too stereotyped in our portrayals of ancient people. Not to say 'the Romans were barbarous, cold and callous and regularly practiced infanticide', or to flip the other way and argue that they never killed babies at birth. It's a false dichotomy. Human experience is always more diverse than that.

And this is the thing about the Ancients. They are much more like us than we like to think. They were shaped by their culture just as we are shaped by ours today. They were diverse, just as we are today. We each respond to life events in lots of different ways – and we might respond differently at different times in our own lives. Some of us will be more stoical, more practical. Some will be more sanguine about difficult choices. Some may be able to move on and forget, or at least accommodate a loss – planned or unplanned – more easily. Others might need time to pause, to mourn, to contextualise and understand what the loss of a fetus or an infant means. It's important not to paint those ancient people as having *one* particular mentality. Even at Yewden – that single locality – those babies would have been born to women who all had different reactions and different experiences. And we need to remember that diversity. This is what links us back to them.

We might say that, generally, our sensibilities are different to those operating back in Roman times. But that is generalising. The broad-brush picture masks the diversity and complexity that would have existed. Some of those babies may have been victims of infanticide, perhaps for economic reasons, because a family couldn't afford to support any more children. Some of them may have been pregnancies that were unwanted for other reasons. Some may have been stillborn. Some may have died naturally soon after birth. We just don't know, but what we can be sure of is that the stories for each of those lost infants would have been different, and the stories of each of their mothers would have been different as well.

It can be so difficult to escape our own cultural lens, to remember that there are so many rituals and practices that we engage in, sometimes for no other reason than 'it's just what we do'. Rituals that are dissimilar to our own stand out – and it may be hard to shake off the idea that those other people are doing something weird, irrational, callous, or even macabre – because it's so different to what we'd do. To Alfred Cocks, the burial of infants in and around the villa seemed so strange, he simply couldn't accept it as a normal practice.

Perhaps it's easier for us to imagine, today. There's been a recent shift in our approach to memorialising perinatal mortality in Britain. This may be influenced by the use of ultrasound scans – where, for the first time in history, parents are able to *see* their baby before it is born. There's also been an increase in ceremonies, sometimes including a burial, for dead fetuses. Before the 1980s, it was standard practice for hospitals to dispose of miscarriages and stillborn babies, sometimes with the mother not even being asked whether she wanted to see or hold her baby. Many were buried in unmarked plots or even mass graves. Now parents are better supported, and can make their own choice about how to say goodbye.

My friend Pip lost her third baby before he was born. She knew that her baby was dead before she gave birth to him. Pip and her husband hadn't thought about what they were going to do afterwards. But then, when they were asked, they realised that what they wanted to do was bring him home. It wasn't a funeral, she said — it was a homecoming. They buried him in their garden, in the orchard. Their other two children helped to bury him and plant a tree on his grave.

An echo of an ancient practice. The baby was part of the family, part of the family tapestry. And he is not forgotten.

3.

OFF WITH THEIR HEADS

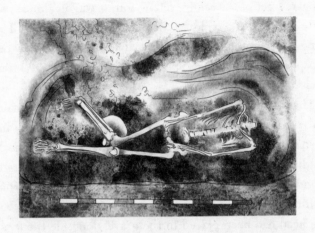

In the summer of 2018, archaeologists were excavating a field near the village of Great Whelnetham, near Bury St Edmunds in Suffolk. The site had been earmarked for a new housing development. The team, from Archaeological Solutions, were expecting that they might find some Roman archaeology – but they hadn't anticipated at all just how strange and macabre their finds would turn out to be.

They'd started with some preliminary investigations the year before, when they'd found pits containing occasional pieces of Roman pottery, and in one, a fragment of a brass or bronze bracelet. And they'd also come across a number of graves. They were working to the south of a known Roman settlement – so this looked like another one of those typical out-of-town cemeteries.

In 2018, a field team led by Kerrie Bull returned to the site for the full excavation, uncovering evidence of earlier quarrying before the area became used as a cemetery. Five weeks into the excavation and a very odd-looking burial appeared out of the sandy, yellow soil. It was an almost complete skeleton of a child aged three or four. But its skull was lying between the bowed-out legs. The body had clearly been decapitated, with the head placed into the grave in this bizarre position.

Then another headless burial was unearthed, a female – and accompanied by an extra pair of feet, which may have been from another, truncated grave. Then there was another headless burial, and another. Eventually the archaeologists found seventeen decapitated individuals – making up around a third of the burials in the cemetery. In several of these, the head had been placed in the grave alongside the legs or feet. Another third of the burials contained skeletons with skulls in the normal place, but with the bodies lying in unusual positions – flexed, crouched or even prone: face down in the sandy soil. Some of those prone burials were also decapitated.

Most of the individuals in the Great Whelnetham cemetery were adults, middle-aged or older, with roughly equal numbers of males and females. Only six of the skeletons were juveniles, less than eighteen years old (including the young child with its head between its legs), but there were also separated, disarticulated bones which could have been the remains of ten more infants or young children. Altogether, those juvenile remains made up about a quarter of the total number of the individuals in the cemetery, a similar proportion to that seen in other Roman burial grounds in the region.

There were very few grave goods amongst all these burials – but luckily, two double-sided antler combs were distinctive enough to provide a date for the cemetery: the end of the fourth century, towards the end of Roman rule in Britain. But what on earth did all those odd burials – the bodies interred face down, and all those with their heads removed and rearranged – signify?

The normal burial custom in western Europe, from the Roman period onwards, was for bodies to be laid in the grave, with or without a coffin, stretched out and supine – not prone. And not headless. Strange burials like this tend to be referred to as 'deviant burials' – or just 'irregular'. If we want to attempt to understand what meaning accompanied this practice, which seems so ghoulish to us today, we must first look at the wider context. And while the Great Whelnetham cemetery is quite extraordinary in terms of the sheer number of irregular burials it contained, it's certainly not the first time that such odd interments have been discovered in Romano-British cemeteries.

Archaeologist Belinda Crerar was so intrigued by ancient headless burials that she chose to focus on this subject for her PhD. She analysed the evidence from Britain, and looked at how interpretations of these discoveries had changed through time.

Some of the first decapitation burials to be recorded in Britain were excavated by the pioneering archaeologist Augustus Pitt Rivers, from Romano-British sites on his Cranborne Chase estate (there's much more on Pitt Rivers in my earlier book on prehistoric burials, *Ancestors*). Various other decapitated burials were reported in the late nineteenth century – most of them Romano-British. Discoveries continued sporadically in the twentieth century, with archaeologists fairly quick to ascribe spooky motives for decapitation. Excavating a Romano-British cemetery at Guilden Morden, Cambridgeshire, in 1935, the English archaeologist (and parapsychologist) T. C. Lethbridge came across a decapitated burial of a woman with an arthritic hip. In his report, he wrote, 'I suggest, though this may appear fanciful, that this lame woman had been decapitated after her death to ensure that her spirit – perhaps bad-tempered owing to her infirmity – should not walk and haunt her relatives.' He went on to discover another decapitated female burial. 'One wonders', he wrote, 'whether both these women had been witches.' In 1947, the archaeologist J. B. Calkin excavated two Romano-British burials at Kimmeridge, on the coast of Dorset, including one where the lower jaw or mandible had been removed – which he suggested might have been done to prevent the dead individual from speaking to the living.

In the 1960s and 1970s, archaeology was changing – in a more scientific direction. And those working in the field were very aware of this shift. Perhaps more than most disciplines, archaeology has developed an acute self-awareness of its own philosophical underpinnings, verging on the shoe-gazingly introspective. The new theoretical framework emerging in the 1960s was snappily called 'processualism', and its proponents, the 'New Archaeologists', began to look at burials from a socio-logical perspective, attempting to understand how funerary rites might have related to social identities during life. This was when the word 'deviant' started to be used, to describe burials which were seen as a departure from the 'norm' (whatever that

72

was at the time). But it also implied that the deviancy went further – that a deviant burial reflected deviant behaviour during life. And this is particularly difficult because the word 'deviant' has that double meaning in modern English – it means something that deviates from the norm, but it can also mean something sinister. Just using the word could encourage us to think about these burials as not just unusual, but in some way troubling. So the New Archaeologists may have made some progress, but in reality this doesn't get us much further than Lethbridge with his cry of 'Witch!'

During these same decades, several large Roman cemeteries were excavated in Britain, and within them, more evidence of decapitated burials came to light. At Lankhills, in Winchester, excavation revealed 451 graves dating to the late Roman period, the fourth century CE. Amongst them were seven decapitated burials which seemed to be associated with higher-status graves. It was suggested that the headless burials could have been symbolic human sacrifices, perhaps involving ritually 'killing' an already dead person, to somehow honour another, more eminent individual. At Cirencester, six decapitated individuals, with their heads placed back close to their necks, were interpreted as victims of execution. But although archaeologists were coming up with new theories, each site seemed to be its own island of interpretation, without any systematic attempts to link up the evidence and look for wider patterns.

In the 1980s and 1990s a new fashion swept through British archaeology: the even more snappily titled 'post-processualism'. Its adherents rejected straightforward links between burial practice and social patterns, recognising the agency of individuals to create culture – not just to slavishly reflect it. And they also questioned just how objective archaeology could ever really claim to be. We always peer at the past through our own, inescapable cultural lens, after all.

What post-processualism did for burial archaeology was important. It encouraged a much more nuanced approach, suspicious of uniformity. One-size-fits-all explanations were out of vogue – instead, there was now an expectation of a diversity of cultural expression. Before this, ethnographic studies – drawing on different cultures around the world – had been used to suggest particular interpretations for burial archaeology. Now, those ethnographic examples were used to draw attention to just how *difficult* it was to draw inferences – without knowing a whole lot more about the structure of past societies and their belief systems.

And yet the whole exercise of interpretation was not considered to be entirely futile. Particularly when it comes to Roman burial rites, we do have some documentary evidence to draw on, which tells us about social systems – and beliefs, too, of course. It's true that much of this written evidence relates to life (and death) in Rome itself, and may not be simply transferable to the far-flung edges of the Empire – but at least it's a useful lead. Indeed, in some cases it can be extremely useful – as it did for the interpretation of the pipe burial at Caerleon. Unfortunately, when it comes to prone and decapitated burials – it's no help at all. Roman authors were silent on these practices. Into this void, a great range of different explanations have been put forward as suggestions. In recent decades, analyses of Romano-British deviant burials have unleashed a plethora of varying theories, each new discovery being grasped as an opportunity for fresh interpretation.

In a Romano-British cemetery in Stanwick, Northamptonshire, excavated in 1991, one grave contained the skeleton of a man in his thirties, buried in a prone position – and with a stone wedged inside his mouth. This was something completely unique – never seen before. Simon Mays (yes, him again) investigated the case and looked for clues in the literature, tracking down later Germanic laws which prescribed cutting out the tongue of an offender who had spread malicious gossip. But the replacing of the tongue with an object – if that's what had happened in this grave – takes it a step further. Was the stone in the mouth intended to replace a missing body part, in a seemingly respectful way, or was it an insult – replacing living flesh with an inanimate object, sealing the punishment in the grave? Regretfully, I don't think we'll ever know.

Individual burials – even clusters of irregular burials within a cemetery – have each added a little more to the picture. But some researchers attempted a more systematic approach. In 2005, Swedish osteologist Caroline Arcini became intrigued by a photograph from a Viking cemetery excavated in the 1950s. The photograph showed a prone burial, the skeleton 'lying in the grave in a position like a frightened spider', as Arcini put it. She checked her own reaction to the burial – 'Why did I react as if there was something wrong with this position?' she asked herself. Presenting the case to other people, outside archaeology, she found that 'the reaction was the same: buried face down did not appear to be culturally acceptable. Buried face upwards, on the side, or sitting was accepted, but face down was unthinkable.'

And so she started to search more widely, realising she was the first person to attempt a systematic survey of such burials – through time and across different countries. She ended up looking at data from 615 cemeteries – tracking down reports of prone burials in many different cultures around the world, from prehistoric times to the twentieth century. The earliest example she could find was an astonishing 26,000 years old, from the Czech Republic. The most recent was from a First World War grave in Flanders. Once she'd collected all the data, Arcini could clearly see that there were periods of time when prone burials were more common in the archaeological record – with a particular peak in the first millennium CE.

Through time, most prone burials were of adult men – but there were also women and children amongst them. Most graves were single, but some were double or even multiple. In cemeteries which contained several prone burials, they tended to be clustered together, often around the periphery. Although the graves dug for these prone burials were often shallow, they didn't look 'careless'. So they didn't seem to represent bodies which had been hastily thrown into graves – just happening to fall face down – as you might expect during an epidemic, for instance. Instead, the positioning of the body in most prone burials appeared to be a clear decision, a deliberate act.

More recently, anthropologist Marco Milella and his colleagues conducted another large survey, but focusing in particular on the centre of the action: the Roman period, from the first to the fifth centuries, in western Europe. They tracked down nearly 400 irregular burials – and then looked for patterns which could provide some level of explanation for the phenomenon.

They found that, while decapitated bodies had sometimes been buried with grave goods, and with evidence of coffins being used, prone burials were more often coffin-less and unac-companied by any artefacts. Milella argued that the inclusion of grave goods implied a certain consideration for the dead – so perhaps we shouldn't assume that decapitation is always a disrespectful act. The lack of grave goods with prone burials, though, could suggest that this type of interment was usually denigratory.

Importantly, what this study revealed was a very definite geographical focus for these burial practices – with around three quarters of these Roman-period irregular burials found in Britain. Prone burials were seen across western Europe, though more frequently in Britain – and with the removal and rearrangement of heads being something that was particularly concentrated in southern Britain. Occasionally, the two practices overlapped – just as they did at Great Whelnetham.

Is it possible that this concentration of irregular burials means that these strange burial rites actually *originated* in Britain – perhaps even before the Romans arrived? Could this be a surviving Iron Age cult?

For a very long time, there's been a theory that head-hunting – with heads being taken as battle trophies in particular – was rife in Iron Age Britain. This 'Cult of the Head' idea comes from the Romans – writing about their barbarian neighbours, the Gauls.

The Greek historian Polybius, writing in the second century BCE, described the Punic War of the previous century. The Carthaginian general Hannibal led his army through what is now modern Spain and France, picking up more Gallic forces on the way, and into Italy – to take on the might of Rome. When Hannibal reached northern Italy, other Gallic troops, who had been fighting alongside the Roman army, saw the way things were going and decided to switch sides. Early in the morning, they fell upon the Roman soldiers camped next to them. Having slaughtered their previous comrades, the Gauls proceeded to cut the heads off the betrayed slain, before walking over to the Carthaginian side.

In the first century BCE, the Sicilian historian Diodorus described various aspects of Gallic culture, including their penchant for cutting off the heads of vanquished enemies. The Gauls would return from battle with those cadaveric heads strung from the necks of their horses, he reported, and then they'd nail them up on their houses, just like hunting trophies. But if the enemy had been held in particularly high esteem, the dead head would be preserved in cedar oil and kept in a chest, to be shown to guests – how delightful. And the Gaul would emphasise just how precious that head was – and that it would not be parted with, not for its weight in gold.

In the following century, the Greek geographer and historian Strabo wrote a very similar description – almost word for word. He revealed his source for this information: the earlier Greek writer Posidonius, who visited the southeast corner of Gaul in the early first century BCE. Posidonius's original works are all sadly lost – perhaps in the book burnings that accompanied the spread of Christianity through the Roman Empire – but some of his content is thankfully transmitted through later writers, like Strabo. And we have to presume Diodorus had a copy of Posidonius on his shelves as well.

Diodorus also wrote that, after the Battle of the Allia in 390 BCE, just before they ransacked Rome itself, the Senones (Gauls originally hailing from the Seine basin) spent a day cutting the heads off the dead – as was, apparently, their custom.

Yet another mention of Gauls taking heads as trophies comes from Livy, in his *History of Rome*. He describes how, in the third century BCE (three centuries before he was writing), the general Lucius Posthumius and his army were attacked by a Gallic tribe called the Boii in the forest of Litana in northern Italy. Of twenty-five thousand men entering the forest, scarcely ten escaped, writes Livy – and Posthumius was not one of them. The Boii cut off his head and carried it, along with other spoils of war, to their sacred temple. There, they cleaned up the head – presumably stripping it down to bare bone and breaking off the skull cap or calvarium – covered it in gold, and made it into a cup to be used by priests for libations, and for drinking out of.

These mentions of head-hunting and rituals involving the heads of enemies are shocking to us today – and would have been just as shocking for civilised Greeks and Romans. (Although Strabo does mention that Posidonius loathed the head-hunting when he first saw it, but then got used to it!) But can we really trust these Roman authors? It's certainly possible that these accounts are embellished, or even fabricated, to create a stereotype of Gauls as dreadful barbarians desperately in need of being civilised. It could simply be Roman propaganda. Even if they are at all factual, they focus on specific cultural practices in what is now France and northern Italy, taking place in the latter half of the first millennium BCE. And yet those sources have been used to argue for a Cult of the Head extending right across northern Europe, and persisting for centuries. It's perhaps pertinent that other classical writers who describe historical events in both France and Britain don't mention any such practices. There's no account of head-hunting, or anything which sounds like a special Cult of the Head, in Julius Caesar's memoirs of the Gallic Wars. Neither does Tacitus allude to any traditions like it in his biography of his father-in-law, the governor of Britain, Agricola.

But while the documentary evidence is dubious or lacking – especially for Britain itself – there is actually some pictorial evidence for heads of enemies being carried off. Osteologist and anthropologist Katie Tucker – who also did her PhD on headless burials – tracked down Iron Age images of decapitations. A coin of the king Cunobelinus, who ruled in southeast England in the early first century CE, shows a male figure carrying a head. There's a very similar coin of Dubnorix from nearby Gaul, dating from the first century BCE. And a fragment of pottery, also from Gaul, shows a horse rider, carrying a spear, with a severed head hanging from his horse's neck – just as Diodorus and Strabo recounted.

Whether or not all this represents a somewhat mystical or sinister Cult of the Head depends on your perspective. Polybius and Posidonius seem to have viewed the collection of enemy heads as barbaric – when barbarians were doing it. But there's actually plenty of evidence that the Romans were at it too. There are mentions of heads being chopped off, and stuck on lances to be paraded around, in the writings of Julius Caesar, Livy, Suetonius and others. There are also some gruesomely detailed descriptions of beheadings. Lucan goes into some detail in his epic poem about the Civil War which ends with Pompey's beheading and that inadequate cremation on the Egyptian shore. Pompey boards an Egyptian boat, where he's assassinated by two men, Achillas and Septimius. Achillas drives a sword into Pompey's side. Septimius grabs Pompey's head – he's still breathing at this point – and bends his neck back over one of the seats in the boat, before hacking through from the front with his sword, severing blood vessels and tendons, until he reaches the spine and cuts through that. Then the head is handed over to a lackey to be taken off and presented to the Egyptian king, leaving the headless body on the shore.

There are numerous other reports of execution by beheading – a fate which befell traitors in the Roman army, criminals and Christian martyrs – and even one Roman emperor, Constantius Gallus, in 354 CE. Most beheadings were carried out with a sword, some with an axe.

As well as this documentary evidence for Roman beheadings, there are plenty of graphic images too. Trajan's Column shows soldiers cutting the heads off slain enemies and presenting them to the emperor, as well as heads being carried by auxiliary troops in battle and skewered on poles on the walls of Roman forts. Other friezes and columns depict similar scenes. And a coin of the Republican official M. Sergius Silus, dating to 116 or 115 BCE, clearly shows a soldier on horseback – carrying a severed head.

Statues of particularly unpopular leaders, or old deities indeed – once Christianity takes hold – appear to get the same treatment, with their heads being knocked off – or being literally de-faced. In Britain, a bronze head of Nero was found in the River Alde near Saxmundham, Suffolk, in 1907. It's tempting to imagine – though impossible to prove – that it was knocked off a statue by one of Boudica's fellow revolutionaries. There's a difference between defacing statues and beheading humans, of course. But there are graphical records of what looks undeniably like decapitation from Roman Britain, too. Among them, there's a stone slab from West Lothian, showing the body of a decapitated Briton being trampled by a Roman cavalryman; and a tombstone from Lancaster that depicts a Roman cavalryman managing to control his horse whilst holding both a sword and a severed head in his right hand.

And a strange little brass or bronze knife handle from Lincolnshire depicts a curious little erotic, fetishistic scene, in 3D, with a woman and two men — one of whom appears to be holding a severed head.

I may have started by being sceptical about the tales of headhunting told by Roman authors, but in fact there's a mass of evidence, both documentary and graphical, which points to a practice of removing heads from bodies — usually in a military context — not only in Roman Britain, but elsewhere in the Roman Empire and earlier, in Iron Age Britain too. Archaeological evidence seems to corroborate the texts and images, to an extent. And some of the finds are very weird indeed.

One curious burial discovered in Rome in the nineteenth century contained a body with its head cut off and placed between the legs – but a plaster mask of the dead man's face lay where the head originally belonged. Four burials in a vault in Cumae, from the third century, were found with the original skulls completely missing, replaced by wax replicas with glass eyes. These seem to represent an entirely separate class of decapitated burials – ones which could perhaps reflect a less martial, more mysterious of Cult of the Head.

Several other decapitation burials have been found at various sites in Italy, with heads lying at the hips, between the legs, or at the feet – like so many in Britain. There are a few similar examples from France, a completely headless burial from Germany, and one from Serbia – again, with the skull nestling on the legs. Some from Israel have been interpreted as victims of executions. Skulls found in pits or ditches around settlements at various locations could have ended up there after being displayed.

Looking around for disconnected heads in British prehistory, Tucker found very little evidence for decapitation or heads being moved around in the Bronze Age. But in the Iron Age, which lasted from 800 BCE up to the Claudian invasion in 43 CE, she found 112 instances, across 61 sites. In nearly half of the cases, the decapitations were represented by isolated skulls and mandibles – just what you'd expect if heads were being taken from dead bodies as trophies. Two crania, from two separate sites, had been detached in a very careful way – but there was no evidence that these heads had been kept for any length of time before being buried. Some of the more roughly detached skulls, though, had been modified in ways that suggest they may have been displayed. There are several with holes drilled into them – possibly to allow them to be hung up. There are others where the dome of the skull has been detached from the facial skeleton and skull base – possibly to create a 'skull-cup'. Nevertheless, such examples are rare – it's still hard to argue for a widespread Cult of the Head in Iron Age Britain. Other instances of decapitation from the Iron Age involved burials without heads. And then, in around a third of cases, heads had been severed, but buried with the rest of the body. Around three quarters of the individuals in question were adult men. In most cases, the head had been chopped off the body with blows to the back of the neck.

So there's evidence – textual, graphical and archaeological – of heads separated from bodies in the British Iron Age, in Roman Britain – and elsewhere in the Roman Empire. But what do all these separated heads and decapitated burials mean? That's a tricky question. We get some perspective on it from those broader studies which bring many examples together, through time and space. But it may be that this amassing of the data also throws us off course. In particular, by sticking all the headless burials, decapitated burials and isolated skulls together – all our eggs in one basket – we may be missing important clues. As already hinted at in the old texts and the images on coins and gravestones, we could be actually be looking at several different types of funerary or mortuary practice, and different causes of death.

There's surely one very important distinction to be drawn – dividing these archaeological cases into two broad categories, before we go any further. That distinction rests on whether the individual in question was alive or dead at the point when their head was cleaved from their body. Some heads may have been removed from dead bodies as trophies, as evidence of the death of a particular enemy, as warnings to remaining enemies, and perhaps some were even curated as relics, and kept in cedar boxes. But the separation of other heads may have been the cause of death itself. How can we possibly tell the difference between decapitation of a dead body and execution by beheading?

Looking at a skull which has become detached from the spine in a grave, we must first be sure that we really are observing human intervention. What has to be ruled out initially is a skull moving around in the grave, without any human help. And they often do, especially in coffins, where the body may decay extensively before the wood crumbles, falls in and disintegrates. The decay of soft tissues – the muscles, tendons, ligaments and fascia – that bind everything in place during life renders a skeleton into a set of separate bones which may simply settle into a final resting position with gravity. That might explain why a mandible falls away from the cranium, or why the skull rolls to one side. But other living organisms – not only humans – can play a role moving things around as well. Maggots can rearrange a body quite effectively, if flies have managed to lay their eggs in it before it is sealed away. Worms can move things around and bring soil in. Larger organisms like rats or even otters (see my book *Ancestors* for examples of both of these potential tomb dwellers) can cause even more mixing and muddling. There's a great word for this taphonomic phenomenon where living organisms interfere with a burial like this: *bioturbation*.

But a skeleton that looks otherwise undisturbed – with its

skull between its legs? The only real bioturbating agent to reasonably suspect in this case is a human one.

The next question to answer, then, is whether the head really was removed from its body *post mortem* – or whether decapitation was the cause of death: a beheading, in other words. This is actually quite a tricky question – and one that Katie Tucker tackled as part of her PhD, examining over 500 Romano-British 'decapitation' burials. There aren't always any cuts to see, and when there are, it's impossible to tell the difference between cuts made on the skeleton just before death and those made soon after. Neither will show any evidence of healing, even when examined close up, under the microscope.

The direction of approach has been suggested as providing a clue – with beheading more likely to attack the back of the neck, and decapitation more likely to be done from the front. But that distinction is untrustworthy. There's more than one way to skin a cat, and more than one way to cut off someone's head. But the degree of force employed and the type of weapon used are important clues. A beheading is very unlikely to be carried out delicately, with a knife, and much more likely to involve a sword or an axe deployed with violent force.

The most extreme example Tucker found was the skeleton of an individual who'd had his head – and there really is no other word for it – hacked off. The burial was in a small Roman cemetery in Andover. The bones were those of a middle-aged man, in his late thirties or early forties, who had been interred in a coffin, positioned on his left side. There were some objects in the grave – hobnails at his feet, from his boots, a couple of coins and an iron knife. This all suggests he was placed into the grave fully clothed. His skull was placed down level with his knees in the coffin.

Tucker described the trauma on the skeleton in appalling detail:

> There were at least two separate incisions to the anterior of the bodies of C_3–C_5 [the third to fifth cervical vertebrae in the neck] at a sharply right-superior to left-inferior angle, as well as ten separate chops affecting C_3–T_3 [from the third cervical vertebra down to the third thoracic vertebra], five chops to the mandible, four chops to the right clavicle, as well as chops through the manubrium and corpus sterni [parts of the sternum or breastbone] and the right rib 1 [the uppermost rib], which were delivered from a number of different directions . . . [and] a chop to the anterior of the right glenoid fossa of the scapula [shoulder blade].

The violence recorded in those bones, severing the head from the body, and which may well also been the cause of death, is quite shocking.

Tucker found around fifty other examples – from both rural and urban cemeteries – where the head had been removed with similar multiple chopping blows, if not as extreme as the example from Andover. And there were a further fifty or so examples where heads had been removed with a single chopping blow. In around two thirds of these cases, the severing blow had been to the back of the neck. In a small number, the pattern of the chop marks showed that the neck was flexed when the blow fell – a position that is, as Tucker writes, 'virtually impossible to achieve in a corpse lying prone on the ground'. In such a case, we can reasonably infer that decapitation was the cause of death – a beheading. The position of the head lends weight to that interpretation: in some cases, following the single-blow decapitation, the body was placed in the grave with the head lying on the chest, or even back in its anatomical position: the skull may have still been attached to the neck and torso by soft tissue. The aim in these cases was not the detachment and rearrangement of the head *per se* – but the death of the individual. (In contrast, for whoever dispatched the man from Andover, separating that head from the body was clearly extremely important.) The Romano-British examples are also very similar to later medieval skeletons from what have been interpreted as 'execution cemeteries', where heads have almost always been cut off by one or more blows to the back of the neck, and where skulls are often found placed in the grave by the knees or feet.

Some of the skeletons that Tucker surveyed showed evidence for traumatic wounds in other places on the skeleton – on forearms and hands, which are likely defensive injuries; a blunt blow to the skull; a piercing injury through the abdomen, leaving a stab mark on the front of the sacrum. Again, the violence recorded in these particular skeletons strongly suggests beheading as the cause of death, rather than something which was carried out *post mortem*.

Amongst the skeletons, there seemed to be clear distinctions between different types of decapitation. There were those where the head was separated by one or more chopping blows, usually to the back of the neck – which Tucker thought probably represented judicial executions. But it's also possible that some violently chopped decapitations may have been carried out – not as the cause of death, but as a '*post mortem* punishment' after the individual had been executed in another way. Some skeletons showed signs of heads being roughly detached, even violently wrenched off – damaging the skull, mandible, spine or clavicle in the process.

There's also a possibility that decapitation could have been associated with human sacrifice. A small number of cases show evidence of the throat having been slit, with the blade just cutting into the front of the vertebrae of the neck. On the other hand, those cuts could have been made as a head was detached from a dead body. And even if some were indeed sacrifices, this evidence is very rare. Strabo described the Gauls performing human sacrifices – something the Romans stamped out once they took over the territory, apparently. But this really could be Roman propaganda – it's certainly not an eyewitness account.

Not all of the decapitated burials showed such signs of violence or extreme force – far from it. In fact, the large majority revealed something completely different: very careful dissecting of the head from the body; the paring away of soft tissues until the bones could be separated. This type of decapitation reminds me of the process for removing a head in the dissection room – a precise operation involving cutting away layers of muscle and fascia, until the joints and ligaments around the spine in the neck are accessible and can be divided. Seeing evidence of careful dissection in some of these archaeological skeletons – leaving shallow, incised cuts on cervical vertebrae – suggests that decapitation in these cases was a meticulous process, almost certainly carried out after death, rather than being the cause of death. In these cases, it doesn't appear a violent act, intended as an insult or punishment, but part of a more respectful burial rite, perhaps.

Although decapitated burials peak in the Roman period, Crerar suggests this type of practice could have evolved out of a wider tradition in the Iron Age of fragmenting dead bodies. Her own analysis supported a more rural focus to some extent;

she found more decapitation in one of her case study sites, along the Fen Edge in Cambridgeshire, compared with London. Perhaps we're more likely to see ancient traditions persisting in rural areas, rather than in the Romanised cities. Are we also glimpsing a difference here between the pagan countryside and civilised Romans in cities as they adopted the new religion of the Empire, Christianity? That argument is problematic, as Crerar points out. It involves an assumption that Christian burials would never involve dismemberment of a corpse – that the integrity of the body was always important, to all Christians. But in fact those decapitated burials appear to have become *more* frequent at precisely the time when Christianity was spreading in the Roman Empire, in the third and fourth centuries. And anyway, burial customs and religious beliefs do not go along so neatly hand in hand. The devil is in the detail, as always: there was actually plenty of other evidence of bodies being fragmented in Roman London – just not quite so much decapitation. Other studies have found less of a difference between rural and urban settings. With that potential lead drying up, the peak of decapitated burials in late Roman Britain – with at least five hundred examples known, not even counting isolated skulls – is still a phenomenon which demands explanation.

Back in 1991, another researcher, Robert Philpott, also completed a PhD looking at Roman burial practices. In it, he dedicated a whole chapter to decapitated inhumations, and he'd also divided up decapitations into different categories, proposing a simple system of interpretation: a skeleton missing a skull implied that a head had been taken as a trophy in battle; a decapitated head restored to its anatomical position in the grave represented an executed criminal; a cranium that had been carefully cut off, from the front, and placed elsewhere around the body was evidence of a funerary ritual carried out on a dead body. Some decapitated and rearranged burials also contained grave goods – again suggesting the deceased was being treated with respect, rather than with fear. (This is tricky, though – as those interring the body – and its head – may not have been those who performed the beheading or decapitation. You can imagine, for instance, the family of a beheaded criminal burying their executed relative with care.)

Other researchers picked up on the potential for positive interpretations of decapitated burials. In 2000, decapitated burials discovered in Kempston, Bedfordshire, were described as either possible guardians of the cemetery, or symbolic 'warrior burials'. But despite those more positive spins, decapitated burials are still very often interpreted in a negative light – either as symbols of social deviancy in life, or invoking fear of something much more sinister. It seems we can't quite escape the abhorrence *we* feel when we see them, just as Caroline Arcini had articulated when she saw that photograph of the Viking decapitated burial. They just seem *wrong* to us.

But as the post-processual archaeologists realised, we have to be self-aware when trying to understand past cultures (or indeed, other contemporary cultures around the world today that diverge from our own). We bring our own culture with us when we look at any others. What might seem odd, unusual or even macabre to us may not have been seen that way in the past. The Ashanti people of west Africa used to deflesh their dead kings, rendering them skeletal, before reassembling their bones with gold wire. Members of the Hapsburg-Lorraine royal family who died away from home were reputedly boiled in wine before being gutted and defleshed, leaving just their skeletons to be conveyed home. (This is probably a very sensible alternative to attempting to transport a complete corpse that would have started to rot fairly quickly.) Although these customs strike us as bizarre, the Ashanti and Hapsburg-Lorraine royals would undoubtedly have raised an eyebrow at our most common funerary custom in Britain today: burning the dead in gas incinerators and grinding up their calcined bones to a fine powder afterwards.

Language stymies us too. Using the word 'deviant' implies that burials we label in this way are somehow 'not normal'. But then, what *is* normal? There's not a single approach to funerary rites from which those burials represent a departure. They represent particular variants within a range of diverse approaches.

It's very possible that what strikes us as unusual today – prompting us to label it 'deviant' – was simply not seen that way at the time. Decapitated burials are relatively common in third- and fourth-century Roman Britain – common enough to be considered as a variant of normal, rather than deviant or even 'irregular'. This is exactly what Belinda Crerar argues in her PhD thesis, having carefully analysed decapitated burials from three regions of Britain. What she found in each case was that the decapitation was often the only difference marking out the individuals in those graves – in all other ways, they had been buried just like other people in each of those regions. This could suggest that we're just looking at a particular burial rite – one that seems so odd to us today, but which may indeed have been carried out with care and respect, rather than in vengeance or fear. The widespread nature of decapitated burials may also suggest that this is a variant, rather than a deviant rite, with decapitations making up a third to a half of burials in some Late Roman cemeteries; in some areas of the country it's rare *not* to find at least one decapitated burial in a cemetery of this age.

But who were those decapitated people? Belinda Crerar's conclusion, that they just represent part of the range of perfectly normal funerary rites in those Late Roman centuries, still leaves me wondering why they were chosen for such treatment – particularly in the case of decapitated, rather than beheaded, individuals. They weren't anonymous. Somehow, to the people burying them, it made sense to take off their heads.

Amongst the interpretations for the bodies which are decapitated after death, there's one theory that refuses to die – and it's nothing if not sinister. It's the theory that came so readily to mind for those early twentieth-century archaeologists, looking for explanations: fear of the evil dead.

———

T. C. Lethbridge, reaching around to try to interpret that decapitated burial in Guilden Morden in 1935, found an answer – not in contemporary, Roman texts, but in later literature. He wrote, 'The method of laying a ghost by decapitating the corpse was of course well known in later times, and is often mentioned in the sagas.' He was right; there's plenty of documentary evidence from the Middle Ages to show that the idea of someone coming back from the dead to haunt the living was taken very seriously indeed.

The dead could take many forms, from invisible spirits to shape-shifters. But sometimes the manifestation was recognisable – either as an apparition, which looked just like the dead person when they were alive, or as a zombie-like (but still recognisable) revenant: a reanimated corpse. Even royalty could get involved. In the twelfth century, William of Malmesbury wrote about the revenant corpse of Alfred the Great, which used to 'wander at night through its lodgings'.

Simon Mays – we meet him again – has combed through medieval texts from territories covering modern England, France, Belgium and Germany, and he's discovered important differences between the respective ways that apparitions and revenants were viewed. Apparitions were essentially religious phenomena, appearing with permission from God, and they were invariably benign in their intent. They might be looking for someone to help them atone for their own sins during life, so they could finally shuffle on from purgatory to heaven, for instance. Or they might appear to someone in order to warn them to mend their ways and turn away from sin. Revenants, on the other hand, were considered to be unusual natural, rather than spiritual, phenomena. And like zombies in modern horror films, they were unfailingly malevolent. They might have come back to life through some residual energy trapped in their bodies, or they might have been reanimated by demons. Either way, they were bad news. They could spread disease, or cause more direct harm – launching terrifying, violent attacks, and even killing people.

It seems that both apparitions and revenants had a limited window of opportunity to either assist or terrify the living. In a spiritual way, that related to the period of time when souls were thought to hang around the grave – for about thirty days after death and burial. In a physical way, this was linked to the decomposition of the body: fleshed corpses, while rotting, could still climb out of their graves; skeletons, it seems, could not.

Those medieval ghost stories also contain useful information about how to successfully terminate a revenant. You might be able to do it with a less invasive, religious approach – officially absolving the dead of their sins, for instance. But if you really wanted to be sure, physical interventions were recommended: you had to dig up the corpse and then do something to neutralise it, which could be hacking it to pieces, beheading it, burning it or dumping it in water.

The Icelandic *Saga of Grettir the Strong* describes two reanimated corpses which are neutralised by having their heads cut off – and placed between their thighs. The Danish historian Saxo Grammaticus also mentions a troublesome corpse being dug up and decapitated.

In twelfth-century England, William of Newburgh wrote: 'It would not be easy to believe that the corpses of the dead should sally (I know not by what agency) from their graves, and should wander about to the terror or destruction of the living . . . did not frequent examples, occurring in our own times, suffice to establish this fact, to the truth of which there is abundant testimony.' And he gave four specific examples: the Buckingham Ghost, the Berwick Ghost, the Hounds' Priest and the Ghost of Anant. Those revenants were variously laid to rest by having their souls absolved or their corpses cremated.

The courtier Walter Map created a collection of historical stories and satirical anecdotes during his time at the court of Henry II. He used the meme of the walking dead to mock life at court – but also described what seem to be genuine reports (if not genuine cases). In one, an English knight, William Laudlin, seeks assistance from Bishop Foliot of Hereford, describing how 'a Welshman of evil life died of late unchristianly enough in my village, and straightaway after four nights took to coming back every night to the village, and would not desist from summoning singly and by name his fellow villagers, who upon being called at once fall sick and die within three days'.

The bishop replies with a diagnosis and a remedy: 'Peradventure the Lord has given power to the evil angel of that lost soul to move about in the dead corpse. However, let the body be exhumed, cut through the neck with a spade, and sprinkle the body and the grave well with holy water, and replace it.'

It sounds like a tried and tested solution – not something the bishop has just invented off the cuff. But unfortunately, that particular time, it didn't work. The corpse went roaming again – finding William and calling his name three times. William was having none of it, and chased the revenant, catching it and cutting off its head (which it seems, was back on its neck) just before it fell into its grave. The corpse, now doubly decapitated, was finally laid to rest. (The story of course also contains a jibe at the bishop – whose spiritual advice turned out to be so ineffectual.)

Geoffrey of Burton's twelfth-century *Life and Miracles of Saint Modwenna* describes how two peasants from Drakelow in Derbyshire, who defected from the service of one abbey to another, were struck dead by the spirit of the saint. After they were buried, their corpses emerged from their graves, zombie-like, and returned to Drakelow, spreading disease amongst the living. The bodies were duly dug up and the heads cut off – and placed between their legs, in a hauntingly similar pattern to that seen in the Roman decapitated burials. Just to be sure, their hearts were also removed and incinerated – which seemed to do the job, as the burning hearts 'cracked with a great sound and everyone there saw an evil spirit in the form of a crow fly from the flame'. Job done.

What's interesting about these stories is that they encapsulate that fear of dead bodies spreading disease and polluting the living. The corpses are blamed for what sound like outbreaks of disease in communities – but they are imagined to play a very active role in that contagion. In epidemics – pandemics, even – people have always looked for someone to blame.

In his survey of medieval literature, Simon Mays found that the majority of reported revenants were male – perhaps because living men were (and are) much more common perpetrators of violent crime than women. Female revenants, when they were described, were absolutely terrifying – but not necessarily violent. But Simon didn't find a single story about a juvenile revenant. Children did come back to haunt the living (often targeting other children) – but they returned as apparitions, not zombies. The ghostly child tended to be good-natured but extremely irritating, often popping up to nudge people about minor missteps. The apparition would remind miscreants that God could see absolutely everything they did – and that even something as subtle as whispering in choir practice could set you on the path to hell.

Despite the fact that Simon couldn't find any stories about young zombies, he did come across a German text from 1008 – the *Corrector*, written by Burchard, Bishop of Worms – which mentions a particular, preventative practice. The *Corrector* is a penitential warning against non-Christian beliefs and rituals, including various superstitions about the undead, and prescribing appropriate penances for each of them. In it, Burchard writes that some 'women inspired by the devil' would entertain a belief that dead unbaptised infants could rise and terrorise the living. And these women would 'take the baby's corpse, put it in a secret spot, and impale the little body with a pole'. That act required two years of penance. The same superstition also extended to women who had died in childbirth, in which case, the solution was to impale the dead woman with a stake, to prevent her potentially evil unborn child rising from the dead, which seems a bit over the top.

There were plenty of other mortuary rituals mentioned by Bishop Burchard in his *Corrector* – from knotting a dead man's belt to banging wool-carding combs over a woman's grave. And all these rituals can be seen as having a double purpose – speeding the soul to the afterlife on the one hand; protecting the living from any lingering, malevolent spirits on the other. It's clear that Christians like Burchard viewed such folk beliefs and rituals as persisting, pre-Christian – and un-Christian – superstitions. And indeed, Burchard mentions yet another funerary practice that he disapproves of: memorial banquets – on the third, seventh or thirtieth day after death, or on the anniversary of the death – linking us back again to that pipe burial, and forward to the Russian Parents' Day.

If Burchard was right – that these medieval superstitions had much earlier, pre-Christian roots – then perhaps we can use this later literature to shed light on irregular burials in Roman Britain. With plenty of medieval references to *post mortem* decapitation being motivated by necrophobia, fear of the evil dead, perhaps this could also explain at least some of those Roman decapitated burials. But a note of warning here. Mentions of revenants in the old texts reach their peak in the twelfth and thirteenth centuries – 800 years after the practice of decapitating burials peaks, in the fourth century. Do we really expect beliefs and customs to persist so long? Perhaps, but it would be reassuring to have more evidence from the centuries in between.

Could fear of the dead explain the prone burials as well? It's certainly possible – though, this time, there aren't even any medieval texts which explicitly suggest prone burial in particular as a way of thwarting revenants. There's another possibility – which is that prone burial is a sort of extended *post mortem* punishment, perhaps for an executed criminal. For some double burials, where one body is buried face up and the other face down, it's been suggested that this could have been punishment for what society considered to be sexually deviant behaviour at the time, such as homosexuality. Finally, there is another potential explanation for some bodies that were lain prone in their graves – not because of perceived transgressions, but through piety. That suggestion emerges from one specific medieval reference to the burial of Pepin, king of the Franks, in 768. Pepin, it was said, chose to be buried face down at the church entrance, as a symbol of humility and penitence. The fact that some other medieval prone burials have been found close to or even *inside* churches supports this interpretation – for those particular graves, anyway. But other prone burials from medieval sites are far away from churches and even cemeteries – and those ones do seem to mark their occupants out as excluded from society. The medieval pattern, then, suggests perhaps two major reasons influencing prone burial: personal motives associated with piety and humility, and public motives linked to social exclusion, and even to criminality and execution.

These explanations are certainly not as sensational as the idea of keeping the dangerous dead in their graves. And this might feel like progress compared with the theories put forward in the twentieth century – but we probably shouldn't completely dismiss necrophobia and fear of revenants as a potential motivation for burying someone face down.

There are plenty of other types of burials across Europe, in medieval times and beyond, where that's clearly what was intended – and carried out in a huge variety of ways. As well as decapitated burials, there are those bodies impaled with iron rods, and others with stakes through the heart; bodies pierced through with nails; with sickles placed across the throat; and with stones piled up on them – particularly in medieval eastern Europe. Old stories from Germany, the Czech Republic, Poland, Lithuania, Hungary, Romania, Russia and Armenia illuminate the archaeology, revealing methods thought to prevent corpses from returning as revenants or vampires. And there's a suggestion that eastern Europe could have been where the irregular burial practices we see in Roman Britain originated – spread by migration within the expanding Empire.

Roman military power depended not only on the legions, but on auxiliary forces, or *foederati*, drawn from populations who were outside the Empire itself. Some were allied with Rome under treaties, but the term also applied to mercenaries. Roman Britain was defended against invasion by *foederati* drawn from the lands of the middle and lower Danube basin: Dacia (Romania), Thrace (Bulgaria) and Pannonia (a territory mainly located in modern-day Hungary).

In 2004 and 2005, York Archaeological Trust excavated yet another Romano-British cemetery, across two sites, close together on Driffield Terrace in York, just outside the boundary of Roman Eboracum. The cemetery spanned the first to fourth centuries CE, and contained both inhumation and cremation burials. The general trend in funerary practice across

Britain is that earlier cremation burials give way to more inhumations in the second century. But at Driffield Terrace, the cremations were later — reminding us that practices are always varied and people don't always stick in the boxes we put them in (no coffin pun intended). And in fact, archaeology has shown that cremation remained popular in the more northerly regions of Roman Britain, right into the fourth century CE. But it was the inhumations in this cemetery that demanded close attention. There were a few prone burials, some of which gave the impression of having been carried out in a rush, or at least, with no particular respect for the body. But the most striking feature was that out of eighty-two inhumations excavated, forty-six were decapitated.

In a quarter of the burials, the skulls had been placed back near the neck, and some were placed by the arms or torso. But the most frequent placement, accounting for around a third of the cases, saw the skull positioned, in that now familiar way, down between the legs. Katie Tucker analysed the human skeletal material from Driffield Terrace — in fact, it was this site that first sparked her interest in trying to better understand the practice of decapitated burials.

Things started to get really interesting when results came back from chemical isotope analyses of bones and teeth from some of the burials, which can provide information about where a person lived, or the diet they ate. You make your tooth enamel when you're a child, and the oxygen and strontium isotopes locked into it record a signature of the geology of the place you grow up in, through the water you drink and the plants you eat: your teeth grow to match the rocks you live on. So if we find a skeleton that has a very different signature in its teeth from the place it's buried in, we start looking further afield for a match. It's often not possible to pinpoint a specific homeland, but there'll be areas where the geology is compatible with the enamel isotopes.

The results from Driffield Terrace suggested that the individuals didn't come from Britain or from the Mediterranean – but probably came from further east in Europe: somewhere with a different geological signature, and where people consumed more millet than they did in Britain. Further isotopic sleuthing showed a close match between the isotope signatures of seven of the decapitated individuals from Driffield Terrace and skeletons from Romania.

A somewhat similar pattern was seen at Catterick in North Yorkshire, where a cemetery associated with a small military camp contained individuals buried in strange positions, along with brooches and beads of a Black Sea style. In the south of England, Lankhills Roman cemetery has yielded similar results: evidence of individuals who spent their early years elsewhere, before coming to Britain, buried with grave goods also suggesting connections with other places, in the form of coins, 'crossbow' brooches and footwear. And there are others – one in Canterbury with isotopes matching central Europe, buried with a pair of Black Sea-style silver buckles (with two decapitated children in the same cemetery), another in Gravesend in Kent, and three from the Walbrook Stream archaeological site outside London – with similarly non-local isotope signatures. One decapitated burial from Walbrook Stream – a woman with her skull lying between her legs – yielded an isotope signature closely matching Romania again.

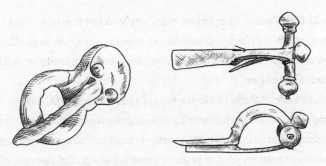

Eastern European-style buckle from Canterbury and brooch from Lankhills

So could those decapitated burials reflect a cultural custom – one that was perhaps more common in eastern Europe, and brought to Britain by the military allies of the Roman Empire, *foederati* from Dacia, Thrace and Pannonia? The picture is complex. (Of course – it's archaeology after all, and archaeology is the anthropology of the past. And people – the subjects of anthropology – are never simple.) Not all skeletons with non-local isotope signatures were decapitated – and some apparently local individuals were. This doesn't destroy the *foederati* hypothesis – those locals could be second- or third-generation immigrants, after all, retaining their cultural heritage in this way.

The real problem with this hypothesis, though, is the high frequency of Roman-period 'deviant' burials, including decapitations – in Britain compared with anywhere else. There are examples elsewhere – but they tend to be fairly sporadic. Crucially for the *foederati* hypothesis, none have been found in Iron Age Dacia. The examples we know of from eastern Europe are later than those in Roman Britain.

The rarity of decapitation burials outside Britain suggests that the practice was 'indigenous' – not something introduced by the Romans, like villas, bath-houses and wine; not something brought in by their allied armies; and not something that was part of a more widespread European culture in the Iron Age, either. And although there's a little less evidence for the practice in the early medieval period, when Britain is no longer part of the Roman Empire, there are still almost four hundred British examples dating from between the fifth and eighth centuries CE. By the following medieval period, the practice is much rarer – even though this is when we start to see mention of it in the literature.

From the numbers, then, this looks more like a home-grown phenomenon in first-millennium Britain, rather than something brought in by a particular group of migrants, or picked up alongside other aspects of Roman culture. One big problem that plagues interpretation, though, is that it's hard to separate *post mortem* funerary rituals from beheadings – occurring in executions or in conflict.

Another possibility that may well be playing out at Driffield Terrace is that it's not really where the *foederati* came from that's important to the burial practices here – but the fact that the cemetery could have been influenced by the Roman military presence in Eboracum. Most of the individuals were young or middle-aged men. Most of the decapitations had been delivered from behind, cutting into the back of the neck. It's been suggested that Driffield Terrace could have been a gladiator burial ground, but another possibility is that it was an execution cemetery.

In her wider survey, Tucker had found that more than two thirds of Romano-British decapitated burials were adult males, while around a quarter were adult females, and less than 10 per cent were juveniles. Her analysis produced results which were somewhat different to other studies, which had found a much wider spread of young and old, male and female, across Romano-British decapitated burials. Incorporating burials from around York – including that Driffield Terrace cemetery – certainly skewed that data: of sixty one decapitated burials from Roman York, sixty were male. (And the odd one out, an incomplete skeleton, was impossible to sex.) But even without those York burials, Tucker found that males still accounted for the majority of decapitated inhumations discovered in Roman Britain. (The pattern is different in rural cemeteries, though, where the sexes are equally represented, and both prone and decapitated burials are often interpreted as forming a small proportion of what may be considered normal burial rites.) Tucker has also pointed out that decapitated burials found in the early medieval period are much more likely to be interpreted as criminal executions, compared with the Roman examples.

And yet we know from documentary sources that execution by beheading was certainly carried out in Roman times, especially in the military. We'd expect to see more men than women suffering this fate – but some women would surely also have been sentenced to death in this way. As the age of criminal responsibility was just seven in Roman law, perhaps the small proportion of juvenile decapitated burials also represent executions. Families were allowed to take the bodies away after execution – so it makes sense that we find the remains of these bodies buried formally, in cemeteries. The pattern of traumatic injuries in the decapitated burials doesn't always fit with warfare – making judicial punishment the most likely explanation in the majority of cases, Tucker has argued.

So where does all this leave us with Great Whelnetham? One thing is clear – each burial needs to be assessed extremely carefully. It's important to ascertain the age and sex of each individual, to take note of other signs of pathology which might hold a clue as to their identity, to analyse the way the head was detached from the body – suggesting either beheading or *post mortem* decapitation – and to look at the wider context.

And I couldn't get that decapitated three- to four-year-old child out of my head. Surely, this was not an executed criminal. Who *were* these people?

The decapitation burials in the Great Whelnetham cemetery were very varied. In one, the skull was completely missing. In others, the head had been repositioned, or placed between the knees, or at the feet, in the grave. Amongst the seventeen decapitated burials, five showed evidence of cut marks to the back of the mandible, suggesting that they had been beheaded with a strike to the back of the neck – slicing right through to the jawbone. The others may have been decapitated after death, rather than executed in this way. But seven of these bore unhealed fractures and other cuts, suggesting that they had been victims of violence around the time of their deaths. The hands of some may have been bound. The graves were arranged in a fairly haphazard way in the cemetery.

That's what we can say about the deaths of these individuals, and their funerary rites – but their bones also hold clues as to what their *lives* were like. In 2018, I had the opportunity to look at one of these decapitated burials. It was the skeleton of an adult female, which bore signs of a hard, physical lifestyle.

At the bottom end of the left humerus, I could see where the joint surface was worn smooth, on the ball-like capitulum which forms a joint with the radius – one of the forearm bones. This smooth surface was so highly polished that it almost looked like ivory – and in fact that's the meaning of the technical name for a lesion like this: eburnation. It happens in the final stages of osteoarthritis, once all the cartilage has worn away from an articular surface, and bare bone rubs against bare bone. There was other evidence of osteoarthritis in her skeleton, including at one wrist. And one of the finger bones or phalanges had been fractured. Although she didn't appear to be elderly – from the rest of her skeleton – the woman had also lost all her upper teeth, well before her death. She looked like someone who had led a hard life. And she wasn't alone. The levels of degenerative joint disease were unusually high in this cemetery: almost every adult had some signs of arthritis or bony growth around joints, particularly in the spine, but also affecting shoulders, wrists, hips and ankles. Now, this could just reflect a particularly elderly population, but osteoarchaeologist Sue Anderson, who carefully examined all these bones, believed that demanding lifestyles had played an important role. And there were plenty of fractures too – especially to ribs and arms – indicating a high level of violence.

There was one particularly chilling find amongst these bones. One of the juvenile skulls appeared to have been burned in a very specific way on one side. This child appeared to have been branded, with a V-shaped iron, on the side of the head. And there was another potential clue to the identity of these people that had been discovered close to the burial site: an iron manacle, from a similar period.

There's one group of people in Roman society who are very

difficult to detect, archaeologically – and yet we know they were there. They are the enslaved – the workforce of empire, labouring out in the fields, down the mines, in the villas of the rich, stoking the hypocausts, and attending to the various personal needs of their owners. Across the Empire, it's estimated that slaves made up some 10-15 per cent of the population. It's possible that the people buried in the Great Whelnetham cemetery represent enslaved individuals. That might explain the high level of degenerative joint disease amongst their bones, reflecting a physically arduous lifestyle. The possible branding mark on the child's skull is another potential clue.

Reading the literature, gazing at archaeological remains, our ears delight in Roman myths and poetry, while our eyes are drawn by the lovely villas that started to grow up in the landscape, the bath-houses, the temples. And so we end up focusing on the lives of the elite, partly driven by the inherent bias in written sources, as only a tiny proportion of the population would have been literate. Historically, archaeology has also tended to focus on forts, cities and villas, only relatively recently switching to an exploration of the bigger picture, and finding out about more ordinary lives and the experiences of those who didn't occupy the higher echelons of Roman society or come here as part of the army. Death is the great leveller, and the information gained from analysing pathology in skeletons, investigating migration and diet through the use of isotope studies, and looking at patterns of ancestry using aDNA, all helps to provide a physical picture of Roman society, to stand alongside the material culture unearthed in archaeological excavations and the written evidence from contemporary literature. And the lavish lifestyles of the few came at real human cost.

The productivity of the Roman Empire, including its rural economy, depended on slavery. In Britain, some of those enslaved people would have been brought from other parts of the Empire, but some would have come from Britain itself. In fact, that trade had already been operating in the Iron Age, when slaves represented a major export from Britain. The trade then increased after Britain fell under Imperial rule in 43 CE, as agriculture boomed.

In Roman times, you could end up enslaved in many different ways. You could be taken captive in a military campaign. You could be captured on the margins of the Empire and sold somewhere far away – too far to ever think of returning home. You could be born into slavery. You could be abandoned as a baby – and enslaved in infancy. You could be sentenced to slavery for all manner of crimes. In extreme circumstances, in destitution, you could opt to sell yourself into slavery. As a slave, you might be owned by the emperor or the state, by a wealthy individual, or a freeperson, or even by another slave. It's estimated that the Roman Empire required new slaves at a rate of between 250,000 and 400,000 a year. Most slaves are thought to have been white Europeans, but ethnicity wasn't a barrier to entry. The status of enslaved humans was legally equivalent to that of livestock. And some owners did indeed keep slaves as pets – *deliciae* – whose unpaid job it was to delight their masters, in all sorts of ways. Slaves could be beaten, maimed and sexually abused with impunity.

It wasn't necessarily a life sentence. Good slaves, Cicero said, could be freed after just six years. Most were probably kept for about twenty years. Others were in it until they died – though many a prudent slave owner would have opted to free their elderly or ailing slaves before they became a real burden.

Biological anthropologist Rebecca Redfern has studied the importance of slavery to the economy of Roman Britain, as well as the potential to archaeologically identify enslaved individuals. As she has noted, many of the names of the enslaved – when we glimpse them in epitaphs and on writing tablets – are indigenous, not Roman.

The range of occupations and roles served by the enslaved makes it difficult to tell them apart based on patterns of pathology in skeletons, although some researchers have pointed to high frequencies of fractures and osteoarthritis in some burial grounds as indicative of the types of hard physical labour carried out by some slaves. At Ostia and Portus in Italy, where slaves would have been used to work in the docks and to extract salt, the Roman cemeteries are full of men who died in their twenties and thirties, riddled with injuries and arthritis. The most likely explanation is that those men were enslaved. In other cemeteries, though, the evidence is not so clear – and the types of pathology we might expect to see written into the bones of enslaved people are also likely to be present in the poorest – yet free – sections of Roman society.

Ancient DNA holds the potential of telling us something about ancestry – but someone with traces of African ancestry, for instance, may not be a first-generation immigrant. And with so many slaves drawn from European populations, it's nigh on impossible to tell the enslaved apart, genetically, from those who were poor but free. Isotope studies can pick up evidence of long-distance travel within an individual's lifetime – but neither aDNA nor isotopes come with a label to say whether any journeys were carried out freely or under conditions of enslavement.

There is another way in which isotope studies can be

illuminating, though, and that's by revealing information about past diets. Elevated nitrogen-15 levels in skeletons from the Roman period compared with Iron Age Britain have been interpreted as evidence for a change in diets to include more marine resources – fish and shellfish. But Rebecca Redfern has also drawn attention to another possible reason for such high nitrogen-15 levels: starvation. It's possible that those isotopic signatures, trapped in the bone for hundreds of years, record lives of deprivation – deprivation that could have been linked to enslavement.

In very rare cases, enslaved people are buried with restraints in place. But even the interpretation of such apparently obvious signs of slavery is more difficult than it might seem at first. Some 'restraints' are simple iron rings – are they really shackles? If they are indeed restraints, are we looking at slaves or criminals? A skeleton of a young man, excavated from a Romano-British cemetery in York, was buried with iron rings around the ankles – and had also been decapitated. The skeleton was marked by a range of pathologies, from osteo-arthritis of the spine to signs of inflammation affecting his legs and ribs. So – is this is a maltreated enslaved man, decapitated after death to prevent his revenant corpse from hounding his master? Or a prisoner, beheaded and buried in his shackles?

For individual burials, it may be that we will never know whether a particular person was enslaved or not. But an inference of enslavement becomes more reasonable at a population level, looking at a whole cemetery, or a significant portion of a cemetery. It's possible that the style of burial also provides a clue. And it's been suggested that prone burials, and perhaps decapitations too, could have been reserved for the enslaved in Roman society – particularly in Britain. Whether or not that combines with a possible fear of the revenant dead – the victims of enslavement seeking their vengeance – I'm not sure we'll ever know.

It's hard to escape from Peter Salway's conclusion about decapitation, in his *History of Roman Britain*: 'The truth is we cannot be sure about either the origin of this rite or what it meant. We can only record it, with the observation that it ought to remind us of just how much that is very alien to our ways of thinking lay beneath the superficially modern and familiar appearance of the Roman world.'

But imagine being a slave owner who has not treated their slaves well. When they die, you wouldn't want them coming after you. You'd want to make sure they stayed in the ground. And at Great Whelnetham, they did, for centuries. Until the archaeologists came along, to examine their bones, and to try to learn their untold stories.

4.

THE BEAUTIFUL BUCKETS OF BREAMORE

First contact

On a wet and windy morning in October 1999, Steve Bolger was metal-detecting in a field on Shallows Farm, close to the River Avon in Hampshire. The field was being used for pasture but had been ploughed in the past. But still, in the west of the field, a subtle, oval mound remained – about 70 metres long, and rising just 70 centimetres above the level of the ground around it. The ground was pockmarked with small pits – metal detectorists had clearly been here before, though nothing had been reported.

Bolger's prospecting turned up a coin-weight and two broken pieces of brooches. But then there was a stronger signal. Something big, Steve thought, and dug down to reveal it.

Steve Bolger knew he'd found something special, and he took it to the museum in Winchester to show the Finds Liaison Officer, Sally Worrell. He placed a box on the table between them, and Sally opened the lid. She lifted out the mud-encrusted object – it looked like a small metal bucket or pail. Nothing particularly exceptional. 'It was really only when the object was X-rayed that we began to realise its importance,' she later said.

When the Breamore bucket was cleaned up by specialist conservators, its hidden beauty was revealed. Greenish with verdigris, it would have been bright and shiny in antiquity. It had been made from a single sheet of copper alloy – probably brass – hammered into shape, until the sides were almost vertical, with a swing handle attached through raised lugs. Traces of tin on the surface showed that the bucket would originally have been 'silvered'. The lower parts of the sides had crumbled away and its base had become detached. But on the outside, its decoration had survived the ravages of time. Punched and stamped into the surface of the metal, three warriors – bravely naked, except for their flowing cloaks and boots – battle it out with two spotted beasts, possibly a leopard and a hyena.

The design on the Breamore bucket, "unrolled"

And, close to the rim of the bucket, there was an inscription in Greek, punched in with rows of tiny circles creating the shapes of the letters:

ΥΓΙΕΝΟΥCΑΧΡΟΥΚΥΡΑΠΟΛΥCCΕΧΡΟΝΥCΚΕΚ ΑΛΥC

It looks like one, immensely long word, but it breaks down into:

ΥΓΙΕΝΟΥCΑ ΧΡΟΥ ΚΥΡΑ ΠΟΛΥC CΕ
ΧΡΟΝΥC ΚΕ ΚΑΛΥC'

Or Ὑγιένουσα χροῦ κυρὰ πολῦς σε χρόνυς κὲ καλῦς'. And just in case you still need a little help with that – it means, 'Lady, use this in good health for many happy years.'

This bucket had travelled a long way to end up in that field in Hampshire. When Worrell started looking into its provenance, she found that only seventeen similar buckets were known of. Two had been discovered in England – one on the Isle of Wight and another in Suffolk, close to Sutton

Hoo – with others being found in Spain, Italy, Saudi Arabia and Turkey.

The other buckets of this type bear similar inscriptions, and the spelling and formulation suggest a sixth-century CE date. Seven of the other buckets also depict hunting scenes, which also appear in mosaic pavements – in Antioch. And it's thought that all these buckets may have come from a single workshop in that ancient city, the predecessor of modern Antakya, in southern Turkey. A few of the buckets show Christian scenes – which is pertinent as Antioch was an important centre of Christianity in Roman times.

One scholar has suggested that these buckets could have been part of a bathing kit issued to Roman soldiers. But if that were the case, why does the inscription on the Breamore bucket refer to a woman? Perhaps they came in pairs, a 'his and hers' set of kits, given as a gift to a couple. There's another possibility: the bucket could have been picked up originally by a pilgrim travelling to the Byzantine Empire. But then again, the bucket could have changed hands many times between Antioch and Breamore.

Steve Bolger's discoveries on Shallows Farm sparked the interest of local archaeologists and English Heritage, and the following year, seven 'test pits', each 1 metre square, were dug in the area of the low mound where the bucket had been found. In one test pit, fourteen sherds of pottery were found. They looked like pieces of a Bronze Age pot, of a type called a 'collared urn' – with an overhanging rim or collar – often used for cremation burials. Collared urns were in vogue from around 2000 to 1500 BCE. Other pieces of pottery and flint also suggested a Bronze Age date for the original mound. In a test pit dug on the spot where Steve had found the bucket, a few tiny fragments of copper alloy were found – probably missing bits of the bucket. But there were small pieces of human bone as well.

At the time, I was working at the University of Bristol as an anatomy lecturer – teaching in the dissection room but also doing some research on archaeological human remains. I was part of a small clique of researchers spread across the departments of Anatomy and Archaeology, and we called ourselves the Bristol Osteoarchaeological Research Group (BORG). As well as working on our own projects, BORG provided an osteological reporting service. Occasionally the police would call in with a piece of bone someone had found in their back garden – often turning out to be deer or badger, rather than human. More rarely, we'd be asked to analyse much more recent human remains: a skeleton washed up on Ladye Bay near Clevedon; a decomposed body found wrapped in a sheet on Exmoor; a piece of bone taken from the skull of a man who suffered a blow to the head and an internal cranial bleed which had eventually proved fatal, despite the craniotomy. Sometimes, museum curators would ask us to reanalyse old collections of human bone – such as the Caerleon cremations. And local archaeologists would ask us to write bone reports on human remains found in their excavations in Bristol, Gloucestershire and Somerset. There always seemed to be a cemetery excavation happening, somewhere. Some of the bones were retained in our collections, for teaching and research. Others were reburied, depending on the project and the antiquity of the skeletons.

Channel 4's long-running archaeology series *Time Team* had offices in London and Bristol. And one of the Bristol team, archaeologist-turned-producer Kate Edwards, asked me if I could prepare reports on various skeletons discovered in *Time Team* digs. There was a bit of a backlog, so I got stuck in.

After I'd been writing bone reports for *Time Team* for a while, one of the producers rang me. 'We're planning an excavation in Hampshire and wondered if you could come along to the site.'

The timing worked for me, so in principle, I'd be able to join the dig. 'Are you anticipating finding human remains, then?' I asked.

'Well, it's a cemetery site,' came the laconic reply.

———

And that's how I ended up in a field in Hampshire, in August 2001. In the somewhat disappointing Trench 3.

Over just three days – as was the *Time Team* tradition – we excavated seven trenches. Five were on the mound itself, one of them over the test pit that had itself been sited on the original find-spot of the Byzantine bucket, the year before.

Walking onto the field, the mound was barely visible. 'This has got to be the flattest, most unprepossessing field we've ever dug on *Time Team*!' exclaimed the presenter, Tony Robinson, striding out into it.

'What about this big mound in front of us?!' dig director Mick Aston joked, waving his arms about.

'I see no mound. I see this vague rise,' replied Tony.

He was right. It was so subtle – not an obvious barrow at all; the ploughing had seen to that. And from the previous test pits, we expected to find archaeological remains lying only a few centimetres under the ground surface. Mechanical diggers rolled in to take off the turf and just a very thin layer of top-soil underneath it. Meanwhile, the geophysics team started a magnetometry survey in an attempt to map out any buried iron artefacts. And metal detectorists would start survey-ing the field — and the trenches — for any other, non-ferrous metal objects.

In Trench 3 — under the watchful eye of trench supervi-sor Jenni Butterworth — we had only trowelled down about 10 centimetres when we started to find human bones. I was disappointed — they were extremely crumbly and fragmen-tary. I switched to using wooden pottery-sculpting tools to remove the clay-rich soil next to the bones — gently prising the crumbs of earth away, taking care not to damage the fragile bone any more.

We uncovered two skeletons lying very close to each other: one larger, one smaller. They were too close to be two sepa-rate burials — in fact, the arm of the smaller skeleton lay above that of the larger individual. This appeared to be a genuine double burial. Anglo-Saxon specialist Andrew Reynolds was on site to advise, and he suggested that the pair could have been victims of disease — perhaps even the plague. Forensic anthropologist Margaret Cox was also there to provide expert opinion. The bone was in extremely bad condition — the skulls had survived in part, though they'd suffered plough damage. The shafts of the long bones of the limbs were there — but the ends of the bones had disappeared, as had all the vertebrae, the ribs and most of the pelvic bones. But in one of the skel-etons, part of the pelvis had escaped destruction — and it was an important part: a piece of the lower ilium that includes a natural notch which is very useful for determining sex in skel-etons. The shape of this notch — technically the greater sciatic notch – varies from being a narrow J-shape to a wide C-shape. A narrow notch is a good indicator of male sex, while a wide notch is more typically female.

We'd excavated an iron shield boss from above this skeleton, in the chest area. A shield boss, or umbo, is a central metal dome in a shield – useful for deflecting blows, but also providing an anchor for a bar grip on the inner side. In this grave, the rest of what had presumably been a round, wooden shield, perhaps covered in leather on the front, had long since rotted away. All that was left was a round, rusty lump that had once been a bright, shiny shield boss. And there had also been a spear laid in the grave, alongside the right arm of the individual.

It's easy to assume that shields and spears are 'male' grave goods. They are indeed often found with male skeletons. But in the past, antiquarians often determined the sex of a skeleton based on grave goods – rather than the bones themselves. This creates a circular argument, of course: weapons are found in male burials; a burial is male because it is buried with weapons. It's best to start with the skeleton itself, and though some may not be either clearly male or female – as all the features used to determine sex vary on a spectrum – others are. The crumbliest fragment of pelvic bone remained – with what Margaret thought looked like a C-shaped greater sciatic notch. But had it eroded into that shape? Possibly. When we attempted lifting the bone, it fell apart – into fine, chalky fragments attached to lumps of mud.

Biological sex and gender don't always neatly coincide, though. We know from many cultures around the world today that some societies recognise more than two genders. If this pelvis really was 'female', what we couldn't tell from looking at that grave was whether this was a man who happened to have a female-looking pelvis, an individual whose body may have been female but whose social identity was male, or – perhaps the most obvious and likely interpretation – a woman who identified as female, but was also a warrior. Is it our own preconceptions that mean we're surprised by the idea of a warrior woman? A 'warrior' identity may be more complex than it seems, though – does it really mean the individual took up arms and fought – or was it more symbolic?

The same debates arise when we see female burials with swords in the Iron Age. It seems a bit of a cop-out to assume that these women were buried with their dead husbands' swords, as has sometimes been suggested. The written histories are full of references to female leaders and warriors in the Iron Age – including the queens Cartimandua and Boudica. So perhaps this high-status female warrior identity re-emerged after the Roman period. In the end, this is probably too much to read into one small piece of crumbly pelvic bone.

Once we'd lifted what remained of the two skeletons, I could get a closer look at them in the on-site 'bone lab' – which was actually a small, white events marquee, complete with clear plastic windows. The teeth of the skeleton identified as female revealed her to be a young adult, in her late teens or early twenties. The other individual was younger – around twelve years old, judging from the pattern of tooth eruption.

Another juvenile grave appeared just south of this double burial. This child was younger – around eight years old. And a final burial saw us extending the side of the trench – as this grave was positioned east–west, perpendicular to the others. When we found the skull (with a shield boss lying over it and a spearhead beside it), we knew the rest of the skeleton would lie beyond the eastern edge of the trench. The bones were very fragmentary, but the teeth suggested an age of seventeen to twenty-five at death. The skull had an unusual feature: a metopic suture – a joint line running vertically up the frontal bone, which underlies the forehead.

Over in Trench 5, another double burial had turned up. One of the individuals was a tall, adult man, aged thirty-five to forty-five, buried with an iron spearhead, a shield boss and a knife. The other skeleton was less well preserved. I could tell the person had been younger when they died – probably in their late twenties or early thirties – but I could not determine the sex. There were a couple of brass or bronze buckles found with this skeleton – one an extremely fine example inlaid, cloisonné-style, with blue and red glass. There was also a shield boss near the feet, and another bucket, made of wood and brass, which looked as though it had been placed on top of the shield in the grave.

In Trench 1, an iron spearhead was found – less than half a metre away from the spot where the original bucket had been discovered. And then, fragmentary human remains began to emerge. A skull lay right next to the spearhead. And then another bucket turned up, buried a little deeper, behind this individual's head. This one was made of wooden staves with bands and strips of bronze or brass holding it together, like a miniature barrel. The leg bones of a second skeleton were discovered – thought to be the only remains of the individual buried with the Byzantine bucket. And then two more buckets were discovered in this same trench; from their position, they must have been placed close to the head of the individual represented by just those leg bones. When those buckets were later cleaned and conserved, a miraculously intact glass bowl was found inside one of them. Frustratingly, with so little bone preserved, there was absolutely nothing I could say regarding the age or sex of the person who'd been buried with these buckets and the glass bowl.

This cemetery would have remained unknown, were it not for the discovery of that beautiful Byzantine bucket – which was so responsibly reported. But all that previous digging into the mound had clearly disturbed the burial, speeding up its disintegration, so now nothing diagnostic was left – just the crumbly remains of a pair of legs. Yet another bucket was discovered against the eastern edge of the trench – presumably accompanying yet another grave, though no bones were found.

After I'd finished lifting the skeletons from Trench 3, I moved over to Trench 7 to help one of the most experienced archaeologists on site, *Time Team* regular Phil Harding. He'd already dug down about a metre – and exposed two skulls. It looked like yet another double burial. The skeletons were extremely close to each other – and not only that, the right arm of the skeleton on the left reached across, the finger bones of the right hand overlying the right forearm bones of the other skeleton. This burial was much deeper than the others – and it was much better preserved. Most of the bones of the two skeletons were not only identifiable, they were relatively intact. Both individuals were clearly male – and both in their late twenties or early thirties when they died, judging from the degree of wear on their teeth. Associated with one of these male skeletons was a shield boss, a spearhead and ferrule, and a bucket – this time made more simply, of wooden staves. The other was buried with an iron knife and a pair of copper-alloy tweezers at the hip. But down towards the legs of those skeletons, we came across a surprise – the fragmentary remains of another skull. Proceeding carefully, Phil and I uncovered what remained of the skeleton of a young child – around three years old – buried between the legs of the adult males. We found a central shield boss at the feet of one of the adult males. The wooden shield itself – long since rotted away – would have almost completely covered the small body of the child.

By the end of day three of excavation, we still had several buckets and skeletons to lift; we couldn't just cover them back up – the bones and objects would deteriorate very quickly, having been exposed. So we did something unusual for *Time Team* – we carried on into a fourth day. By the end of this extra day, I had boxed up all the bones – wrapping them in acid-free tissue paper before nestling them into large cardboard boxes, also acid-free, ready to take them back to the lab in Bristol for further analysis.

The metalwork, pottery and soil samples had been separately boxed and bagged up, and these would also be sent off for specialist analysis. Kate Edwards collected up all the site plans and notes, which she would later assemble into a report. The mechanical diggers moved in again to back-fill the trenches, and then we relaid the turfs and trod them down. Finally, Phil Harding walked over the field, with a bagful of various metal washers, broadcasting them like a medieval farmer sowing seed: a cunning plan to discourage any unscrupulous metal detectorists from prospecting on what we now knew was a high-status Anglo-Saxon cemetery.

That Breamore dig exhumed far more questions than answers. Years later, Sally Worrell and archaeologist David Hinton would pull together all the reports on all the bones, artefacts and groundwork at Breamore, and try to tackle some of those questions.

Over those four days in 2001, we'd also managed to collect almost fifty pieces of smashed-up pottery. When those were properly analysed, they turned out to range from late Bronze Age, through the Iron Age and Roman periods, into Anglo-Saxon times. Phil Harding had looked at all the flints that had been found, most of which were from the late Neolithic or early Bronze Age. It's in the Neolithic, or 'New Stone Age', which starts around 6,000 years ago, that farming arrives in Britain. This is probably when the forest on the west bank of the Avon was originally cleared – for timber, certainly, but also to make room for fields for the first farmers' crops and livestock. Later on, in the Bronze Age, it seems a burial mound was created on the site, perhaps accentuating what was already a slight natural rise in the land. Just a few fragments of collared urn provide the evidence for this Bronze Age funerary use of the site. The field may have been ploughed and cropped in the Iron Age and Roman periods, then just used as pasture or hay meadow in the medieval period, before being ploughed again in more recent centuries – reducing the mound to the subtle bump we see now.

There are many, many Anglo-Saxon cemeteries across England that reused prehistoric burial mounds. This might have been about symbolically claiming territory – a connection with ancestors in the landscape. And while there are much more visible barrows in the landscape around Breamore, it may be that this particular site was favoured because of its proximity to an Anglo-Saxon settlement in the fields to the north of The Shallows. Archaeologists had carried out field-walking there – literally walking over fields, scouring the ground for surface finds, best done just after ploughing. This survey had revealed a hotspot of Anglo-Saxon finds – including pottery sherds – in this nearby field. Around the modern Shallows Farm, there was a loose cluster of homes and other farms. At the time of the dig, Mick Aston had described it as 'a classic dispersed settlement – cottages all over the place, bits of green, lots of bits of woodland – it's what you'd expect from a Saxon settlement pattern that never turned into a village'.

The burial mound itself was sited on a promontory of gravel projecting into the River Avon's flood plain, just to the south of the focus of Anglo-Saxon settlement. That position in a river bend might have been important too – other Anglo-Saxon burial sites are close to rivers, including the famous royal site of Sutton Hoo, with its magnificent ship burial.

It's difficult to map the true extent of the cemetery. Geophysics didn't reveal the position of graves under the ground – which wasn't surprising as, even when we dug them, it was impossible to see the edges of graves in the sandy soil. But we'd found graves in four trenches, and if there had been just as many graves between the trenches as there were *in* them, that would imply at least fifty on the mound. Alternatively, we could just have been lucky – guided by the metal-detecting and magnetometry signals – and there may have only been twenty or so graves.

Accepting that we'd only excavated a sample of the cemetery, it does look out of the ordinary. First of all, there were the buckets. The decorated Byzantine bucket was exceptional, of course – with only two other similar examples in England. But then our limited excavation had turned up another *six* buckets. None were as spectacular as the first, metal-detected find, but clearly these buckets had been important to this particular group of Anglo-Saxons in Hampshire. Five had all been made in a similar way, with wood staves – yew in four and ash in one – secured with bands and strips of brass. The one in the triple burial, in Trench 7, was made entirely of yew staves, with no brass fittings. This type of stave-built bucket is most common in England – with over sixty examples having been discovered. They've been found accompanying cremation burials as well as inhumations; at Spong Hill in Norfolk, where twenty-four such buckets were found, all but one accompanied cremations. The type with wooden staves and copper-alloy rings are most common in the early sixth century; by the end of that century, the fashion changes and buckets with iron fittings appear. Yew seems to have generally been the wood of choice – a dense, fine-grained timber that can be polished to a high shine, holds water and resists decay.

Making buckets like this required skill – to shape the staves with bevelled edges so that they would fit tightly enough, and to make the brass hoops and decorations. The six buckets we discovered during the excavation at Breamore are similar in many ways to those found at other sites – there's nothing particularly outstanding or special about them. One had been well used by the time it ended up in a grave, with a mended handle. Nevertheless, buckets like this tend to be found in graves marked out as high-status in other ways – often containing weapons. And it's notable that no other cemetery in southern England has ever been found to contain quite such a high density of these curious grave goods, relative to the number of graves.

We'd hoped that analysis of the soil taken from the insides of the buckets might hold clues as to what they'd contained when placed in the grave. But unfortunately, the bottoms of the buckets had all rotted away, and the contents had been thoroughly turned over by the action of roots and worms. There were some seeds, a charred hazelnut shell and even some frog bones in the samples – but all these were all thought to be later intrusions – complete red herrings – not the original contents.

But then there was that one bucket that had been found to contain a glass bowl, when it was delicately cleaned up in the lab. The bowl may suggest that the bucket was used to hold a drink, rather than food. The glass bowl is a lovely object – and it is somehow magical that it passed through the centuries, unscathed. Just under 13 centimetres in diameter and 4 centimetres tall, it is made of the palest green glass, with tiny bubbles trapped in it. Faint white lines have been applied to it, concentrically, around the turned-out rim. It has a flat bottom, unlike the round-based 'palm cups' which are more common Anglo-Saxon finds. One similar bowl has been found at Carisbrooke on the Isle of Wight, and three in Kent, and they're thought to have been made in northern France or Belgium, some time around 525–50 CE.

The cloisonné buckle found with the younger individual in the Trench 5 double burial looks similar to some found in Kent – but it's a style seen right across Europe, from Spain to Hungary, in the late fifth and early sixth centuries. It's probably an import – but it's not known where the centre of manufacture of these buckles was, if indeed there was just one. One of the brooches that Steve Bolger had originally found in the field was similar in style to others found in Kent, on the Isle of Wight and in northern France. It was silver – making it an unusual find. Away from Kent and the Isle of Wight, only six silver objects from this era have been found in southern

England and the Midlands. The other brooch from Breamore was gilded brass or bronze, of a type thought to originate in Kent, and becoming very commonly used by women across southern England, in the sixth century.

The little bronze weight that Steve found with his metal detector was just over 9 grams – six times the standard Byzantine unit weight of 1.5 grams. It's a small but extremely interesting and informative object. It has punch-marks around the perimeter – perhaps a precaution against being shaved down, like Roman coins. It also has a central hole, so could have been carried on a string. Only two others like it are known in England, both from a cemetery in northern Lincolnshire, but many other types of Anglo-Saxon weight sets have been discovered, some using recycled Roman coins, and sometimes even found along with sets of scales.

When Britain exited from the Roman Empire, domestic coin production ceased – and only started up again in the seventh century, when Eadbald, king of Kent, started minting his own coins. But this doesn't mean that money wasn't changing hands at all in fifth- and sixth-century Britain. Early Anglo-Saxon weights imply a familiarity with both Byzantine and Frankish systems of currency – in other words, with the two economies developing in the eastern and western ends, respectively, of the old Roman Empire. That little weight is like the block-chain for a crypto-currency – maintaining the standard. Coins were not tokens like ours today: what made a coin valuable was the metal it was made of – it was effectively a small ingot of gold or silver.

Taken together, all the artefacts from the graves indicate that the cemetery was in use in the first half of the sixth century. And they speak of ongoing connections between Britain and the European continent, its power structures and its economies. This is important – but a theme we've come to expect in Anglo-Saxon archaeology. And yet Breamore stands out.

The Byzantine bucket aside, the weird thing about Breamore isn't the type or nature of the grave goods, but their sheer density. *All* those buckets. And the ubiquity of the weapons is exceptional. Every single adult we discovered was buried with weapons – which is really unusual in Anglo-Saxon cemeteries. One individual had *two* shields – again, this is extraordinary. What also seems odd is that, while there were fairly typical iron spearheads, shield bosses and knives in the graves, there were no swords – which are so often part of weapon sets in other Anglo-Saxon burials. But could we still be looking at some sort of 'warrior cemetery'?

Looking at all the skeletons back in the lab, those that were well preserved enough to determine biological sex were all male. There was that one fragile skeleton that had been interpreted on site as a possible female – but that was a tentative interpretation. Anglo-Saxon weapon burials are usually male; burials with buckets are more often male than female, the books will tell you – but are we getting into that familiar circular argument again? As a biological anthropologist, I steadfastly refuse to determine the sex of a skeleton based on associated grave goods, so I can't say that all the individuals – including the ones I couldn't sex – were male, just because they were buried with spears and shields. On the other hand, the two brooch fragments that Steve found are more often associated with female burials, where sex can be determined from bones. It's all rather disappointingly inconclusive. But remember it wasn't just adults that we found in those graves. The three children don't fit that idea of a warrior cemetery – their presence perhaps suggests that this was more of a family burial ground, and not just reserved for male 'warriors'.

The other odd aspect of Breamore was the preponderance of multiple graves. Of the eleven individuals we had discovered, four had been interred as double burials, and then there was that triple burial, with the two men and the young child. The range of ages and these multiple burials suggest something catastrophic befell this community. That could have been a virulent disease, wiping out young and old. Or it could have been other humans – in a battle or a massacre.

There are two prime suspects here. One is the Battle of Cerdic's Ford and the other is *Yersinia pestis*.

The *Anglo-Saxon Chronicle* records a battle taking place at Cerdices Ford (Cerdic's Ford) on the River Avon in the sixth century. (Actually, it records it taking place twice, once in 508, and then again in 519 – undoubtedly a clerical error.) The battle was apparently between the Anglo-Saxon invaders Cerdic and Cynric, and the local king, Natanleod. The problem with early events like this, recorded in the *Chronicle*, is that they are somewhat cobbled together. Dates are provided and seem very precise – but the duplication reminds us how unreliable these dates actually are. Cerdic – as a founding Anglo-Saxon king – is problematic himself as his name sounds much more British than Germanic; it's cognate with the Iron Age name-forms Caratacus or Caradoc.

But maybe there is a grain of truth in what seems like an origin myth: a battle taking place at Cerdic's Ford in the sixth century. By the time of the Domesday Book, in 1086, there were two manors called Cerdeford, and they evolved into today's North and South Charford – in the parish of Breamore, and just north of Breamore itself, on the west bank of the Avon. So it's possible that the Shallows cemetery contains warriors – and their families – killed in that battle.

Another explanation is that the myth attached itself to the cemetery later on – connecting the story of a battle with a sacred and high-status burial mound. But then that wouldn't offer us an explanation for the multiple graves. The human remains themselves don't help us much here. There were no obvious weapon injuries on any of the bones, but most of the skeletons were so badly degraded, there would have been nothing left to see.

The other suspect for these untimely deaths, with the bodies piling up into multiple graves, is pestilence – and the most infamous pestilence of them all: the plague.

Working with archaeological human remains, geneticists can sequence human genomes – but they can also look at DNA from the pathogens that plagued our ancestors. Palaeogenetic analysis has pushed the origins of plague infection in humans – caused by the bacterium *Yersinia pestis* – right back into prehistory, into the Bronze Age, more than 4,000 years ago. In 2013, geneticists confirmed that the Plague of Justinian, which ripped through the Byzantine Empire in the 540s – and then persisted for some 200 years – was caused by *Yersinia pestis*, making this the first historically recorded outbreak of the disease.

In 2019, researchers isolated *Yersinia pestis* DNA from early medieval cemeteries across western Europe, including one cemetery in Britain – Edix Hill in Cambridgeshire, dating from between 500 and 650. This was the first evidence that plague had reached these shores before the outbreak in the fourteenth century that we know as the Black

Death. Archaeologist Craig Cessford, at the University of Cambridge, was involved with the study. He said, 'There are no documentary sources that definitely record that the Justinianic Plague of the 540s reached Anglo-Saxon England, so its identification at Edix Hill represents a major discovery. It is unlikely that this site is unusual in being affected by the plague; more probably most, if not all, of Anglo-Saxon England was ravaged by it.'

Edix Hill was a large Anglo-Saxon cemetery excavated in the late 1980s – having been threatened by both plough damage and unscrupulous metal-detecting. The archaeologists found 149 individual skeletons, but estimated the whole cemetery was twice that size. Around half of the male burials were accompanied with weapons – mostly spears and shields. Female burials were accompanied with characteristic jewellery: brooches and girdle hangers. The Historic England record for the site reports that the cemetery was thought to have been in use for around 150 years, and that 'the population was revealed to be healthy with several long-lived individuals'. But amongst the graves at Edix Hill, eighteen were multiple. And – as the aDNA analysis had shown – that apparently 'healthy' population had fallen prey to the plague.

Could the multiple burials at Breamore mean that this burial ground, too, was used for victims of the Justinianic Plague? Arguments against this being a plague cemetery are the formality, density and richness of the graves. The burials seemed shallow, but this was just because the mound had almost been ploughed out. And although we'd found examples of two or three individuals buried in a single grave, the grave pits themselves were not that close together. Finally, they were extremely well furnished with grave goods – perhaps not something you'd expect for hasty burials of people who'd died from an aggressive disease.

Which brings us back to our beginning, to that beautiful Byzantine bucket. What did it mean, when it was placed in the grave? David Hinton and Sally Worrell suggested it may have been used for feasting, even if it was originally intended as part of a wash-set. They also observed that 'no-one in Breamore would have known what the Greek inscription on it meant, though the letters might have been regarded as possessing special power, like . . . runes'. The beasts depicted on it must also have seemed remote and unfamiliar, magical or mythological; it seems unlikely anyone in Britain would have ever seen a real hyena or a leopard.

Perhaps the buckets were used for drinking at the funeral. Maybe they had been used on other occasions too, other feasts. Or perhaps they were solely reserved for the dead – possibly filled with food or drink to sustain them on their journey into the afterlife. The buckets are beautiful, showy items, particularly that tinned beauty from Antioch – that would have glittered in the grave. The impression of a maggot pupa on one rusted spearhead in the Shallows cemetery suggests the graves were open for a while before the people buried in them were covered with earth and sealed in the mound. The funeral was a visible demonstration of identity, opulence and status – it was just as much about those who were still living as it was about the departed.

The rarity of these buckets suggests that they weren't routinely traded. That might seem like a tautology – but it's important when we consider how that Byzantine bucket might have ended up in Hampshire. It's been suggested that they might have been diplomatic gifts – given to individuals who spent time at the Byzantine court, perhaps. The Breamore bucket seems to have been buried fairly soon after it was manufactured, around 550 – so perhaps it does represent a journey made by one person, rather than being an object which passed from hand to hand on its journey from the workshop to the grave.

The two similar buckets found in Britain come with implications of prestigious connections and social elites. The one from the Isle Wight came from a high-status burial of a woman, whose grave also contained three beautiful brooches, a gold braid and a gold finger-ring. The other one, from Suffolk, was raked up by a harrow in a ploughed field, less than a mile away from the famous Sutton Hoo cemetery, with its splendid boat burial. That means we don't know the original context of the bucket – but it could well have been from a grave. Its find-spot was also close to the Tranmer House Anglo-Saxon cemetery, discovered in 2000, which is thought to be a sixth-century predecessor to the Sutton Hoo mound cemetery.

That Tranmer House cemetery provides us with an interesting comparison for Breamore. The bone preservation there was even worse, but thirteen weapon burials accounted for more than a third of the graves excavated. There were only four burials with stereotypically female artefacts accompanying the body to the grave. There were also cremation burials, where the bone was better preserved, though of course fragmentary – and these were mainly female. Perhaps the same funerary customs pertained at Breamore – and we just didn't find the female cremations in our small excavation.

It's been suggested that the Tranmer House cemetery served a royal household – including troops. So could Breamore also have been a royal stronghold? Just 4 miles west, in Roman times, there was a palatial villa at Rockbourne. Sally Worrell and archaeologist David Hinton have suggested that the power base could have moved from Rockbourne Villa to the nearby Whitsbury hillfort, which was redeveloped in the post-Roman period – and then to Breamore itself.

Another possibility is that Breamore was some kind of frontier community – where relatively new settlers were emphatically demonstrating their identity in these elaborate burials. Although we usually focus on (incoming) Anglo-Saxons battling it out with (indigenous) Britons for supremacy, not all the Anglo-Saxons were necessarily on the 'same side'. We use the term now as a catch-all to describe cultures with Germanic links – but various medieval histories tell us that there were incursions of different, discrete groups: Jutes, Angles, Saxons and others.

The Venerable Bede, who is thought to have finished his *Ecclesiastical History of the English People* in the 730s, informs us that Jutes – originating in Jutland, Denmark – occupied the Isle of Wight and Hampshire in the sixth century. Sally Worrell and David Hinton followed Bede's lead, suggesting that the 'Anglo-Saxons' in the Shallows cemetery could actually have been Jutes, arriving in the Avon valley from the Isle of Wight – before Saxons swept in a little later and conquered the whole area in the seventh century. Perhaps the cemetery reflected a battle between Jutes and Saxons, then, rather than a bust-up between local Britons and invaders.

But there's a very real possibility that historians like Bede have seriously led us astray. Bede was, after all, writing about that fifth-, sixth- and seventh-century history somewhat later, in the eighth century. How much of that history can we really trust? And who *were* the Anglo-Saxons anyway?

It's a very good question. Focusing on Breamore, the way that these people were buried and the artefacts buried with them are broadly what we'd recognise as 'Anglo-Saxon'. But looking more carefully, those graves at Breamore contained objects and fashions reflecting connections near and far. The brooches and glass bowl speak of links with people on the Isle of Wight, in Kent, and in northern France or Belgium. The Byzantine bucket represents long-distance trade or diplomatic links with the centre of power that developed out of the eastern Roman Empire. There's nothing particularly Germanic about those fashions. And there's nothing to tell us whether those individuals or their proximate ancestors were locals or immigrants into Britain from Germanic regions. So why do we even label them 'Anglo-Saxon'? The answer must be: because history tells us to – or at least, it used to.

In the early medieval literature, the two groups most often referred to, in what is now England, are the Angles and the Saxons; some references compound them as 'Anglo-Saxon' – which may also be a way to differentiate the Saxons in what would become England from those on the continent. By the ninth century, the term 'Anglo-Saxon' was being used generically to mean 'English'. As for more modern usage, the language of Old English is sometimes described as 'Anglo-Saxon'. And then there's the archaeological sense of the term. We divide history up into manageable chunks, labelling particular periods and specific groups of people with characteristic customs. When we talk about 'Anglo-Saxon' archaeology, we're referring to a time period in England, between the fifth and eleventh centuries. (Confusingly, it can also be used to describe contemporary populations – in Britain but also in the US, where it's used to denote broadly

English ancestry. This modern ethnic use of the term is hugely problematic; labelling people living now with 1,500-year-old names strongly suggests a coherent and exclusive identity or ethnicity persisting through time – and has also become intertwined with appalling ideas about white supremacy.)

For now, I'm continuing to use the term in its archaeological sense, though I must acknowledge it's far from ideal – because of all these other connotations, but also because it carries with it an implicit idea of ethnicity, linked to the assumption that Bede was right and that a new group of Germanic folk (those Angles, Jutes and Saxons – and others, too) really did move in en masse, to occupy what would become known as England. This is how historians and archaeologists have traditionally explained the cultural change in southern and eastern Britain after separation from the Roman Empire. For a long time, we've tried to shoehorn archaeological evidence into the traditional historical narrative. But it doesn't fit well. And a new generation of historians and archaeologists is now questioning the long-accepted story – the story that is still in many of the history books. Were those cultural changes really down to mass migration, or could it be that they were more home-grown? This has been hotly debated for decades, with scepticism about the neat picture that Bede gives us steadily growing.

Now geneticists have arrived on the scene too, sticking their oar in. It's possible to sequence entire genomes from ancient skeletons now – and this is exactly the sort of information we need in order to resolve these debates about migration and population replacements in the past. If we can see particular genetic variants appearing in Britain at a certain time, that could be a clue to an influx of people arriving from another country. If we can sequence enough genomes, through time and with a good geographic spread as well, we should be able to get an idea of how large any migration was – or wasn't. And looking at individuals, we should be able to tease apart how much of their own ancestry goes way back in Britain, and how much looks like a relatively recent import from elsewhere.

Unfortunately, the Breamore skeletons were mostly badly degraded – but it may just be possible to extract DNA from at least some of them. That DNA may hold part of the answer to the puzzle of their origins – revealing genomic connections – and could help us with understanding the wider picture, too. And there's yet another conundrum that it could also help to solve – the riddle of the multiple burials at Breamore. When you sample DNA from an ancient skeleton, you may be mostly interested in the fragments of human genome that you put back together and decode. But there'll be other DNA there too – non-human DNA. And if an individual died while infected with a pathogen – it's possible to pin down the identity of that infection.

Twenty years after I wrote the first bone report on those Breamore burials, I'm looking at a photograph of a double burial from Edix Hill, where the bones held those genetic clues to the cause of death: *Yersinia pestis*, the plague. That double burial really reminds me of the graves we dug at Breamore. The similarity shimmers in my mind. And I know who to contact.

Pontus Skoglund is a geneticist with a keen interest in archaeology. He's heading up a hugely ambitious project at the Crick Institute in London, which is setting out to fully sequence a thousand ancient genomes from archaeological human remains spanning the eras, right across Britain. I'm already working with Pontus and his team on an interesting sample of skulls, from sites on Cranborne Chase that were excavated in the nineteenth century by Pitt Rivers. Working in Pontus's lab, on that Thousand Ancient Genomes project, infectious disease specialist Pooja Swali is focusing on metagenomics: looking for genetic traces of pathogens alongside the human DNA.

I talk to Pooja about Breamore and she sounds interested in investigating. I just need to find out where the bones ended up; they could be in the stores at Wessex Archaeology, where the *Time Team* archive is kept, or they could be in the collections at the University of Bristol, where I was working back in 2001. They were delivered to me after the dig had finished, and the skeletons had been washed, for me to analyse and write my report. But what happened to the bones after that? I'll have to dig out the records. If I can track them down, we might be able to answer this question: was Breamore an Anglo-Saxon plague cemetery? And – we might even have a better idea about who those people really were.

5.

THE MEANING OF BLING

The centuries after Roman rule in Britain and elsewhere were once called the Dark Ages. There was the sense that the benign light of Roman civilisation had dimmed; societies and cultures had collapsed. Most modern historians now baulk at the term, pointing to the richness of material culture in these centuries. But it's certainly a period for which we have few records – so very little in the way of contemporary accounts. And so, in this textual darkness, we search for physical texture. Archaeology must work hard to help us peer back through the gloom.

We find graves packed full of clues to the identity of the people who lived in what would eventually become

England – if we can but decipher those clues. New science comes along to shine a brighter light on centuries-old bones and age-old puzzles. And we're enthralled by gleaming, glittering new discoveries, treasures that hold secrets to this shadowy era, shining a light into the darkness.

I remember the excitement the Staffordshire hoard ignited when it was discovered, and when the first pieces were cleaned up and put on display, with eager visitors queuing round the block at Birmingham Museum to see the first exhibition. The hoard was discovered by metal detectorist Terry Herbert in a field in Hammerich, near Lichfield, in 2009. And it was clearly something exceptional right from the start. Herbert knew exactly what he must do – he contacted the finds liaison officer at Birmingham Museum, and an archaeological dig was carried out to recover the whole hoard and check for any other remains close by. The artefacts were spread through the plough-soil in the field – the original pit had been completely ploughed away. And there were no other traces of Anglo-Saxon activity – no buildings or graves – in the area. A further eighty-one artefacts turned up three years later, when the field was ploughed again.

When the hoard was cleaned up and conserved, it shone with forgotten glory: a huge haul of golden sword hilts and pommels, pyramid-shaped buttons, and other decorative gold and silver plaques and bands.

Dated by its style to the sixth and seventh centuries, the Staffordshire hoard is the largest collection of Anglo-Saxon treasure ever found in a single location – reeking of royalty, a warrior elite. Surfaces decorated, cloisonné-style, with red and pink garnets inlaid into golden cells, embroidered with filigree, engraved and stained with black niello. Stylised animals compete with geometric patterns, pagan symbols with Christian. Around a third of the 4,600 fragments come from a single original artefact – a splendid helmet, made up of richly decorated panels. Many of the other fragments come from the hilts of what must have been around a hundred different swords. It's very military, very *male* – dominated by those sword fittings. There are none of the objects that typically turn up in female graves, such as brooches. There are no drinking cups or coins as you might expect in a more general haul of treasure. And there are certainly no ordinary items. It's all treasure – prised off the weapons that it would have graced, buried in a hole in the ground.

Where did it all come from and why was it buried? The first question is easier to answer. Some of the early silverware is thought to be British in origin – though not local to Staffordshire, where it ended up – but one sword pommel probably came from Sweden. Many of the golden objects, dating from the later sixth century into the first half of the seventh, are thought to have originated in East Anglia. Some of the raw materials would have come from further afield; the silver could have been from Britain, but the smaller garnets are probably from what's now the Czech Republic, and the larger ones from India. The gold itself could have come from many sources, and it's likely to have been recycled – and alloyed with other metals – so many times that we'll never be able to track down its origin. In total, there's about 4 kilograms of gold in the hoard, 1.7 kilograms of silver – and thousands of garnets. It's the largest hoard in Europe, let alone Britain.

Why would anyone consign all this wealth to the ground? There are several reasons someone – or a group of people – might want to do this. One might be as a 'votive offering' – a gift to the gods, to the ancestors, or to other mysterious entities. This would have been an extremely generous offering. Another reason might be to take that metal out of circulation, or to obliterate the power or status linked with it. And yet – it could have been melted down or recycled in a much more pragmatic approach to scrubbing it clean of old associations. A final possibility – and I think the most likely, for the majority of hoards, in fact – is that this treasure was buried in a time of unrest – sealed in an earthen 'safe' – and that whoever hid it simply never had the opportunity to return and dig it up. The conservators painstakingly removing the mud from the artefacts and analysing the composition of the pieces found a tiny piece of linen which may be all that is left of the sack that once contained the hoard.

It was buried in the mid-seventh century. By this time, the political turmoil of what had been the Roman province of Britannia had resolved into different political units: the Anglo-Saxon kingdoms. There were seven major kingdoms – East Anglia, Kent, Essex, Sussex, Wessex, Mercia and Northumbria – and plenty of minor ones, though this gives a false impression of stability. The boundaries of the kingdoms were constantly in flux (by the eighth century, for instance, the former kingdoms of Kent, Essex and Sussex would all become subsumed into the powerful Wessex). In the first half of the seventh century, Penda, king of Mercia (roughly corresponding to the Midlands today), had fought Cynegils, king of Wessex (in southern England), and they seem to have settled on an uneasy truce. But then Mercia was also embroiled in battles with Northumbria, and in 655, Penda – who was the last non-Christian king of Britain – was killed. Northumbria got the upper hand for a while, then Mercia grew powerful again, under Penda's son, Wulfhere – who was committed to expanding his territory.

The battles go on and on. The ninth-century *Anglo-Saxon Chronicle* is full of them. But the point is – this is the historical context of the Staffordshire hoard, in the middle of the seventh century: those Anglo-Saxon kingdoms battling for supremacy – and perhaps it's even related to that particular battle where Penda, the pagan king of the Mercians, was slain. Somewhere, in the midst of all that brutality and bloodshed, someone gathered together this treasure.

We don't know who buried it – but we can make an educated guess about who all this gold and silver originally belonged to: Anglo-Saxon kings and princes, their royal troops and their priests. One of the largest gold pieces is a pectoral cross, worn on the chest – a very unsubtle religious symbol. It speaks of that Christianisation of Anglo-Saxon kingdoms. But was the person who buried it a Christian? It may well have been loot from a battle – it's been very carefully dismantled.

Perhaps all these glittering pieces represent the spoils of war, stripped off the weapons and chests of slaughtered enemies. Perhaps they were gathered up from slain warriors by their comrades, on the same side – a mass of gold and silver for bargaining with, for sealing new alliances. The archaeologists examining the hoard have suggested that it might have come from a whole series of battles; some of the pieces would have been quite new in the mid-seventh century, while others would have been nearly a hundred years old already. But we'll never know who it was that finally brought all these pieces of metalwork together and hid them away. All we do know is that this treasure was collected up and buried in a time of strife, when kings were riding into battle with each other, when the kingdoms were often at war.

It was hidden in a place which was at once away from other people – but close to them. The hoard was buried on a hill near one of the principal roads across Britain, Watling Street, within the Anglo-Saxon kingdom of Mercia. The hill isn't far from Lichfield, which had become an important religious centre around this time. (Unlike his father, Penda, Wulfhere clearly saw the usefulness of Christianity to an Anglo-Saxon king.) Not too far away is Tamworth – the capital of Anglo-Saxon Mercia. And yet the burial place of the hoard is remote enough from settlements to have been a safe hiding place. Too safe a hiding place.

While the Staffordshire hoard gives us an astonishing insight into the skill and artistry of Anglo-Saxon metalworkers, and the riches that were earned by or bestowed on the soldiers whose collective military might underpinned the power of kings, it is, in the end, an isolated haul of treasure. This is the problem with most hoards: they simply have no physical context. We think we know the broad political context, from the written histories, but we're missing the really important details.

Hoards like this are buried away from any other clues, any other archaeology. We can draw information out of them by finding connections – in materials, in style and in date – with other finds. But they are divorced from the people who would have made them or used them. They have no social or personal context: they are just buried objects – without a burial. Without their people.

Grave goods come to us with a social context. They're buried with someone for a reason. Some are offerings placed in graves, others are artefacts that would have been carried or worn by people.

In 2008, a large plot of land was being prepared for the development of a new housing estate to the northwest of Sittingbourne in Kent, on an area known as the Meads. The area had been fairly thoroughly dug over for brick-earth extraction – so it was expected that most traces of archaeology would have been obliterated long ago. But there was one aerial photograph, taken in 1982, showing a large, circular crop mark – and this was enough to ensure that archaeologists would be on site, watching and supervising as mechanical diggers moved in to strip away the topsoil. The circular crop mark turned out to be the ghost of an ancient ring-ditch – probably all that was left of a Bronze Age round barrow. The remains of a few Bronze Age Beaker burials turned up. But then, it became clear that – right across the entirety of the site earmarked for the housing development – there existed a huge, early Anglo-Saxon cemetery. The watching brief quickly evolved into a full-scale excavation, carried out by a team from Canterbury Archaeological Trust, led by Tania Holmes. They worked on the site from May to December 2008, uncovering more than 200 burials. But the earth was free-draining and slightly acidic; over the centuries, the mineral had been leached from the bones, leaving the protein open to bacterial destruction. A handful of graves contained the crumbling, friable remains of long bones and teeth. But most contained no bones at all. In contrast, the great majority of the graves included grave goods – with more than 2,500 artefacts emerging from those boneless graves.

The cleaning and conservation of these objects posed a massive challenge. The cemetery had been completely unexpected – and its excavation hugely expensive. There was no extra funding for post-excavation processing, let alone analysis. Conservator Dana Goodburn-Brown came up with the idea of involving local people to help conserve the huge collection of artefacts. Two years after the site had been dug, I was filming the first series of *Digging for Britain* for BBC Two, and I visited Sittingbourne to find out how the project was going. I found Dana in an unlikely place: inside the Forum shopping mall, in the town centre. Together with the local heritage museum, Dana had commandeered an empty shop and transformed it into a high-tech conservation lab. She'd called it 'CSI Sittingbourne: Conservation Science Investigations'.

'Have your volunteers ever done anything like this before?' I asked Dana.

'No, no-one's done anything like this,' she said. 'They go through a training session, and work on some practice pieces. And then they start working on the real thing.'

Dana was working on a huge block of sediment with a large, ornate, gilded brooch sticking out of it. But there were metal rings embedded in it too – showing up clearly on an X-ray of the whole block. Some graves contained multiple objects – there were dress fittings and brooches, knives, vessels and weapons, all in need of conservation.

Dana's lab had drawn enormous interest, enticing thousands of people away from their clothes shopping to see accessories from 1,500 years ago instead. And many of them had stayed to learn more, returning as apprentice conservators, to help with the project.

'Normally, conservation work goes on behind closed doors

in a museum,' said Dana. 'And I love my work so much – it's wonderful to share it with other people.' Drawn in by Dana's enthusiasm, and by the wonderful artefacts themselves, the volunteers toiled away, peering through microscopes and removing dirt from the objects, crumb by tiny crumb.

Opposite the lab was another shop which had been turned over to archaeology – this one had been transformed into a mini-museum, a gallery displaying just some of the cleaned-up objects from the Meads cemetery. And they were stunningly beautiful. There were brooches gleaming with inlaid garnets, buckles with ornate patterns, sword and belt fittings, and even delicate glassware.

Anglo-Saxon expert Andrew Richardson had started work on interpreting the finds. He showed me a plated disc brooch with filigree detail and inlaid with garnets – a fine piece of jewellery, amongst the finest that anyone could possess in Anglo-Saxon England. But alongside some outstandingly high-status pieces from the richer graves, there were other, much simpler burials too, containing just the odd, quite ordinary item – such as an iron knife. So this didn't look like a cemetery which was reserved for just the higher echelons of society. Richardson believed he was looking at a graveyard used by an entire community, rich and poor.

Plenty of the graves contained weapons – including iron spearheads and swords. There were pyramidal sword-belt fittings – made of silver, inlaid with gold and garnets – very similar to the examples in the Staffordshire hoard. One grave had contained a sword, a shield boss and a spearpoint, together with two, intact, conical beakers. Andrew interpreted them as designed for communal feasting – and drinking. You can't put down a conical glass – you have no choice but to drain it, or to pass it on. (That theme of funerals and feasting again.) There were several female-gendered burials, including brooches and beads – of glass, amber and amethyst. One grave contained an incredible three hundred beads.

The finds from Sittingbourne suggest the cemetery was in use from the mid-sixth century through to the end of the seventh century. But, with the exception of the garnet-inlaid brooches and some belt fittings, the objects in the graves were not much like those found in earlier Anglo-Saxon cemeteries, in Kent. Did this community see themselves as separate to the kingdom of Kent, further east? Or had fashion moved on by this time?

Delving into the literature, I tracked down some earlier mentions of Anglo-Saxon discoveries, at Sittingbourne. There's an elaborate Anglo-Saxon dagger in the British Museum – just the blade, inset with panels of silver, niello and brass. A note published by the journal *Archaeologia*, in 1874, records this knife being discovered as foundations for a new house were being dug, close to the *Daily Chronicle* paper mill. That mill was at Kemsley, just north of Sittingbourne itself.

The dagger is believed to have been made in Britain – in Northumbria. In the eighth century, two letters were written in the monasteries of Monkwearmouth, on the River Wear, and Jarrow, on the Tyne, making mention of small knives being sent as presents to the Rhineland. They must have been exceptional, as the Rhineland itself was a renowned centre for metalworking and weapon manufacture. One of the letters says 'the knives are made in our style'. This type of knife was known as a 'sax' or 'seax' – a word which might contain the etymology for 'Saxon' within it – and was often worn with swords, and found in burials alongside other weapons. The seax from Sittingbourne bore two inscriptions:

Biorhtelm me worte
S[i]geberiht me ah

Biorhtelm made me
Sigbert owns me

There's a similar inscription on an eleventh-century Viking sword from Norway, this time written in runes – but on a band of metal around the grip. Other sword hilts bear similar 'maker's marks'. A hilt from Exeter bears the words 'EOFRI MEF'. It reminds us that abbreviation has a long history, going back centuries before mobile phones and texting were invented. The long version is thought to be:

Leofric me fecit
Leofric made me

Some later hilts bear single names, usually Germanic: Hartolfr, Hiltipreht, Hliter, Ulfberht. Are these the names of the owners? Perhaps, more likely, they are the names of the smiths or workshops that made them. (I have a small axe from the Swedish Gränsfors Bruk axe factory – and its blade is stamped with the smith's initials. The custom continues.) It seems much rarer that the owner's name is included in an inscription – though with a single name, it's hard to be sure. The Sittingbourne seax leaves us in no doubt, though, recording both the names of smith and owner. Perhaps it was a special commission, or a blade made for a wealthy patron by a smith who worked for him.

Such beautiful weapons – the Sittingbourne seax, the Staffordshire hoard – and all those weapon burials seem to suggest that Anglo-Saxon men took their warrior identity extremely seriously. And the burials with spears, swords, shields and knives do tend to grab our attention. The idea of a lost 'warrior identity' – ancestral heroes – somehow still seems to resonate today. It's often assumed that the weapons were personal belongings, and represented the status of the dead man – the warrior – in life.

But there are various clues which suggest this most obvious interpretation – that weapon burial = warrior – just can't be true. Firstly, the frequency of weapon burials doesn't track with episodes of violence – as far as we can accurately map these from the literature, which is, admittedly, a little sketchy. Providing us with one of the very few contemporary sources, the monk-historian Gildas characterises the sixth century as relatively peaceful – but this is precisely when weapon burials reach their zenith. When the Anglo-Saxons were busy fighting, they weren't burying so many people with weapons. (Maybe there's an economic imperative at work here – perhaps you simply can't afford to bury useful military equipment if you're actively battling it out with other tribes or kingdoms.) The relative paucity of swords in graves, even when weapon burials were at their most frequent, suggests that these particular weapons *were* too precious not to be passed on; they probably would have been kept as heirlooms, rather than being taken to the grave. It's also very rare to see complete 'weapon sets' being buried with their owners – presumably some weapons were selected to be passed on, while others could be disposed of, fulfilling a symbolic role in the grave. Indeed, many of the weapons turning up in graves seem to have been second-hand, adapted and modified: they may have reached the end of their useful 'lives'.

Defining any burial with any number of weapons in it as a 'weapon burial' implies a certain consistency, a standard practice. But these burials are actually very diverse – as we glimpsed at Breamore. Four out of five Anglo-Saxon weapon burials contain a spearhead. Half contain a shield boss. Other weapons – a sword, a knife or seax, an axe, arrows – each occur in about one in ten weapon burials. And were all these objects really weapons? Spears could have been used more often in hunting than in battles. Seaxes, often of a narrow-bladed type, are found on their own in some graves – but surely no-one could have been considered well armed with just this one small knife?

And what about the identity of the individuals in the weapon burials – we assume they were all men, but can we be so sure? In fact, the answer to that is: yes, most of the time. Where it's been possible to sex the skeletons in these weapon burials, they've proven to be almost exclusively male. Having said that, there's a whole group of skeletons whose sex cannot be accurately determined. These are the bones of juveniles. Some of them may have been boys old enough to have borne arms. And some of the weapons accompanying children to the grave appear to have been scaled-down versions, even toys. But then, some of the 'warriors' in those burials were clearly too tiny to have ever held even a toy spear or shield. Weapons have even been found buried with one-year-old infants. So that 'warrior' identity must surely have been symbolic, for some. These infants and children must have inherited that status rather than earned it.

And there are often additional markers of high social status in weapon burials – which, on average, tend to be richer in other ways than other burials. They are more likely to include other grave goods, especially metal objects, and more likely to involve a coffin or wooden chamber. Status and wealth seem to go hand in hand here. Men buried with weapons also tend to be relatively tall – another possible indicator of a wealthier-than-average lifestyle. Stature – like every aspect of biology, in fact – represents an interplay between genetics and environment. Your genes may provide the potential for you to grow to a certain height, but if you are underfed during childhood and adolescence, you will never reach that potential.

There are these hints of social stratification in the cemetery at Sittingbourne, but where did all these people actually live? It's a cemetery without a settlement. Or at least, a cemetery with no known settlement.

The 'ing' in Sittingbourne could be an important clue. Place names containing this Old English *ingas* element were once believed to reach right back to the earliest Anglo-Saxon settlements. Later on, analysis of place names together with archaeology cast doubts on that simple chronology, and on the usefulness of place names for dating the origin of settlements. There didn't seem to be any particular association of 'ing' places with the earliest Anglo-Saxon cemeteries, for instance. But with its early, large and well-endowed cemetery, it's clear that Sittingbourne really was a significant early Anglo-Saxon population centre. The *ingas* means 'people of' – so the first part of the name refers to the people of Sed (whoever he was). Many Anglo-Saxon place names contain references to natural features in the landscape – *dun* is 'hill', *mere* is 'lake', *feld* is 'field' (open land), *cumb* is 'valley', *ford* is, well, 'ford'. And *burna* is 'stream'. The people of Sed, on the stream or burn. Or the Stream of the People of Sed, perhaps. The stream is hard to track down today; it runs under the town.

The Anglo-Saxon settlement at Sittingbourne wasn't a completely new foundation. Like so many other towns, it had grown up over time, with evidence of prehistoric people camping there in the Mesolithic, and settling there to farm in the Neolithic. The Romans created a port at nearby Milton Regis – which has become subsumed as a northern suburb of Sittingbourne today. The settlement lay on Watling Street – the southern end of which connected Londinium to Dubrae (Dover). Local legend has it that invading Saxons made their own fortress close to the ruined Roman fort – perhaps at Castle Rough. This is also said to have been where invading Vikings later set up their camp, in the ninth century, before it became a moated medieval manor. The *Anglo-Saxon Chronicles* says that Vikings landed at 'Middletune' – thought to be Milton Regis – in 892. An earlier episode in Anglo-Saxon history sees Queen Seaxburh becoming regent after the death of her husband, King Eorcenberht of Kent, in 664 – and staying on the throne until her son Ecgbehrt was old enough to take the reins of power. Seaxburh founded abbeys at Milton (reportedly the first abbey for women) and on the nearby Isle of Sheppey, just across the Swale channel to the north. Seaxburh herself became a nun, later moving to become abbess of the double monastery at Ely. In doing so, she founded a tradition where royal women could retain power and prestige by securing top jobs in the hierarchical Anglo-Saxon Church. Like the Romans before them, the Anglo-Saxons were realising the exceptional political – and economic – utility of institutionalised religion. Religious plurality and tolerance were out, Christianity was (back) in. Seaxburh's husband, King Eorcenberht, gets a special mention in the *Anglo-Saxon Chronicle* for overthrowing 'all devil-idols in his kingdom' and being 'the first of the English kings to establish the Easter festival'.

But that was all to come when the people interred at the Meads were laid in their graves, with all their finery. Those people, buried in their clothes, were most likely 'pagan' – the disparaging and derogatory term used by Christians for non-Christians. It comes from the Latin *paganus*, meaning 'rural', 'rustic' or 'villager'. So there's a sense that pagans – from a late Roman, Christian perspective – would have been people living out in the countryside, not in the civilised towns. (In this way, it's similar to 'heathen' – the people living in the open country, in the heath.) But the term 'pagan' was also applied to those who still followed pre-Christian Greek and Roman polytheistic belief systems – for whom the label 'Hellene' (Greek) was also used. The Hebrew Bible had a catch-all term for everyone who wasn't a Jew – *goyim*, which means 'nations' and, in practice, usually meant 'all those other nations'. The Greek Bible has the corresponding *ethne*, which gets translated in to Latin as *gentilis*: 'gentile'. All of this goes to show just how good the Abrahamic religions were at what we might call 'othering' today, as well as infecting our language so deeply that we still use the term 'pagan' to describe people in the past who weren't Christians – defining them in a very negative way, as non-Christian, uncivilised country folk. The value-laden words we use to describe people in northwest Europe who practised religions other than Christianity in the first millennium – and earlier – are derived from Christian and Jewish writings. The old religions of northern Europe were promulgated through an oral tradition – largely lost as Christianity became dominant. Fragments are preserved in collections of Old Norse poems from Iceland, the medieval German 'Song of the Nibelungs' and the Old English epic poem *Beowulf*.

These texts provide us with precious glimpses of the myths and religions which were part of the culture of northwest Europe before Christianity jealously swept them away. There are resonances with Greek mythology that we are – strangely – more familiar with today, including the idea of an underworld and of a hall for the worthy, for slain warriors. The underworld in Norse mythology is Hel, presided over by a goddess of the same name. The underworld of the Greeks was Hades, presided over by its eponymous god. The Norse Valhalla, the Valour-Hall, the Hall of the Slain, seems conceptually close to the Greek Elysium, the Elysian Fields or Isles of the Blessed, where the righteous and heroic would live out their deaths. These two, opposing destinations would become Hell and Paradise in a Christian edit of earlier belief systems.

So often, we assume that, because these ideas were written down, they were taken literally. We know that in certain times and places – and particularly in a Christian context – they were. Undoubtedly, these ideas would feel very real to some. But there's surely something more lyrical, metaphorical and philosophical here, too. I often wonder how many people in the past actually embraced these ideas as rich metaphors: the kind, noble and worthy would be in a good place after death; the malevolent and selfish would rot in a dark hell. Death is so arbitrary: we find ourselves wishing that the souls of the departed will somehow gain from lives lived well – or pay the price for mortal sins. We might acknowledge that life stops at death, and still have these thoughts.

While we can glean some insights into what early Anglo-Saxons thought about what might happen to them after death, from those ancient poems, what we can see quite clearly from the archaeology is that the burial rite involved inhumation of a body, fully clothed. And quite often the body would be accompanied by additional objects – like the shields, spears and buckets at Breamore. It's easy to leap to conclusions about this – to imagine that the clothing and objects were included in the grave for that individual to use in an afterlife. But once again, we should be cautious about such assumptions, because we know how varied our attitudes and beliefs are today. It's all too easy to reduce those ancestors to stereotypes, cardboard cut-outs – a cartoon idea of a 'typical Anglo-Saxon'. But ‚imagine the scene of the funeral, and all the people gathered there. The guiding principle for the mode of burial is surely driven much more by tradition than by a fresh interrogation of beliefs: 'It's what we always do, what everyone does.' And when someone has died, disturbing the pattern, the fabric of the community, there's some comfort in carrying out familiar traditions. Some of the mourners may be of a more mystical bent, imagining the soul of the departed already heading off, dressed just as their body is in that grave, to Valhalla or Hel perhaps. Children might wonder if the person is really just sleeping, and might wake up, or come back in bodily form at some other time. Some may think that life stops at death, whatever the myths say, and that this is just a respectful way to treat a dead body. We tend to think that this is a modern idea, tied up with a more secular view of the world. But we know that humanist perspectives like these existed way back, in antiquity. Some people had a very rational, natural view of life and death. The Roman emperor, Marcus Aurelius, in the second century CE, certainly believed that death was the cessation of existence – for everyone. He saw it as a rule of

Nature: that change was inevitable; that life forms died and other life forms would take their place.

Particularly in places and times where the literary sources are so thin on the ground, we must be careful about making generic assumptions and lumping everyone together – 'The Anglo-Saxons believed . . .' In all times and all places, there are some people who are more deeply religious, others who engage with religion as part of culture, and yet others for whom religion is largely irrelevant. So even those objects in the grave are open to interpretation. We can know that someone placed them in there; we don't know why.

But those artefacts, including clothing, still have the potential to tell us something about the identity of the dead person: who they were in their society, and in turn, how that identity was represented through material culture. Rare finds like the inscribed seax from Sittingbourne let us glimpse a unique individual, not just 'another Anglo-Saxon'. Strangely, perhaps, the bones in those graves are relatively anonymous. It's the artefacts buried with them that let us glimpse these people, these individuals, most clearly.

By the time Dana Goodburn-Brown packed up the CSI Sittingbourne lab and gallery in the Forum shopping centre, nearly twenty thousand visitors had seen the Anglo-Saxon finery from the Meads burial ground. And volunteers had contributed an amazing six thousand hours to the conservation effort between them. One artist-volunteer, Rob Bloomfield, was inspired by the project to create images which captured what he felt and described as an 'aura of mystery and magic' in the lab. Conservation work focuses the attention on tiny details: crumbs of verdigris on bronze, glinting garnets enclosed in tiny metal prisons, filigree curls and flourishes. The intensity of the gaze connects the conservator back through those centuries to the metalworker, the goldsmith, the gem cutter in the Anglo-Saxon heartland of England.

Travelling some 200 miles north from the Swale, past East Anglia, we land in the Lincolnshire Wolds, and track down another metal-detecting discovery – this time, from 2017. Jim Hoff was exploring fields close to his home in Scremby, on the edge of the Wolds. Following the signals from his detector, he found some pieces of Anglo-Saxon metalwork: a broken brooch and a strap-end. He duly reported his finds, and Hugh Willmott, from the University of Sheffield, set off with a small team to carry out an exploratory investigation. Jim's discoveries were just the tip of the iceberg. The trial excavation uncovered richly furnished Anglo-Saxon graves full of metalwork and other artefacts – and the following year, Hugh was back with a larger team, to explore the extent of the cemetery.

From the very beginning, Hugh wondered about who these people were; their graves were classic 'Anglo-Saxon' – but were they born in Lincolnshire or were they immigrants from the continent? It was that enduring question again. 'Perhaps their ancestors had always lived here, and they've just adopted new styles and fashions of the incoming Anglo-Saxons,' he'd suggested at the time. But the question was impossible to answer just by looking at the artefacts – Hugh knew that he would need to call on other techniques, such as isotope and aDNA analyses, to resolve this question.

Just as at Breamore, ploughing had reduced the ground

level so that the graves were covered by a very shallow layer of earth. Once Hugh and his team had stripped the topsoil away, across three large trenches, they could see the shapes of graves standing out. As they dug down within the grave-cuts, skeletons started to appear – accompanied by more metalwork. In one grave, a huge spearhead lay parallel with the femur, or thigh bone: a long blade, some 30 centimetres long, rusty orange with corrosion, shaped like a long, pointed leaf. Hugh recognised the style immediately and knew it dated to the second quarter of the sixth century. In another grave, that of an adult female, a bangle-like ring lay next to the hip. And yet, at around 15 centimetres in diameter, it was too large to be a bracelet. Again, Hugh's knowledge of Anglo-Saxon culture meant that this mystery was quickly solved; he thought it most likely to be a ring which formed the support for a purse-bag. And it appeared to be made of ivory. Where the bag itself – which may have been cloth or leather – would have been, there were other artefacts that had once been contained within it. More ivory rings turned up in other graves. These bag-rings are known from other cemetery sites, especially in Norfolk and Lincolnshire – but they are usually few and far between. Hugh's team had found seven at Scremby – accompanying more than a quarter of the women they found in those graves.

Aside from the bag-rings, the female burials were unusually lavish, even for Anglo-Saxons. Plenty of jewellery was emerging. Many graves contained small, dull brown beads, looking like nothing much perhaps at first glance. But these drab beads would once have been clear, bright, shiny orange: they were amber. One grave contained a multitude of these amber beads, settled amongst the bones of the neck and thorax – this individual must have been buried wearing multiple necklaces.

Another grave presented the poignant scene of a woman who had been buried, resting on her left side, with an infant lying in the embrace of her left arm. Over and amongst the infant bones lay some five hundred beads. All this from a cemetery that was completely unknown, long forgotten – until Jim Hoff found the telltale metalwork in the field.

'At first, we thought this would be a standard Saxon cemetery,' Hugh explained to me, when I met up with him after the excavations had been completed. 'But these are extremely richly furnished graves. Of the twenty four – we excavated, only one had no artefacts in it. That's very unusual.'

Hugh showed me some of the finds that had been discovered in just one grave, containing a female skeleton. This woman had clearly been laid in the grave fully clothed, with all her accessories. One of the items was a fine, decorated buckle.

'This is where the finds get even more special,' commented Hugh. 'This is a very unusual design that you don't normally find in Lincolnshire'.

'Where do you normally find it?'

'Well, not many buckles like it have been found – but the ones we know of are from Kent or the south coast of England.' A buckle that would have been more at home in Sittingbourne, then.

I was intrigued to find out more about the great quantities of amber beads that had been found in the graves. I asked Hugh if he knew where the amber came from. And he did. If I'd asked him this question twenty years ago, it would have been completely impossible to answer. The techniques for pinning down the origins of materials such as amber were just not available. But now spectroscopy – which uses the scattering of light to probe the structure and composition of matter – is proving

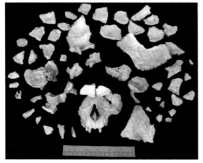

Some archaeological human remains can emerge in a highly fragmented state. This skull was a real jigsaw puzzle – I need to know the detailed features in order to be able to work out where each piece belongs.

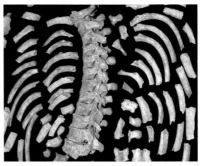

Thoracic vertebrae and ribs: analysis of human remains begins with laying the bones out in the lab – in an anatomical position.

The Roman amphitheatre at Caerleon.

The colour of cremated bone relates to the temperature and duration of burning. Brown or blackened bone is only slightly charred, while blue and grey fragments have reached higher temperatures. White fragments of calcined bone are well cremated. In pyre cremations, different parts of the skeleton may be variably burned – as shown here.

The lead canister which contained the Caerleon pipe burial.

Jill Eyers reviewed the archive of finds from Cocks's 1912 excavations of Yewden Roman Villa, as well as carrying out new fieldwork on the site in 2008–10.

The recycled boxes containing the infant bones from Yewden Roman Villa.

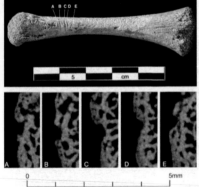

An infant femur bearing cut marks from Roman Hambleden, England (from Mays *et al.* 2012).

A tiny, perinatal skeleton from Yewden Roman Villa. Notice the ends of the long bones look 'unfinished'. At birth, these are still made of cartilage, which does not survive.

Excavation of the Romano-British cemetery at Great Whelnetham, Suffolk.

Decapitated burial from the Great Whelnetham cemetery.

The beautiful Byzantine bucket from Breamore – which prompted an investigation of the cemetery.

Two adult male skeletons in Trench 7, with planning frame in place ready to record the grave by drawing it. Later, we would find a child's skeleton buried between the two adults.

The extremely fragmentary remains of two skeletons from a double burial, Trench 3, Breamore.

Phil Harding and Margaret Cox in Trench 7, Breamore.

Dana Goodburn-Brown's conservation lab in the shopping mall, Sittingbourne.

Dana in action – carefully cleaning beautiful Anglo-Saxon artefacts under the microscope.

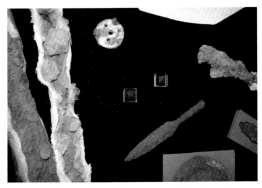

A selection of just a few of the grave goods found in the Meads cemetery, including a sword, a disc brooch, two pyramidal sword-mounts and a spearhead.

Two copper alloy brooches and a pin from one of the Anglo Saxon graves at Scremby, Lincolnshire.

An X-ray of a cruciform brooch from Scremby – revealing hidden details (image courtesy of Pieta Greaves/Hugh Wilmott).

A girdle hanger overlying an ivory bag ring, lying next to the femur of a female skeleton in a grave, Scremby.

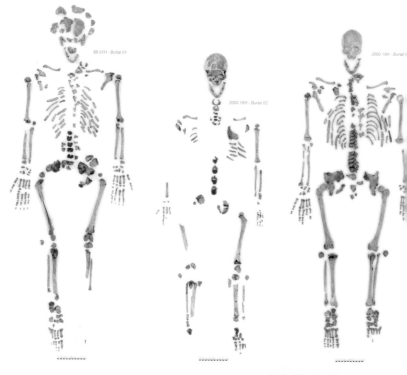

The dig at Glyn Llanbedrgoch, Anglesey.

Excavating the early medieval burial at the bottom of the midden – the author and fellow digger, Llanbedrgoch.

The midden burial, Llanbedrgoch.

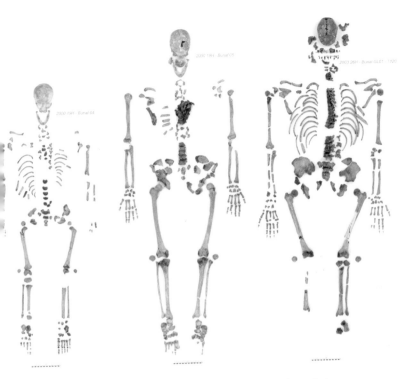

The skeletons from Llanbedrgoch, laid out ready for analysis.

The skeletons (burials 2, 3 and 5) in the ditch beyond the western wall, Llanbedrgoch, 1999.

The sixth skeleton in the group outside the wall, discovered in 2012; the metal-detected coin that sparked investigation of the Llanbedrgoch site.

The author and Mark Redknap, examining skeletons at National Museum Wales.

The cut mark on the back of the male skull (Burial 3) from Llanbedrgoch.

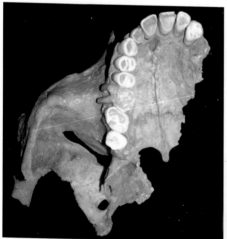

The upper jaw of one of the Llanbedrgoch skeletons, showing heavy wear on the anterior teeth, with yellow dentine exposed on the surface.

The author's husband, Dave Stevens, planning at Llanbedrgoch.

On the Pembrokeshire coast path – on the Penlledwen headland, looking south towards Porth Mawr/Whitesands Bay.

The excavation at Whitesands Bay.

extremely useful. A particular technique called Raman spec-troscopy, named after the Indian scientist C.V. Raman, involves firing a laser at a sample, and analysing the pattern of scattered photons produced. The resulting 'fingerprint' can reveal the chemical composition of materials – in an entirely non-destructive way. It's not surprising that it's gaining the approval of archaeologists – and art historians. And it had pro-vided Hugh with an origin for the Scremby beads. 'This amber comes from the Baltic,' he told me. 'Perhaps not all that sur-prising, as we know the Baltic was a major source of amber.'

Anyway, I was impressed. But I did think there was a chance this Baltic amber might have made its own way to British shores. It could have arrived, borne on the currents of the North Sea, washing up on a beach in East Anglia. But, then again, it's perhaps more likely that it came from Baltic shores and was traded into Britain. We know such trade links existed at the time. And then I wondered if the bag-rings had travelled along a similar route. Hugh thought this was an interesting possibility. 'In the past, people have speculated that perhaps, because you've got an amber trade coming from the Baltic, ivory may have come that way too, from Siberia. It could be mammoth ivory, preserved in the permafrost.'

I knew that it was possible to distinguish mammoth and elephant ivory by its microscopic structure – using Raman spectroscopy. I suggested this to Hugh as a possible line of investigation. But he was one step ahead of me.

'Actually, we've done radiocarbon dating on this ivory and it's clearly contemporary with the Anglo-Saxon cemetery. It must be elephant ivory.'

There you have it. No spectroscopy necessary; there were no mammoths alive in the sixth century – they'd been extinct for some 10,000 years. The next challenge was to work out – if possible – whether that elephant ivory had come from the tusks of an African or an Asian elephant. Hugh pursued this question, and he was later able to give me a definitive answer: the ivory had come from an African elephant, from the Rift Valley.

I was amazed that he'd been able to pin it down so precisely. Hugh had called on the expertise of Michael Buckley, head of the ancient biomolecules laboratories at the University of Manchester, who had undertaken isotope analysis on the ivory. The same technique that is used to trace the childhood home of humans, from the elemental signatures in their teeth, could be used on elephants too.

There was another toothy revelation from Scremby. Hugh told me that one of the female burials contained not only plenty of rock-crystal beads but also a pendant made from a beaver's tooth. 'There's a suggestion that she might have been a cunning woman,' Hugh said, enigmatically.

Hugh wasn't making a comment on this individual's character. Later texts and traditions suggest the existence of the role of the 'cunning woman', perhaps some kind of priestess or shaman, in early Anglo-Saxon society. The word 'cunning' comes from the Anglo-Saxon *cunnon*, meaning 'to know' – so the cunning woman was more wise than devious.

Another potential archaeological example comes from Bidford-on-Avon in Warwickshire, where a woman was buried with thirty-nine glass and amber beads, as well as a leather bib with tiny bronze buckets attached to it – interpreted as amulets. Female shamans or folk healers are also thought to have been important in Viking society – and continued to be active in the far north of Siberia, even through the

Soviet period, right up to the present day. (Later on, of course, such women would be persecuted as witches – considered to be either antithetical to Christianity or, post-Reformation, too dangerously close to being Catholic!)

Hugh sent the beaver tooth, from the Scremby 'cunning woman', for stable isotope analysis. It turned out not to be British – but from a Scandinavian beaver. Perhaps the woman herself had come from Scandinavia.

Some of the Scremby burials contained artefacts which bore stylistic links to southern England: a finger-ring and some brooch types – and that buckle, which looked similar to ones usually found around the south coast and Kent. 'It will be really interesting to see if the isotope data suggest we have local people from Lincolnshire together with people from other parts of Britain or even further afield,' Hugh said. The geologies of Lincolnshire and Kent are sufficiently different that stable isotope studies should be able to differentiate people who had grown up in either of these two areas.

Hugh had also jumped at the chance to enrol the Scremby skeletons in Pontus's Thousand Ancient Genomes project at the Crick Institute. He was keenly anticipating the results – once those genomes were fully sequenced, they should help shed light on the origins of these Anglo-Saxons in Lincolnshire.

While we wait with bated breath for the genomic data to roll in, careful analysis of the style of artefacts in graves – particularly metalwork – can provide us with important clues. Exhaustive analyses of particular artefact types, scrutinising their styles, categorising them by type, seem a bit – old fashioned. They're the sort of thing a nineteenth-century antiquarian or early archaeologist would have done (someone like Pitt Rivers, indeed, who loved to catalogue changes in the style of objects over time). But this kind of analysis can be incredibly useful – far from being just a stamp-collecting exercise – if you trace the evolution of a particular object over time, in its social and historical context.

Toby Martin did just this, spending years poring over the entire collection of more than two thousand cruciform brooches from the UK, and comparing them with others in continental Europe. 'Cruciform brooches', he writes, 'are among the most abundant and important examples of decorative early Anglo-Saxon material culture. They are often the standout objects from cemetery excavations, they dominate the early medieval records on the Portable Antiquities Scheme database [the record for metal-detected finds] and they are frequent display pieces in museums throughout England.'

All this is true, but until Martin started his survey, very few people had tried to work out what these brooches *meant* for Anglo-Saxon society, other than being ornamental dress fixings worn by women. But this new analysis would shed light on how they'd evolved over time, and how they were linked to an emerging sense of identity.

Cruciform brooches seemed to have developed out of a particular type of Roman fibula, the crossbow brooch, but they represent a very definite, Germanic development of this form. They also hark back to Iron Age bow brooch designs. And although the brooches found in England are of a unique, regional style, the wider fashion for wearing big, blingy brooches stretched right across Europe from Iberia, Britain and

Norway, all the way to the shores of the Black Sea. In Britain, and elsewhere in Europe, the appearance of these characteristic brooches has traditionally been linked to incursions by Germanic groups – the Franks into France, the Visigoths into Iberia, and the Ostrogoths into southeast Europe.

But it surely can't be as simple as Bede (however Venerable he was) portrayed it. Group identities may have drawn on these ideas of migratory origins – but ethnogenesis is much more complicated than this. People can adopt ideas and adopt aspects of culture. They can clothe themselves with a social and cultural identity. As Martin points out, there are very few dependable, historical examples of discrete groups of people migrating en masse. And migration always involves change – with new identities emerging. People and cultures aren't hermetically sealed off from each other. Thinking specifically about what the brooches represent, you don't wear something simply because you happen to be from a certain place; you choose to wear it as an expression of your identity. A group's identity feeds into its style; the style crystallises that group's identity. You might adopt a certain style because it's attractive in itself, or because its associations are attractive. As Martin so eloquently and succinctly puts it, 'what if Angles only became Angles by wearing such objects?'

Put like that, we start to see the style as something which speaks of an individual affiliating themselves with a group. Wearing a football shirt not only shows support for a particular club, it expresses a sense of community with all the other supporters of that club. Wearing religious symbols does something similar. But what about all the other clothes and accessories we wear? What are we expressing there, in what seems like a less deliberate choice – but is a choice nonetheless?

It makes you think. What are you wearing today — and why? What do you think your choice will mean to others?

The earliest cruciform brooches in England do appear to be direct imports, in the 420s, and probably were worn by migrants themselves. But very quickly, designs acquired a local flavour, and it's clear that brooches were being made in Britain. They were cast in bronze, using a lost-wax technique. As symbols of identity, it seems important that they *looked* Germanic — but they didn't need to have been made abroad. Again, the football shirt and religious jewellery analogy comes to mind. It doesn't actually matter where the shirt or the crucifix is made, it's what the image represents that's important.

The reason the cruciform brooch became such an iconic Anglo-Saxon artefact may be specifically because ambitious, powerful people chose to wear them, as status symbols. Having a powerful influencer backing a certain style always helps to drive its popularity up. In the early fifth century, cruciform brooches were relatively rare. By the end of the century, they were much more popular and there was an explosion of different styles. By the sixth century, they've become massive and elaborate — but we don't find as many. And in the later sixth century they disappear, replaced by daintier fashions with Frankish and Byzantine connections. (This is surely associated with England reconnecting with what had developed out of the old Roman Empire — which would see those later Anglo-Saxon kings, like Cynegils, converting to Christianity.)

There's a particular concentration of cruciform brooches in East Anglia, but over time they spread, and are found, albeit in lower densities, further north, west and south in England — though never as far west as Cumbria or the southwest of England, and never in Wales. If we can see that spread as linked to an idea of Anglian identity, this does seem to echo the story from history; the *Anglo-Saxon Chronicle* relates how the first king of Mercia backed up his claim to power by saying that he was descended from Anglian royalty, going all the way back to Angulus in Germany.

But it's women, not men, who are potentially signalling their Anglian identity with these brooches. They're just one component of Anglo-Saxon female high fashion – which involved layers of clothes fastened with brooches and clasps, and a belt which could be used to suspend keys, girdle hangers, knives and purses – like the ivory-ringed bags at Scremby. Standard female clothing involved a garment which was worn widely across Europe in antiquity: a simple, peplos-style dress – essentially a tube of fabric which would be held up by being pinned at the shoulders, with cruciform brooches if you were wealthy enough to have them. (It always makes me wonder why they didn't think of sewing a short seam at the shoulders, to hold the dresses up. But I suppose you would then miss out on the opportunity for showing off your best brooches. And perhaps this style was useful for breast-feeding, too.) The peplos was sometimes worn over an under-dress with sleeves, which could be fastened with wrist-clasps: small pairs of metal plates bearing a row of hooks and eyes. Over the peplos, or instead of it, a woman might wear a mantle dress: a square of cloth wrapped round and fastened on one shoulder. And then a cloak could be worn on top of everything. The mantle dress and cloak might also be fastened with cruciform brooches. From the number and position of cruciform brooches in graves, it can be possible to work out which layer of clothing they were used to fasten. A single cruciform brooch at a shoulder suggests a mantle dress;

one at each shoulder, a peplos dress; one or two on the front of the chest, a cloak.

Burying someone fully clothed might seem a little odd to us, today – especially wrapped up in so many layers. In modern funerals, a choice might be made to clothe the body if it's going to be visible to mourners, in an open casket. Or families might want the dead to be dressed in favourite clothes, whether or not they're going to be visibly on display. Sometimes – perhaps rather strangely – brand-new clothes might be bought for the dead person; a bespoke funeral gown might be chosen. But people nowadays certainly don't tend to be buried in layers and layers of clothes, including overcoats.

It seems that, for the Anglo-Saxons, the identity of an individual expressed through their clothes and accessories was quite inseparable from the body itself. Toby Martin points out the contrast between the long and layered nature of Anglo-Saxon clothes for women and those for men, who would have worn tunics over trousers or leggings. Not only were male clothes more practical, you would have seen much more of the shape of the body underneath, especially the limbs. The female body is swathed in cloth, hidden away – with jewellery pinned on those layers – forming a 'social skin'. The clothes and objects, Martin argues, were probably seen as part of that *person*. They had to stay with the body, in the grave.

The clothes may have rotted away long ago, but the objects that survive in the graves contain clues to individual social identities. And this seems to be highly gendered. We've assumed all the graves containing brooches were female. But of course, if we then classify graves according to the artefacts they contain, we enter into a circular argument. What do the bones themselves say? Sometimes it's impossible to assign a sex to a skeleton, and osteoarchaeologists like me will then put the individual into a useful fence-sitting category of 'indeterminate sex'. This doesn't mean that the individual was intersex – though, in rare cases, of course, they may have been – it just means that it's impossible to tell their sex from looking at their skeleton. All the bony features we look at, to determine sex, vary on a spectrum, and some people have skeletons which are in the middle. (This is another area where geneticists can be useful – they can determine sex from aDNA when the skeleton itself is ambivalent.) Toby Martin looked at graves and cremations in which cruciform brooches have been found, and for which there's a record of osteological determination of sex – and astonishingly, more than half turned out to have been classified as indeterminate. Of the remaining skeletons, where sex had been determined, most were female – but 9 per cent were recorded as definitely male.

We can be fairly certain that some of the assumed 'mismatches' between biological sex and gender (expressed through grave goods) may just arise from errors in sexing the bones – that assessment isn't 100 per cent accurate. But in any case, it's important not to approach the evidence with *any* preconceptions – whether those are the expectations that women will always be buried with brooches or beads, and men with spears or swords, or indeed if you're setting out to find 'mismatches' – male skeletons buried with 'female' artefacts and vice versa. Once again, we do have to be very careful not to impose our modern preconceptions on the past – to be as objective as possible, while recognising that we can never entirely escape our own subjectivity. It's also important to recognise the limitations of the data. The actual numbers are low – in Martin's survey, the 9 per cent of graves with cruciform brooches where the skeletons were determined to be male is actually just five graves. One of these 'male' cruciform-brooch wearers was only ten years old – and we don't usually attempt sex determination in juveniles anyway, as the differences between the sexes don't really develop until puberty. Of the others, who were adults, two may be examples of men wearing cloaks fastened with cruciform brooches. The other two were accompanied with other items of feminine dress. Were these anatomically male individuals who had chosen to represent their gender as female? Or were they women who had been mis-categorised by the osteologist? We may never know – though DNA would certainly be useful here. A third possibility is that when these individuals were buried, wearing early forms of cruciform brooches, this fashion wasn't seen as exclusively feminine. Brooches had been worn by both men and women in Roman times, certainly. So perhaps these Anglo-Saxon men could wear their cloaks fastened with cruciform brooches without appearing feminised or even emasculated. We should also look at the wider picture here. After all, we're choosing to look at just two things: biological sex of an individual, and one particular accessory – which we're assuming carries a gender label with it. But what if those men had been given those brooches as gifts, or had inherited them? All we see is a brooch buried with a man – a single point in time, frozen for centuries – we don't know anything else about the life story of that person, or the 'life history' of the brooch either.

I caught up with Hugh to find out more about his analysis and interpretations of the Scremby burials. He'd received the initial screening data from our geneticist friends working on the Thousand Ancient Genomes project at the Crick Institute. This included information on sex, and Hugh was pleased that this had matched up very well with the osteological determinations of sex.

'Well, that's a relief to hear, for an osteologist!' I laughed. 'In the early days, there were quite a few cases when the genetic determination of sex was opposite to what the osteologists had concluded. But the DNA techniques have improved – and we have much better agreement, thankfully.'

Modern genetic techniques now involve thousands of short sequences being read, which can be mapped onto X or Y chromosomes – and the correlation with osteological techniques (in those cases where we can be sure of sex) is now practically 100 per cent. This means we can now be much more trusting of genetic estimations of sex – and even rely on them in those cases where all I'd be able to say about a skeleton was that it was of 'indeterminate sex'.

The pattern of grave goods at Scremby also echoed what Toby Martin had found in his survey – there was a good match between biological sex and the binary-gendered nature of dress and accessories. 'There are no surprises there,' said Hugh.

'What about weapon burials? Were there any at Scremby?'

'Yes, but they're very boring. That's why I always tend to talk about the female graves!' Hugh laughed. 'There are no swords. The men are all buried in a very similar way. They have a spear; they have a knife; they have a shield. That's it.'

'The classic triad.'

'Yes, all boringly similar. No differentiation to speak of. There was one burial with a bird-shaped shield fitting. But apart from that, they were all very uniform. And dull.'

This is not something which is restricted to Scremby. In particular, there's not much regional differentiation in objects buried with men – in contrast with the varying styles of those cruciform brooches in female graves. Male grave goods say 'We're men, and we're Anglo-Saxons.' Female grave goods say 'We're women, and we're Anglo-Saxons, *and* we're from this particular region.'

'What do you think these weapon burials represent, though? Are they all warriors, or is it more symbolic?' I asked Hugh.

'I think they're men. And that's just what you bury a man with. If you're an Anglo-Saxon man, you probably have a shield and a spear, whether you use them or not. If you're spending all your time farming, you've probably got a shield in the cupboard, and then when you die – that's what you're buried with.

'What's interesting is why you don't get more objects in male graves at this time. They're not demonstrating status by adding in anything else. So I think they were just buried in what they were wearing – with their own weapons. It's only later, in the seventh century, when you get flamboyant princely burials full of treasure.'

It was always very refreshing talking to Hugh. He looked at those rusted remnants of weapons in the graves, and wondered what these had meant to the person they were buried with; what it might have been like to live in Anglo-Saxon Lincolnshire. The weapons suggest a general right to bear arms, and may have been a marker of a freeman, as well as suggesting some degree of wealth.

Hugh also paid exquisite attention to detail – and he'd noticed something particularly important about brooches. 'What always strikes me, digging up brooches – and something that isn't discussed much,' he'd said to me, 'is that they're always used and worn. The gilding isn't perfect. They're rubbed; they're repaired. Sometimes there's a suggestion that the brooches would have been special objects placed in the grave – but I think they're simply burying people in what they were wearing, the day they died.'

There's an inclination to use the number of brooches buried with someone as a way of ranking their status. But Hugh thought there could be an alternative explanation. At Scremby, there was a particular woman who had been buried with a pair of annular brooches at her shoulders, fastening her tunic dress. But then she had *four* cruciform brooches as well. 'She was obviously wearing another outer garment or cloak, pinned in place. There's a tendency to think: she must have been special, she's wearing all these brooches,' said Hugh. 'But perhaps she just died in winter, buried in her winter cloak.' Maybe even two cloaks – if it was very cold.

It makes sense – perhaps varying numbers of brooches just reflect the season of death and burial. 'It does feel as though, with these early Saxon burials, they're just buried with what they have. There might be food offerings placed in the grave, but otherwise, it's very much life reflected in death,' remarked Hugh.

It's interesting to look at the ages of people buried with cruciform brooches. It seems that girls began to wear peplos dresses around the age of twelve – and this is perhaps when they began to be viewed as young women. But showy dress items, like cruciform brooches and girdle hangers, begin to be worn in the late teens – and are most commonly found accompanying women in their late twenties, thirties and forties. What's important to recognise is that, while cruciform brooches are such recognisable, eye-catching Anglo-Saxon accessories, they would still have been quite rare – worn by just a few women, perhaps around one in seven. Were these older women seen as matriarchs, as founders of lineages and guardians of Anglian identity? Toby Martin certainly sees them as 'part of a network of elite groups throughout Europe who all dressed in closely related, if regionally distinctive, costumes'. (It will be fascinating to see whether we can pick up these lineages by sequencing the genomes of women buried with brooches across England – another question that the Thousand Ancient Genomes project might be able to shed light on.)

If Martin is right, it wasn't really the cruciform brooches as such that represented the group's identity, it was the women themselves – in their dresses, their mantles, their cloaks, pinned through with those symbols. And this was a new, visibly un-Roman, distinctively 'Germanic' identity. Symbols are powerful, and this identity made great use of this material, visual language. It was important in life – and remained important in death. 'There is no other period in Europe's history,' Toby Martin writes, 'when quite so much property was put into so many graves.'

The culture that spreads across southern and eastern England in the fifth and sixth centuries – a culture in which those iconic cruciform brooches are embedded – seems to fit so neatly with the traditional historical story of mass migration from Germanic homelands; why would we even doubt this narrative?

The doubt, the devil, lies in the detail.

The link between material culture and ethnic identity is much more tenuous than we may assume. We interpret Anglo-Saxon style as Germanic, but we don't know if the people buried with cruciform brooches and enamelled buckles, or with swords and spears, saw *themselves* as Germanic. We should be cautious about projecting an ethnic identity onto them. In his *Ecclesiastical History,* Bede gives us a neat picture where whole ethnic groups move into Britain, bringing their culture with them. But perhaps he and other chroniclers were trying to make sense of a cultural change they knew had happened in preceding centuries – and to them, the most obvious way of explaining it was the arrival of a whole new group of people in Britain. But which came first – the ethnic identities (whatever they were) or the myths?

In some ways, it's as though post-Roman Britain was returning to an idea of itself that it had before it became part of the Empire. Perhaps we could even start to see Roman Britain as an aberration – being part of the Empire in some ways obscured long-standing connections between Britain and neighbouring polities and cultures (especially at the more eye-catching elite level of villas and higher-status burials). And then those connections became much more visible again as Britain fragmented away from the shrinking Empire.

Ancient genomics holds out the promise of finding out how much this cultural change, this new identity, was linked to change in the population itself. And one day very soon, we'll know the ancestry results for the people in the cemetery at Scremby. 'I really didn't expect Scremby to turn into such an interesting project,' Hugh Willmott confided to me. 'It's yet another Anglo-Saxon cemetery amongst hundreds. But I do hope it can shed light on some of our big questions about the Anglo-Saxons.'

With a new excavation of a cemetery, carried out using modern techniques, Hugh knew the context of every single object – not just which grave each came from, but where in the grave. And he could use the very latest scientific methods to interrogate the evidence, to tease out the answers he was after. 'We can look at the material culture very carefully, going beyond simply cataloguing different types and styles – and try to understand what it tells us about networks of trade and communication. Those ivory bag-rings, for instance – rather than just saying "It's an ivory bag-ring", we can think about *how* that ivory comes from the Rift Valley and makes its way to Lincolnshire. And of course, we have the opportunity to look at the ancestry of these people, using ancient DNA.'

Hugh was still waiting for the more detailed results of the genome analysis. But he'd heard back about the results of isotope analysis – for the woman buried with the decorated buckle. And it had provided a surprising answer.

'She's not from Lincolnshire,' said Hugh. 'But neither is she from further afield – across the North Sea. She grew up on the south coast, we think, somewhere around Kent or even Brighton.'

It was just extraordinary – to be able to unlock such biographical details from bones, so many centuries later. As a young girl, this woman had lived down in southeast England, then – and this is a part of her story we will never unearth – made her way north to Lincolnshire.

The composition of her teeth matched the origin of her buckle.

'She's wearing things still, which hark back to her childhood in Kent, then,' I observed.

'Absolutely,' agreed Hugh. 'There's a memory that lingers.'

6.

THE VIKINGS IN THE DITCH

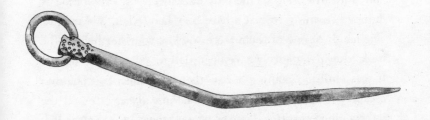

So many late summers, digging on Anglesey, at a site on a farm called Glyn Llanbedrgoch, near Benllech on the northeast coast of the island. I was there with the man who would eventually become my husband, who was working as an archaeologist for Amgueddfa Cymru, the National Museum Wales. He was there supervising students in the trenches, surveying the site. I went along as a volunteer – I could be useful, armed with a mattock or trowel, and even more useful if any human remains turned up. And they did.

One year, we found an early medieval burial. The body had been laid into the ground with care, but we found that grave a metre deep, at the bottom of a midden, with rubbish piled up on top of it. Another year, we found an Iron Age burial, close to a freshwater spring. The body had been tucked up into a crouched position. Those individuals have their own stories to tell. But it was the five skeletons we discovered over two summers in particular that have kept intruding into my thoughts. And we're still unlocking secrets from their bones.

Those skeletal remains were found just outside the perimeter wall of the settlement. The bodies had not been carefully laid out. They all seemed to have been unceremoniously dumped, coming to rest where they had fallen, awkwardly. The hands of one of them were so close together behind the back, they must surely have been tied together at the wrists. It was chilling, coming across these remains. You couldn't escape the brutality of the end of those lives, after all the intervening centuries. Even as we dug them, it was clear that two of them were children.

I'm voyaging. Island-hopping from shore to shore. On the lookout for the next adventure, with my cousin who is more like my sister. We are closer than our shared DNA would suggest.

We're exploring the Outer Hebrides – taking the ferry from the island of Berneray, north of North Uist, to continue northwards to Leverburgh, on Harris. A rainy squall delays our departure; it's important to have good visibility on this short voyage.

We pull away from the slipway and pier at Aird Ma-Ruibhe, and head off: weaving between McCaskill Rock and Little Sandbank Rock; swinging round the north side of Ceann Na Dige, past three unnamed rocks; another nameless rock west of yellow rocks west of Sursay, to the east of the submerged Sgeir a Siar; west of Sgeir a Chruinn, then Brusda, Narstay Rocks, east of Sgeir an Iaruinn, Sulliven; squeezing between Cabbage South and Cabbage North, past Cabbage Racon off our starboard bow, and the tiny island of Gousman, then between Sgeir Chruaidh and the islet of Eire, west of Groay; turning to port around Rodel Rocks, across a reef line and then across a larger reef, shallowing to just 2.4 metres at lowest of low tides – slow, slow, the green of shallow sand beneath us, darker rocks; past Knight's Rock and west of Langay, close to Mile Sgeir, Grocis Sgeir, swinging around Grocis North, then through deeper waters, around Stumbles Rock, moving into Jane's Trench, between Bo Stainen and Sgeir Mhic Coma west of us, Eilean a Charnain to the east; then slipping in just west of Suam an t-Struth, safe into the port at Leverburgh.

The marine map on the ferry was strewn with this collection of English eponyms and straightforward descriptive words – Sandbank; the lumpy Cabbages; Stumbles. But it was the Gaelic words that caught my eye and settled into place inside patterns of thought that had been running like subroutines amongst the tangle of neurons inside my skull, for some time now.

Sgeir, *skerry*, *sker*: respectively Gaelic, English and Old Norse (and modern Danish) for a rocky island or reef. The Old Norse *sker* is the earliest of these words, the ancestor of the others. It means 'cut' – the rock is cut off from land, fragmenting into the sea.

I knew there were some Old Norse – Viking – words in English. *Gate*, from the Old Norse word for 'street', *berserk* and *husband*, *reindeer*, *skull* and *gift*. But what about Norse connections with Gaelic? The Viking presence in the Outer Hebrides is well attested in the archaeological record – from the Lewis Chessmen to Viking settlements and boat burials. Vikings settled Scotland and its islands – as well as Ireland – extensively in the later centuries of the first millennium CE. And by the ninth century, they had created a Viking kingdom in the northern half of England too, with its capital at York. That Viking kingdom effectively ended when the Northumbrians kicked out Eric Bloodaxe, but the Vikings were back in 1016, when the Danish King Cnut led an invasion and took the throne of all England. Cnut's son, Harthacnut, ruled England until his death in 1042, when the throne passed to the Anglo-Saxon son of Æthelred the Unready, Edward.

Viking interest in the Scottish islands started earlier – and their control in this area lasted longer. Historical sources tell of Viking raids on the Gaelic kingdom of Dál Riata starting in the late eighth century CE – with attacks on the monastery on Iona. Dál Riata was a scattered coastal and island kingdom, encompassing western Scotland (Argyll means 'coast of the Gaels'), the southern Hebrides and northeastern Ireland. By the ninth century, the Irish annals describe Viking leaders who seem, now, to have been based in Scotland. Viking rule was consolidated when Harald Fairhair of Norway took the Northern Isles and the Hebrides, sending a governor to maintain control. But this governor, a certain Ketill Bjornsson, nicknamed Flatnefr, 'Flatnose', turned rogue and declared himself the King of the Isles – including the Hebridean islands, Arran and Bute, and the Isle of Man. At various times, the kings of Norway, Scotland and Ireland clashed over supreme control of these islands, which continued to be locally ruled by kings and lords with very Scandi names – Sigurd, Lagman Godredsson, Olaf Godredsson, Ragnall – right up to the last

King of the Isles, Magnus Olafsson, after whose death, in 1265, the kingdom became part of Scotland.

The Norse influence on place names in this archipelago was extensive and lasting – almost completely replacing Gaelic names, though it's thought that Gaelic continued to be spoken in the southern Hebrides. That's what the historians say. But how much fusion was there between cultures and language? The fact that so many Norse words persist in Gaelic today – not just *sgeir* – suggests that the languages may have merged much more than has perhaps been accepted previously. And perhaps there's an even more interesting possibility – we've assumed Gaelic, and indeed English, to have been quite separate entities from Norse languages at the commencement of Viking contact with Britain and its islands. We may have been led astray by what we see as a very coherent and easily identifiable package of culture that has been labelled 'Viking', both in Scandinavia and further afield. Scandinavian connections across the North Sea and around the coasts of Scotland and Ireland undoubtedly go back earlier than the eighth century: the Vikings may have had great ships, for sure, but they didn't *invent* boats. Maritime links between Britain and the near continent go right back into deepest, darkest prehistory. And the Celtic languages of Britain were not entirely separate creations from the languages of northwest Europe – they are part of that language family, with a common root. They evolved off in their own directions, certainly, but never in complete isolation from each other. Cross-fertilisation – exchange of words and ideas – must surely have happened before the Vikings themselves arrived.

These were the kinds of ideas that had been floating around in my brain – an archipelago of separate ideas, beginning to join up, just as wind-blown sand forms a causeway to unite an islet with an island.

One such islet formed in 2018, when I was in Norway — filming in winter snow with champion dog-sledders. After a long and exhilarating day outside, I sat in a cosy restaurant and looked, bleary-eyed, at the menu. I squinted at it. I could *read* it. Now let me be quite clear about this: I don't speak Norwegian. I can't understand anyone speaking it — though some of the rhythms seem similar to English. But when I looked at those words for foods I was familiar with — it turned out I was sort of familiar with those words as well.

There was *brød* — bread. *Fisk*, which was fish. *Frukt*, which was fruit. *Paerer* — pears. *Steik* — steak. And — *egg*. So was the language I spoke more Scandinavian than I'd assumed it was? English is described as a Germanic language, with its roots in western Germanic languages. Words can travel both ways, of course, but there seemed to be a hint here that there was more of a northern Germanic, or Scandinavian, influence.

Later that year, I met a Norwegian man at an education conference in Birmingham. I mentioned how I'd been taken aback by the similarity between Norwegian and English. Being (at least) bilingual, he was already well aware of it.

'And I can easily read *Beowulf* in the original — not because I know English, but because Old English seems to be even closer to Norwegian,' he told me.

'Do you know,' I said, 'the more I think about these connections — the Viking presence in Britain, for so long — the more I start to see my country from the outside. And it looks like — I don't know — an outpost of Scandinavia, off in the north Atlantic.'

'Ha! That's how we've always thought of you,' my new friend replied.

It's all very complicated. English is meant to have taken hold in southern Britain during the 'Dark Ages', after the collapse of the Roman Empire, when those invading Angles, Saxons and Jutes brought their new Germanic language – and their distinctive material culture – with them. This, the historical tradition goes, is when the earliest version of English replaced the preceding Celtic or Brittonic languages across much of Britain, leaving variants of that language family pushed to the edges, surviving in what would evolve into modern Cornwall, Wales and Scotland – and in the island of Ireland. Old Norse was spoken by the invading Vikings who established their almost-century-long northern kingdom of Northumbria, but then it died out, replaced by English as Anglo-Saxon influence swelled.

In Scotland and its isles, there's a similar tale, of various languages – Scots, Gaelic, Pictish – competing with each other, replacing each other, being overturned. The introduction of Old Norse by the Vikings and their ilk left its mark on place names and people's names, but then died out after the Viking era – like a tide rushing in and then receding – leaving Gaelic, and later, English, to fill the gap.

What seems missing from these too-simple narratives is the mixing of languages that *must* have happened. Just as Viking DNA was mixed into British DNA – meaning the genomes of everyone living in these islands would never be the same again – the language of the Vikings must have permeated any languages that were already here, and surely not just by leaving a few borrow-words scattered in its wake.

So this hunch of mine demanded more investigation, more research. If I was right, English – and Gaelic – would bear much more evidence of Scandinavian influence than is perhaps commonly accepted. Was there any recent research challenging the old paradigms? It turned out there was, and in fact linguists have been pointing to extensive Norse influence in Scotland since at least 1975. I was late to the game. The histories – once again – have led us astray, creating the impression that the Viking presence in Ireland was more extensive than it ever was in Scotland. But language and culture strongly suggest the opposite is true. And linguists think that Old Norse continued to be spoken in the Hebrides up to the sixteenth century, when it seems there was quite an abrupt shift to Scottish Gaelic as the preferred language – perhaps over just a few bilingual generations. The old tongue still echoes in the dialect of Scottish Gaelic spoken in the islands today. Early attempts to quantify the number of words that had passed into Scottish Gaelic from Old Norse produced surprisingly limited results – suggesting that only around 2.4 per cent of words had arisen in this way (compared with 13 per cent coming in from English), although more recent analysis has increased the estimate a little. But it's in place names where Old Norse dug its heels in most firmly. Any island name ending with 'ey' or 'ay' remembers its Norse settlers. Some island names seem to have transformed from older names into Norse versions – including Unst, Yell and Fetlar in Shetland, and Lewis and Uist in the Outer Hebrides. But the vast majority of place names in the Northern and Western Isles are Norse with no apparent incorporation of any preceding Gaelic language – it's a profound linguistic takeover. Something different happens when Old Norse is eventually replaced with Gaelic – as many place names, like Loch Langavat and Ben Tangaval, still contain their Norse elements. Linguists have argued that the Gaelic-to-Norse transition was mediated by a population replacement.

Archaeology seems to support this interpretation – with an abrupt change in culture in the ninth century in the Western Isles. The later Norse-to-Gaelic switch appears to have been a language change without a major population turnover.

The Irish annals offer some clues. They describe the Gaelic kingdom of Dál Riata, encompassing the western coast of mainland Scotland, the Inner Hebrides and part of what is now Northern Ireland, which was in its heyday in the sixth and seventh centuries. They also describe a new group of people, the Gall-Ghàidheil or 'Foreigner-Gaels', who are involved in several conflicts in the ninth century. They describe other foreigners too, the Finngaill or 'Fair Foreigners' (thought to be Norwegians) and the Dubgaill or 'Black Foreigners' (thought to be Danes). So they seem to recognise different groups of Scandinavians. The Gall-Ghàidheil could be either Scandinavianised Gaels or a mixed group of Norsemen and Gaels fighting together. But they're hard to pin down. After appearing in the annals in the ninth century, they evade historical mention until the eleventh century, when suddenly we hear about a king of Gall-Ghàidheil – and now the name seems to refer to southwest Scotland and its people. The name itself persists through to the present – it is Galloway.

A Frankish bishop and chronicler of the ninth century provides us with another view, telling us that the Northmen conquered Dál Riata – taking over islands all around Ireland, with no resistance. And back in the *Annals of Ulster*, one entry refers to the leader of the Gall-Ghàidheil as a certain Caittil Find – thought to be none other than Ketill Flatnose himself.

Place names remain like flags stuck in the map, or graffiti tags: 'Vikings were here'. Almost all place names in Shetland and Orkney are derived from Old Norse. The far north of mainland Scotland – corresponding with modern-day Sutherland and Caithness – is also full of Norse names. And, as well as the Western Isles themselves, the west coast of mainland Scotland is liberally scattered with these names, including many ending with 'dale' from Old Norse *dalr*, meaning 'valley', 'bie' from *býr*, 'farm', and 'sta' from *sœtr*, meaning 'pasture'. Another clue to an Old Norse origin is when the place name includes 'of' – as in the Burn of Forse, the Garth of Tresta or the Clett of Thusater. Many of these place names are essentially descriptions of the location in the landscape. Others tell us what was happening at these places – and especially letting us know where seats of power and government developed. The modern parliament of Iceland is the Althing, originating as the *thingvellir* in the tenth century. Then, from the same root, there's the Tynwald, or parliament, in the Isle of Man, and the place names of Dingwall in the Highlands and Thingwall on the Wirral peninsula. All of these come from the Old Norse *thing vollr* – meaning 'assembly field'.

But the trail of clues doesn't stop there; it continues south, to the Isle of Man, which was part of the Kingdom of the Isles until the thirteenth century (and thereafter, ruled by Scottish and English kings, while remaining quite independent – and it's still not part of the UK today).

It becomes very difficult to separate out the spheres of Scandinavian influence as we move further south. To the east, in the north of England, there are territories that are historically attested as northern Anglian kingdoms. There seems to have been some Anglian intrusion into what is now Dumfries and Galloway, judging by place-name evidence. But then, that territory in the north of England was conquered by the Great Heathen Army (of Vikings) in the ninth century. If we focus on southwest Scotland, the people who have left their language embedded in the landscape could have come from the east, from the Viking kingdom emerging in northern England, but also from the north, from the expanding, Norse-ruled Kingdom of the Isles. There also seems to be a Gaelic influence on Norse names – which suggests the namers could well have been those Gall-Ghàidheil, Scandinavianised Gaels from the Kingdom of the Isles. The same pattern is seen further south, in Cumbria and Lancashire. Linguists have also been able to tease apart the differences between names based on an East Norse (Danish) dialect and those based on a West Norse (Norwegian) dialect. That West Norse dialect includes elements such as *scale* ('hut'), *fell* ('mountain') and *beck* ('stream'). So it seems that Vikings – or at least, descendants of Vikings – named Seascale ('the hut by the sea'), Scafell Pike ('the bald mountain') and Beckfoot ('stream mouth'). And there's also place-name evidence of Norse influence around the coast of Wales, from the Great Orme ('great serpent') and Worm's Head to Swansea ('Sweyne's island' – though this is contested), Skomer ('cleft island') and Anglesey ('Öngel's Island').

By the eighth century, the Anglo-Saxon kingdom of Mercia had expanded westwards, as far as Wales. But whatever England was becoming, Wales was different. It was its own place. The people there would continue speaking a Brittonic language – a language that would eventually become Welsh. The culture was quite definitely *not* Anglo-Saxon. But there has also been a perception that Wales was largely untouched by the raiders, traders, settlers and rulers who made such a huge impact on northern Britain – and Ireland – in the closing centuries of the first millennium: the Vikings. And yet, the scatter of Norse place names suggest that Vikings knew at least the coast of Wales quite well.

There are historical references to Vikings in Wales, too. In the mid-ninth century, Rhodri Mawr – or Rhodri the Great – was the king of Gwynedd, which had expanded to control most of modern Wales. But the kingdom was under assault not only from the Saxons of Mercia, to the east, but from Vikings, who attacked Anglesey. The *Welsh Annals* refer to the Vikings as the *kenedloed duon*, the 'dark foreigners'. In 856, Rhodri fought back – killing the Viking leader Gormr or Orm (another 'serpent'). But just ten years later, Vikings attacked York, and took control of Northumbria. Meanwhile, the Mercians were on the warpath again, and Rhodri was killed in an invasion in the 870s. His kingdom was divided up amongst three heirs, with the northern kingdom of Gwynedd passing to his eldest son, Anarawd. In the 880s, the Mercians attempted another invasion, but this time, the Welsh, led by Anarawd and his brothers, beat them back. (This was the end of Mercia's expansionist ambition, and that Anglo-Saxon kingdom would go on to be ruled by the king of Wessex, Alfred the Great.) Still worried about the Mercian neighbours, Anarawd decided his best bet was to seek an alliance with the Vikings of Northumbria – and it's possible that this alliance was a rather uneven relationship, in which the Vikings essentially gained control of Gwynedd for some sixteen years.

In 902, Anglesey was under attack by Vikings once again. This lot had been expelled from Dublin, and were looking for somewhere else to settle down. Led by Ingimund, these Vikings landed on Anglesey and took over a place called Maes Osfeilion, thought to lie on the north coast of the island, close to Red Wharf Bay. Anarawd had gone off the Vikings by now, and was having none of it. He fought and won Anglesey back, forcing the defeated Vikings to wander off and find somewhere else; the Irish annals record that this 'somewhere else' was the Wirral, then lying within Mercian territory. But occasional raids on Anglesey continued for another two decades. The island was right in the middle of a network of seafaring routes across the northern Irish Sea. Dublin lay to the west – and was seized by the Vikings again in 917. The Isle of Man and the Hebrides, further north, were already under Norse control by this time. And then there was the Wirral to the east, with its Norse-named Thingwall and a port called Meols, from *meir* in Old Norse, meaning 'sand dunes'. It must have seemed like a waste if you were to sail right by without grabbing the opportunity to stop off for a quick raid on a rich farmstead or even a monastery on Anglesey. The fact that the island acquired what seems to be a Viking name might suggest that they didn't just drop by, but eventually put down roots there too. But we should be cautious about this – as the island has a completely different Welsh name, Ynys Môn. The Scandinavian name may have persisted amongst cultures that were around the Irish Sea, but it doesn't seem to have been embraced by the native population – who continued to use their own Welsh name.

Later historical records tell of an increased Viking presence in Anglesey and on the mainland of north Wales in the tenth and eleventh centuries – with a suggestion that part of Gwynedd was even ruled by Vikings for a period. But there has been very little in the way of archaeological finds to back this up. At least, until 1993, when two metal detectorists, Archie Gillespie and Pete Corbett, found some lead weights and a coin in recently ploughed fields on the farm of Glyn Llanbedrgoch, near Benllech.

These finds would change everything.

Archie sent a small package of his finds to Mark Redknap, Keeper of Archaeology at the National Museum Wales. The coins seemed significant. Mark jumped in a car and drove up to Anglesey. He remembers driving down the lane to the farm, all overgrown. 'It was as if we were going back in time,' he told me. And when he stopped the car, he was suddenly surrounded by a pack of enormous Irish wolfhounds. There was an uneasy moment. But the hounds were gentle giants, and in the farmhouse, Mark met Roger and Debbie Tebbutt, who were excited about the discoveries made on their land. They granted Mark permission to dig – and in 1994, he was back, for a brief, five-day exploration. He took a small team with him, and they did as much geophysics across the fields as possible, with some small, targeted trenches to 'ground-truth' any features that showed up on the scans. They found what looked like a massive ditch in one field – a ditch which could well be associated with some sort of defended perimeter to a settlement. Inside that assumed perimeter, a carefully positioned trench reached down to the buried floor of a long-forgotten building. More early medieval finds emerged. Mark knew then that this was a significant site. It would keep drawing him back, every summer, until 2001, and then sporadically thereafter, for even longer.

Over the years, Llanbedrgoch would be dug again and again. A generation of archaeology students, from Cardiff, Bangor and further afield, would cut their teeth and wear down their trowels digging for the Vikings of Anglesey. Mark ran the excavations, with an experienced team from the National Museum. And every year, more discoveries would be made, more mysteries would be solved, and new questions would present themselves.

As the evidence accumulated, Mark could start to tell the story of a forgotten settlement through time. The site had been occupied for centuries before the Viking period, but by the late ninth century, it had developed into an important trading post. Strong stone walls were constructed around the site at this time – probably in direct response to the increased threat of Viking raids.

Within the settlement, there was evidence of daily life and industry – with various different buildings, some of stone, some of timber. There were hearths for heat and cooking, evidence of baking and woodworking, and plenty of evidence of metalworking – bronze, iron and lead. There were piles of animal bones, showing us what meat people were eating at Llanbedrgoch; a high proportion were deer bones – often associated with high-status sites. There were also several pieces of decorative horse trappings, including bridle bits. But in September 1998, we made an unexpected discovery: two skeletons, in the ditch outside the western wall of the settlement. Three more skeletons were discovered, just a little further down the ditch, in the following year.

I helped to excavate those human remains. The bones were incredibly fragile and friable. I used a thin leaf trowel to gently move earth away from them, swapping to wooden pottery tools for even more delicate work. I didn't attempt to clean all the clayey mud away from the bones, though. They were so crumbly, they would have completely fallen apart. Once each skeleton was completely exposed, it was photographed and drawn. The drawings are useful – it's easier somehow to pick out important details, and even to differentiate between bone and stone, when you're looking at the real thing, rather than trying to work it out from a photograph. These bodies appeared to have been thrown into the ditch. There were no grave-cuts that we could see – no evidence of someone having dug a pit to place a body into. The dispositions of the bodies varied, and one skeleton lay on top of another. There were no grave goods with them.

On site, I could tell we were looking at the skeletons of two adults – looking like one younger and one older male – together with three adolescents. I'd be able to tell more when the bones were cleaned up, back in the lab. I lifted each bone very carefully and wrapped it in tissue paper before placing it in the requisite cardboard skeleton box – a different box for each skeleton – to give those remains some chance of surviving the journey down to the National Museum in Cardiff. There, the bones would be washed and consolidated – and once that work was done, I'd have a chance to take a proper look at them, and to prepare my bone report for Mark.

Mark had also sent samples off for radiocarbon dating – and most of the results came back suggesting a tenth-century date, though one skeleton dated to the eleventh century. I was surprised by this spread of dates. I'd expected these five individuals to have all met their deaths around the same time – in a single event. It seemed like the most likely, neat and parsimonious explanation for this group of roughly handled, hastily buried bodies. Mark was immediately wary of the discrepancy in the radiocarbon dates, too, although he thought it possible that the bodies could have been disposed of in the ditch sequentially, with perhaps decades intervening between some burials. If they weren't buried at precisely the same time, though, it was clear that the location of any earlier burials was still known about when later bodies were added – that there was some living memory of the location of earlier graves. The variation in the ranges of the radiocarbon dates drove Mark's conclusion that the graves may not represent a single event in time, but rather, that the bodies had been buried – or thrown into the top of the ditch – within a short time of each other.

Chucking bodies into ditches was not a normal burial practice for this time. Burying individuals in cemeteries was the usual thing. There are conventional early Christian cemeteries on Anglesey, usually with graves oriented east–west, and some lined with stone slabs. But these people had not been treated with any care or respect in death, I was sure. What we were looking at seemed to be about basic disposal of bodies, rather than a funerary rite. They could have been victims of disease, hurriedly thrown outside the settlement, for fear of contagion, I suppose. But with that one individual with his hands – most probably – tied at his back, I suspected foul play. And that body was lying right on top of one of the younger individuals. It looked to me that the most likely cause of death here was not a microbial pathogen, but a human assailant.

The bodies were in very shallow graves – perhaps even natural hollows. There certainly hadn't been much effort put into their burial. Even if pits had been slightly scooped out, this was the merest of preparation. A scatter of limestone blocks and rubble just under and over these burials suggested that the bodies had been deposited around the time the site was abandoned and had started to fall to ruins.

The skulls of the skeletons in the ditch were used as a basis for a forensic reconstruction of the faces of these individuals, which were included in an exhibition several years later, at the National Museum in Cardiff, and then St Fagans Museum.

The reconstruction artist, Caroline Wilkinson, tentatively suggested that she could see family resemblances amongst the skulls.

In 2012, Mark Redknap returned to the site with a skeleton crew – no students this time – to do some more excavation in and around the settlement, in an attempt to resolve some outstanding questions. One trench was put in across the rampart and ditch, just to the north of the 1998/1999 trenches in which the skeletons had been found. And yet another skeleton was discovered, this one in a semi-crouched position. The radiocarbon date range (it is always a range, rather than a precisely pinpointed date) just overlapped with some of the other skeletons, but this individual is likely to have been buried a little earlier, in the eighth or ninth century. And although he was buried just outside the wall, like the others, he seemed to have been interred a little more respectfully, on his back, with his legs resting over to the right, in a semi-crouched position.

When I examined this newly discovered skeleton, I also went back and reviewed the five skeletons from the 1998 season. And I found an important clue that I'd missed, first time around.

Burial 1 contained a person who had died as a teenager. The skeleton was almost complete, though heavily fragmented. The pieces of cranium had been carefully reassembled and glued with consolidate to create a three-dimensional skull. The skill of the conservator was impressive, in restoring the skull's structure, but the glue-like consolidant played havoc with some of the early attempts at radiocarbon-dating these remains. There were thirty teeth present, some in their sockets, some loose where the bone supporting them had crumbled away. I looked carefully at them – the lower third molars or 'wisdom teeth' were yet to erupt. That was a clue to the age of this individual, and the rest of skeleton contained more clues.

Our bones grow when we're young by maintaining islands of fast-expanding cartilage in certain places. Cartilage plates, which lie close to the ends of long bones, persist through adolescence, finally disappearing and being replaced by actual bone tissue when the bone in question has reached its final, adult length. Some cartilage plates stick around longer than others. In archaeological human remains, the cartilage decays away, leaving bones which have appear to have separate ends, or epiphyses. By looking at the pattern of fusion of those growth plates throughout the skeleton, I could estimate the age at death. In particular, some of the metacarpals – the long bones which you can feel within the palm of your hand – had stopped growing; others had 'open' growth plates, and separate epiphyses. The finger bones had finished growing: their bases, separated by a growth plate from the rest of the bone in younger children, had fused. My conclusion was that this individual had been fourteen to sixteen years of age when they died – or were killed.

Determining sex in a juvenile is always difficult, as the differences – many of which are linked to increased muscle mass in men compared with women – only start to emerge at puberty. This skeleton was very slightly built, and key features of the skull and pelvis looked 'female'. In my report, I cautiously suggested that Burial 1 was female, with the caveat that it's impossible to be conclusive about determination of sex in young individuals, based on bony features at least.

Burials 2 and 4 were younger adolescents – one skeleton lying on top of the other. The unfused growth plates of the skeleton from Burial 2 suggested an age of eleven to sixteen years, but I could refine that, looking at the teeth. The second upper molars had erupted, and the third molars had yet to erupt, but I could see that the crowns – still hiding in their crypts in the bone of the jaw – were complete and mineralised. This individual had probably been around twelve or thirteen years old when they died. There were some furrows on the front teeth – evidence of temporarily arrested development, called enamel hypoplasia (literally 'under-growth'), which is associated with periods of physiological stress during childhood. That stress could be either a bout of infectious disease or a period of malnutrition – but I can't say which. There was a bit of calculus on the teeth, but no other pathology.

The individual in Burial 4 looked a little younger; the crowns of the third molars were not yet fully mineralised. Putting the growth plate and dental evidence together gave an age range of ten to fourteen years. The teeth had been glued back into their sockets when I looked at the bones again, for my final report. But I'd had the opportunity to see the skeletons before all the reconstruction and consolidation happened – and I'd made detailed notes at the time. Looking at the teeth when they were still loose, I'd been able to see that the roots of the incisors and premolars were fully grown, but the roots of the second molars were visibly open at their tips. This would suggest an age of around twelve, give or take around six months either way. This may sound like I'm hedging my bets, but growth rates in children can vary quite a bit, depending on genetic factors, but also levels of nutrition and disease.

Burial 2 had some potentially male-looking cranial features, and Burial 4 looked possibly female – but again, I really couldn't be sure about sex in these two skeletons, as they were so young. As a rule, biological anthropologists don't attempt to sex juvenile skeletons – because we know we just can't be accurate. (Our geneticist friends can help us out here, and I'm glad I'd hesitated to assign a sex to these juvenile skeletons in my report: later aDNA analysis revealed Burial 4 to be male.)

Burial 3 involved a fairly complete skeleton – in that most of the bones were present, but very fragmentary. All of the growth plates had fused in this skeleton, and all of the permanent teeth had erupted into the mouth – though there wasn't too much wear on their surfaces. I estimated the age as twenty-five to thirty-five years old. The skull and pelvic bones bore clear indicators of male sex. The bones had been so painstakingly reassembled and consolidated that it was possible to measure the lengths of some of them, and this allowed me to use standard equations to estimate stature: this young man had been around 160–170 centimetres tall (5 feet 3 inches to 5 feet 7 inches in 'old money'). He had not looked after his teeth; they were caked with hard calculus (the mineralised plaque that builds up if you don't brush your teeth regularly – beware!). And he'd also suffered with abscesses around the roots of two of his upper back teeth, one on each side. On the left side, the tooth itself had been completely lost due to the abscess at its roots. Another upper molar had broken away, probably after a large cavity destroyed much of the crown, leaving just one root behind. Looking carefully at the mandible, I could see that there were much more pronounced muscle markings on the left side, where the chewing muscle, the masseter, attaches. It looked as though the abscess on the right – where the tooth was still hanging in there – had been so painful that this young man had shifted to chewing mostly on the left, and that he'd been doing that for quite a while. Although he'd had an abscess on the left side too, the pain of that would have quickly disappeared after the tooth was lost, and the pus had escaped from the bone. That's usually the case with abscesses – drainage is the answer: better out than in. But it was in this skeleton that I noticed a key feature which I'd missed on first inspection: on the back of the skull, in the middle of the occipital bone, was a cut mark. I measured it with a pair of calipers – it was just 36 millimetres long, but this small cut was an important clue. A sharp blade had just bitten into the back of the skull of this young man. There was no evidence of healing at all – the edges of the cut were clean and fresh. It must have happened around the time of death – even though it wouldn't have been the direct cause of death itself. My hunch of foul play, of a violent cause of death for these people, was now more than just a hunch.

Burial 5 was also an adult male: his pelvis and skull were clearly male, all of his permanent teeth had erupted, and all of his growth plates had long since closed. Features of pelvic joints and the wear on his teeth suggested he was older – somewhere between his mid-thirties and early forties when he died. It's impossible to be any more precise, unfortunately – we all age at slightly different rates, and teeth wear down at a faster or slower rate depending on how tough your diet is. Judging from the length of his bones, he was a bit taller than Burial 3: 170–180 centimetres (5 feet 7 inches to 5 feet 11 inches). There was very little pathology to note: some carious cavities in his teeth, and a little bit of extra bone forming around the margins of joints – just a normal accompaniment of ageing.

The sixth skeleton in the group outside the wall, discovered thirteen years after the rest, in 2012, was a male. He'd been in his late teens, or perhaps just into his twenties, when he died.

We puzzled over those skeletons. Were they locals from the trading post, and the victims of a brutal Viking raid? Or were they Vikings who had met their fate at the hands of the Moniars, the native Welsh of Anglesey? I certainly couldn't tell just by looking at the bones. Isotope analysis of their teeth held out the promise of finding out where these individuals had lived as young children. Katie Hemer, a bioarchaeologist at University College London, tested samples of tooth enamel from each of the skeletons, looking at ratios of strontium and oxygen isotopes trapped in the crystalline substance. The results were diverse – but crucially, what they revealed was that none of those individuals in the ditch were born and bred on Anglesey. One individual probably came from mainland Britain, while the others grew up somewhere further afield. The two adult males had isotope signatures linking them to colder, more northerly places – Scotland, Denmark or Norway, perhaps. It's frustrating not to be able to be any more precise, but isotope analysis simply matches up with geology and climate, and it's impossible to differentiate between lands with very similar rocks or patterns of rainfall. Nevertheless, the fact that they were all outsiders, not islanders, was an important finding.

They could have arrived in raiding parties, via the Isle of Man, perhaps – and been captured. They may even have been slaves. They could have been incomers who had joined the community, but who were executed for crimes. The young man with the blade wound to the back of his head and his hands most likely tied together had surely suffered a brutal death. As for the others – there's no evidence of violent injury on the skeletons, but the manner and site of their burials makes me think they could also have been victims of violence. Not all violent assaults leave marks on bones, after all. But my overwhelming impression of these burials is that they are much more about disposal of bodies rather than a funerary rite. That's all speculation, but Mark Redknap believes that the graves signify something important about these people – something we can be quite sure about – and that's that they were certainly seen as *different*. These burials certainly contrasted with the standard burials found in early medieval cemeteries – including one which had been recently excavated near Llanbedrgoch, within a mile or so of the site. These individuals had not been accorded a standard funerary rite – so, once again we're looking at irregular or deviant burials. It could have been superstition, prejudice or fear that saw their bodies buried in this way. They might have been low-status; they might have been accorded these peremptory burials because they were not Christian, perhaps. It could simply have been that they were 'not from round here'.

The links they represent, to England and to the Viking world – either the Norse Kingdom of the Isles or Scandinavia itself – resonate with other finds at the site. There were Anglo-Saxon coins and strap-ends, as well as British- or Irish-style brooches and pins. But there were also more Scandinavian-looking objects (which could have come from Scandinavia itself or from the heavily Norse-influenced Kingdom of the Isles). These included fragments of silver dirhams – Islamic currency from the Middle East which was used throughout the Viking world. The Vikings were prodigious travellers and traders, tapping into trade networks that had been going for thousands of years, extending them, carrying goods across vast distances from west to east, east to west. Alongside the cut-up pieces of dirhams were ingots and other pieces of silver – including part of an arm-ring. The Vikings engaged in a bullion economy – using ingots and 'hack silver', cut up and carefully weighed out, for trading.

There were other artefacts which spoke of a Viking identity: bronze ringed pins, for fastening clothes; glass beads; finger-rings and little cruciform pendants (not necessarily Christian – though possibly so – perhaps worn by some early adopters); lead weights; a bell; and a piece of a brooch. It's impossible to know if these objects were traded in or made more locally, although Mark interpreted one artefact as a lead trial piece for a silver arm-ring – suggesting that manufacture of Norse-style accessories may well have been happening at the site.

For Mark, the settlement at Llanbedrgoch was certainly an important place – possibly a trading hub for Gwynedd. The fact that repeated raids are historically attested implies there were riches worth plundering there. But despite the evidence for Viking culture at the site, Mark does not think that the current evidence points to a Norse colony or entrepôt. He sees it as more of a local development, influenced by its trading connections – and possibly with some Viking settlers adding to the mix. It's a node of contact between Ireland, the Isle of Man, the Wirral and north Wales. And as such, it prefigures deepening connections in the eleventh century. History tells us that in 1055, Gruffudd ap Llywelyn became king of all Wales, having driven the Mercians out of mid-Wales, and beaten and killed a rival Welsh king in the south. He also sacked Hereford – helped by eighteen pirate-ships' worth of allies from Ireland. The later Welsh king Gruffudd ap Cynan, who fiercely resisted Norman rule in Wales, had Scandinavian connections too. He grew up in Dublin, with its strong Viking connections. And when he died in 1137, he was mourned by Welsh, Irish – and Danes.

Was the trading hub at Llanbedrgoch the beginning of that strong Welsh–Norse connection and political alliance? It's certainly possible. But there are often casualties when new allegiances are forged. We still haven't got to the bottom of the story of the bodies in the top of that ditch. There's one more weapon in our scientific arsenal, after my osteological assessment and Katie Hemer's isotope analysis. It's aDNA, and our colleagues at the Crick Institute have taken samples from the bases of the skulls, from the petrous temporal bones, where the DNA is best preserved. We should have answers very soon. Their genomes should tell us how closely related these people were, and they will also hold clues to ancestry which will take us beyond the isotopic signatures of childhood homes, mapping out the family connections of those unfortunate individuals who ended up as bodies, as skeletons, in the ditch.

The timing of those burials in the top of the ditch seems important. With rubble from the rampart under them and over them, they must have taken place just as the site was becoming abandoned. The walls of the settlement were falling into ruin – but still clearly visible.

I started off wanting to know if those people – the two men, the teenage girl, the two children – were 'Vikings'. But this isn't the right question. Their story – as it continues to emerge – is part of the story of people moving around, and of changing cultural identities in Wales and western Britain. Identities that are not in any way insular or isolated, but that are forged through connections – this time, across the Irish

Sea and beyond. Mark didn't see Llanbedrgoch as a Viking colony; the buildings were of a local style. Instead, he saw the settlement absorbing Hiberno-Norse culture, including ring-pins and the use of hack-silver, as well as aspects of Irish culture, including characteristic brooches. But they were also making plenty of cultural artefacts on site – including metalwork, leatherwork and textiles.

Llanbedrgoch in its early medieval heyday, in the ninth to tenth century, was a cosmopolitan centre – a wealthy trading hub. It had much to offer, including the artefacts made on site, but also plenty of grain from the famously fertile fields of Anglesey. Carbonised grain had turned up in the digs. It's the only known site of this type, size and significance at this time on the island – and indeed in Wales. It could have been a wealthy manorial estate – but Mark thought it might have been more than that – perhaps even a *llys* – a site with a royal foundation. In fact, he was sure it must have had some royal connections, as such an important centre of commerce and generator of wealth. He'd always borne in mind the possibility that Llanbedrgoch had been a rich monastery site – it looks similar to some walled early Irish monasteries. But there's no obvious church, no styli, no inscribed gravestones. Instead, it looks more secular, perhaps a wealthy farmstead with roots in the Romano-British period, which grew richer and richer with all the passing trade of the Viking Age, until it was almost a town-sized settlement. But it was also vulnerable. Impressive ramparts were constructed to protect the site – but in the end, they wouldn't be enough.

Llanbedrgoch offered itself as an easy target for attack, just as raids were on the increase. In the 970s, Vikings led by Ingimund, who had been kicked out of Dublin, are recorded as landing at Red Wharf Bay – and sacking a settlement on the north coast. The *Welsh Annals* record the taking of two thousand slaves during this raid. Mark thinks this is wild exaggeration. But perhaps those skeletons in the ditch were at least associated with episodes of raids and slave-taking. The raids seem to have spelled the end for the settlement itself. It had been so successful, but it was not to last. The focus of trade seems to have shifted southeast to the more easily defendable harbour at Llanfaes, near Beaumaris – just where the Menai Strait opens out. In the twelfth century, Llanfaes became the main port of the kingdom of Gwynedd, and its capital. Meanwhile, Llanbedrgoch fell into ruins, faded from memory and disappeared under the fields.

The digs have finished. Mark is writing up the final report, waiting to see what further insights might emerge from the genome analyses before he finalises his conclusions. But I hear a note of longing in his voice. He'd still like to go back and find out more. The site has got into his bones. It's part of who he is.

7.

THE BIRTH OF CHURCHYARDS

The Roman army may have been pulled out of Britain in 407, and the Britons may have expelled the remaining officials in 409, but there were other engines of Empire that were harder to expunge. There was still a network of powerful people and influential families who could hope to maintain their authority and status if they could keep their link to a very important aspect of the Empire alive – and that was its religion.

In the east of Britain, Christianity seems to have largely died out with the end of empire (though we don't know much about the diversity of beliefs that existed, of course). But in the southwest of England, and in Wales, with their ongoing connections with Gaul, the Roman religion persisted – and spread.

Years ago, I dug on the cliffs of Longoar Bay, near St Ishmael's in Pembrokeshire. Now a small village with a pocket-sized parish church, St Ishmael's was once the second most important diocese in Wales, after what is now St Davids.

Now, 'diocese' is an interesting term. It refers to a region controlled by a particular bishop. Its origin is Greek, from *dioikein*, literally 'house-keeping', but also used to refer to an administrative unit. It passes into Latin as *dioecesis,* and in the late third century was used to define an area of the Roman Empire with regional governance, comprising several provinces. Each diocese was governed by a representative or delegate of a praetorian prefect: a *vicarius*. These 'vicars' kept tabs on provincial governors, presided over courts of appeal, and administered taxation.

In the early fourth century, Christianity became legal in the Roman Empire, and by 380 was declared to be the new Imperial religion by the emperor, Theodosius I. Bishops quickly set up an alternative legal system, with episcopal courts. And then, as the Roman Empire started to crumble in the west, local councils lost control, and the Church took on more and more administrative power. As the power of provincial civilian governors waned, the power of bishops grew. Like many of our modern counties, medieval dioceses – still in existence today – were the direct successors, *in situ*, of Roman *civitates*.

Back to St Ishmael's. It seems far too small, today, to have once been an important regional centre of administration. But 21st-century appearances can be deceiving. The church is dedicated to a saint whose name in Old Welsh was Ysmail. He was a sixth-century bishop and not of humble origins at all – being the son of an exiled king of Brittany, according to one of the earliest Welsh manuscripts, the *Book of Llandaff* or *Liber Landavensis*, compiled in the twelfth century. In fact, the name Ysmail means something like 'under-prince'. An eleventh-century biography of St David, *Dewi Sant*, mentions Ishmael as one of three 'most faithful disciples' of this more prominent Welsh bishop. St David was also a member of the royal family of Gwynedd, the king of Ceredigion having reputedly raped David's mother, Non. History doesn't tell us what Non thought about this (of course), but David certainly didn't let his illegitimacy stand in the way of his ambitions. These saints and bishops were part of the governing aristocracy. So the Roman Empire didn't really disappear at all: instead, it morphed into a system of theocratic government. The religion of Empire *became* the Empire.

Ishmael was an important person, a bishop whose diocese comprised much of Pembrokeshire, and he was later to succeed David as Bishop of Menevia in northern Pembrokeshire. But he'd never achieve the same level of fame, and his original diocese in Rhos would be subsumed into the diocese of St Davids, which expanded to include all of Dyfed (Pembrokeshire) as well as Ceredigion (Cardiganshire) and Carmarthenshire – and further, encompassing the area that's now the Diocese of Swansea and Brecon, right up to the English border. It's hard not to see these dioceses as small kingdoms, jostling for power – and that is exactly what they were. State and religion went hand in hand. And the expanding network of churches and monasteries was also starting to influence where people got buried.

The *Liber Landavensis* mentions some burial practices. But I also noticed something else as I was poring through its pages. There are passages which describe the return of St Teilo (uncle of Ishmael and another disciple of St David) to Britain, having emigrated to Armorica (Brittany) for a legendary-sounding seven years and seven months. While in Brittany, Teilo had managed to secure a fabulous gift from God for the Armoricans: equestrian excellence – which would make them indomitable in battle. The chronicler records that this divinely granted ability had persisted through time – the Armoricans were seven times better as cavalry than they were as infantry. (To be fair, we don't know how good the Armoricans were on foot; they could have been abysmal, making them only just above par as cavalry.) Anyway, Teilo eventually resolves to return to his native country as he's heard (he says, from an angel, but we may suspect a more conventional, human source of information) that King Gerennius of Cornwall is terminally ill. St Teilo sets sail in a large ship, with many doctors – and bishops, whose saintly influence will be required to refresh the British 'after the pestilence'. (My metaphorical ears pricked up when I read this. We can't be sure, of course, which specific pestilence is being referred to. But could this be a mention of the Justinianic Plague? It was recorded in Gaul in the sixth century – so perhaps we have here a historical mention of the plague having reached British shores around that time. With the discovery of *Yersinia pestis* DNA in that Anglo-Saxon cemetery at Edix Hill, perhaps this is a hint of a more wide-spread outbreak in Britain. Ancient DNA will help us to see just how extensive this wave of infection really was – in the fullness of time.)

The story in the *Liber Landavensis* then moves on to describe how Teilo is planning ahead for Gerennius's death. He embarks on his voyage back to Britain, and he wants to bring a stone coffin with him for the king. It's a truly enormous coffin. His companions tell him that even ten yoke of oxen wouldn't be able to move it. But Teilo trusts in God to help him transport the coffin, throwing it into the sea in front of the ship, and it magically floats all the way to Britain with them. Teilo arrives just in time to deliver the sacrament to Gerennius, before the king shuffles off this mortal coil and is duly inserted into the miraculous stone coffin. Then Teilo returns home to his bishopric at Llandaff, and remains there until his death, presiding over all of the churches in southern Britain, so the *Liber Landavensis* tells us. It also relates that it was Teilo who made his nephew Ishmael a bishop, and gave him his position at Menevia, as St David's successor. Teilo, it says, created lots of other bishops too, giving them various dioceses and consolidating the power of the Church in Britain. But his own power and authority were granted to him by many 'kings and princes of southern Britain' – and signed off by the Pope in Rome. Again, we see the Church as an engine of state. And yet it stood apart in many ways – the Church at Llandaff got to exercise its own legal system, did not have a governor overseeing it, and was exempt from military service; it had its own market and its own mint. And Teilo could employ the ultimate sanction against anyone threatening the cathedral church of Llandaff and its possessions or its rights – he could have them excommunicated.

We learn so much from the *Book of Llandaff*. It's a masterly piece of propaganda, stating the case for the supremacy of Llandaff over all the other churches of Wales – and particularly over its twelfth-century rival, St Davids. It didn't work in the end – St Davids made its own case, gaining recognition from the Archbishop of Canterbury and the Pope as the top diocese in Wales. But in the pages of the *Book of Llandaff*, we see how the Church and the Welsh kingdoms supported each other: kings and princes gained divine authority and a free pass for their souls from the Church; the Church gained royal approval and support, was granted land, could create its own laws, and was in charge of its own business in return. (All this in the early sixth century, well before 597, when St Augustine was sent by the Pope to convert the Anglo-Saxons over in Kent to Christianity, and to become the first Archbishop of Canterbury. Again, we see that contrast between waning Christianity in the east, in the post-Roman period, and the continuing power of the Church — and its connections to Francia and, ultimately, to Rome — in the west, including Wales.)

The *Book of Llandaff* also makes reference to some funerary rites: it tells of a reputed twenty thousand saints buried on Ynys Enlli, Bardsey Island, just off the Llŷn Peninsula in Gwynedd; of a king called Meurig who founded a chapel and a cemetery at Mathern (just south of Chepstow), where he buried his father — who'd been slain in a battle against the Anglo-Saxons; and of that seafaring stone coffin for King Gerennius.

Islands and magical stone coffins aside, the church-and-cemetery founded by Meurig is notable, as this is one of the earliest records anywhere of a *churchyard*. For pre-Christian Romans, temples and cemeteries were quite separate spatially. Temples were in towns and cities, and in other sacred spaces. Cemeteries in pre-Christian Roman Britain — and throughout the Roman Empire — were, as we've seen, largely out-of-town affairs. The living had their own place; the dead had theirs. (The burial of infants around and within buildings being an important exception, so often occurring within domestic settings.) But burial practices changed with Christianity. The big USP of this Middle Eastern religion was, after all, that promise of an existence after death. (It's such a genius promise as well – completely untestable, unprovable, but for many, the ultimate aspiration.) The business of Christianity was with the dead as much as it was with the living. And if a lifetime of piety, and alms-giving to the Church, was to *mean something* when it came to an end, your body had to be buried in consecrated ground. As close to a church as possible – if not in it.

And so, with the foundation of churches, we also have the origin of churchyards. These seem like such a familiar concept to us now – even though relatively few people are actually still buried in them. Most burials in Britain – of bodies or of cremated remains, when these are interred – now take place in secular, local authority burial grounds. But still, when we think about burials, we may often conjure up an image of a churchyard. There's one in practically every parish after all. And that's the point, perhaps – you can't easily get away from them. Those churchyards are *in* our villages, towns and cities, not relegated to the edges, like Roman cemeteries – or indeed Brookwood cemetery in Woking, the 'London Necropolis' – the largest burial ground in western Europe, once served by its own 'Necropolis Train'.

Churchyards – in the popular imagination – seem like obvious, natural places to find graves, but they only start to appear in Britain from the sixth century – as part of the culture of Christianity. None of the Roman or early Anglo-Saxon burials we've paused to look at on this journey through the first millennium took place inside settlements (apart from those infant burials). And yet, by the ninth century, pretty much everyone living in what had once been the Roman Empire – and where the Roman religion had taken root – was buried in a church graveyard. The preceding centuries saw a gradual transformation of burial practices, as former out-of-town cemeteries fell into disuse, and churchyards became the final destination of choice. The transformation in burial practice maps onto the declining power of the Empire – and the rise of Christianity. These two phenomena are intrinsically linked – as the old state disintegrated, the Roman Church was able to take over many of its functions.

To begin with, Christian doctrine didn't prescribe funerary rituals, and burials continued to follow local traditions. The old Roman law prohibiting burial within the city, as laid out in the Twelve Tables, officially persisted until the ninth century, when it was rescinded by the Byzantine emperor Leo VI. But by that time, the law had clearly fallen by the wayside, as many urban cemeteries had already been operating for centuries, including in Rome itself.

The craze for burials associated with churches seems to have started with saints themselves – bishops-turned-saints being buried in the places they had founded or preached in. And then if you could secure a burial close to a saint, perhaps that would help to ensure your own salvation. But there's another aspect to this which echoes through funerary practices down the ages – going right back into prehistory. And that's the marking of territory and status with the placement of a burial. Some Neolithic chambered tombs – we now know from ancient genome studies – contained related individuals. It may have been that these were the tombs of elite families, connecting with recent ancestors and demonstrating their hereditary land rights, perhaps. In the Iron Age, we often find cemeteries where a single high-status 'founder' burial lies at the heart of a cluster of later burials. Christianity introduces a whole new concept with the introduction of churchyards, but the saint in his (or much more rarely, her) church, surrounded by later members of a community, seems to follow an age-old pattern. Medieval Christianity introduced another dynamic element into this pattern, as the human remains of important religious figures were moved around, often from rural or suburban resting places to more prestigious urban churches. Relics were an incredibly important commodity for churches. The bodies of saints were divided up – a hand here, a leg there – and distributed amongst multiple destinations.

The Church would gradually take over what had been civic rituals and institutions, as it extended its influence over funerary rites. Church and grave were becoming closer – and sometimes the erection of a church would follow an existing pattern of interment; at other times it would create a brand-new place for burial. In fourth-century Rome, shrines and then churches were built in pre-existing suburban roadside cemeteries. Inside the city walls, churches were built in the gardens of rich estate owners, and then these places became burial grounds (and eventually the Church came to own them, by default). The traditional rituals that Roman families had held at the graveside – including those annually recurring feasts like Parentalia and Rosalia – became subsumed into Christian ceremonies. By the third century, there are records of the Christian eucharist taking place at funerals – though some early funerals may not have involved a visit to a church. And by the sixth century, the dead were being commemorated in regular Christian liturgies, with the names of recently deceased members of the community being read out.

The Church would also take increasingly greater charge of

the business of securing burial plots and digging graves – tasks that had previously fallen to families. By the fifth century, in the Western Roman Empire, the Church was made responsible for burying the poor – taking over a function that the government had previously been responsible for. And it knew how to get key workers on side. Whereas the meek were due to inherit the earth, and the peacemakers would be called the sons of God, grave diggers had their own special divine prize to look forward to – being promised a priority pass for the resurrection.

As churches began to monopolise burial rites, there was potential for them to make a lot of money out of this business. But there was also recognition at the very top that the profiteering could be pushed too far. Pope Gregory I wrote to one of his bishops to warn against overcharging, while at the same time saying that any donations to the Church could of course be gratefully received: accepting a donation being completely morally different to charging a fee. As the Church seemed to hold the keys to heaven, making donations may have seemed like a very sensible investment.

There's another big change in burial practice with the ascendancy of Christianity, and that's the disappearance of grave goods. Social status was now displayed by the physical proximity of your grave to a particular church building, and by your financial contributions to the Church as an institution. That relationship with patronage was made explicit in a document emerging from the Council of Mainz in the ninth century, when the assembled bishops decreed that only priests and people who'd made significant donations could be permitted to be buried *inside* a church.

Gradually, then, the Church would take over the business of

death and burial, and while grave goods fell out of favour (to the disappointment of archaeologists, certainly), graveyards literally gained ground. Even on the furthest fringes of what had once been the glorious Empire of Rome, where the Roman religion had only just started to put down roots, before the official end of Roman rule in Britain.

———

So there I was, dangling on a rope, looking at someone's femurs poking out of the 12-metre-high red sandstone cliff at Longoar Bay. It was a complicated challenge. Our mission was to recover any bone which was in danger of being washed out in the next storm – but how far back into the cliff could I reasonably chase the skeleton? Until I got to its toes, or its skull, depending on which way those femurs were pointing? That would mean burrowing into the cliff – and this isn't normally how archaeology is done. We usually dig from the top down, not from the side in. And I didn't want to add too much to the erosion of the cliff that was already happening. In the end, we settled on rescuing any bones which were projecting out, without tunnelling into the cliff. We wouldn't be able to tell all that much from those bones, but we could at least radiocarbon-date them. And later researchers might decide to try sampling them for aDNA.

Up on the top of the cliffs, the geophysicist with our team, Meg Watters, was scanning the ground to see if she could pick up any traces of the cemetery that way – and she could. There were clear signals coming through which looked very much like they could be graves – at least seven of them. We dug down to one, to ground-truth it – and came across a stone slab lying over a grave. Turning over the slab, we discovered a rough cross hewn into its undersurface.

We sent off bone samples for radiocarbon dating, and they came back with a seventh- to ninth-century date. Although we found no sign of it, National Park archaeologist Phil Bennett said that there was a local tradition there had once been a chapel on the clifftop.

Other early medieval cemeteries in Pembrokeshire have recently been investigated more fully, including at Brownslade Barrow, Angle Bay and Whitesands Bay. Like St Ishmael's, these three were all threatened in various ways, prompting archaeological investigation, and they've all been found to contain cist – or stone-lined – graves.

Brownslade Barrow, as its name suggests, is an early medieval cemetery associated with a barrow, or burial mound. It's near the south coast of southern Pembrokeshire. Old maps provide some clues: a 1790 estate map and the 1865 first edition of the Ordnance Survey show an open rectangle – presumably a roofless ruin. It disappears on later maps. On the 1790 map, the field containing both the barrow and the rectangular building is labelled as 'Churchy Bank', the field to the south is 'Churchway Meadow' and the fields to the east are Upper and Lower 'Church Hill'. (It's almost like they're trying to tell us something.) The site was excavated in the 1880s. The barrow was dug into and found to contain a cist in which a human skeleton was found, together with animal bone and what was recorded at the time as 'wheel-thrown' pottery. If that's true, this suggests a Romano-British date at the very earliest, as this is when the pottery wheel first starts to be used in Britain. Those nineteenth-century excavations also uncovered many more cist burials, rather graphically described as 'packed in tiers at least three deep, like pigeons in a pie'. There was no way of dating these graves, at the time, but as they were oriented in an east–west direction, they were presumed to be Christian. Brownslade Barrow is over a mile from the coast, but in recent years, it's been threatened by careless digging – by badgers. It was decided that human diggers should move in to recover precious heritage before it was clawed away. The recent excavations uncovered a jumble of archaeology, including human bones, disturbed and rearranged by the badgers. In the area of the badger sett, archaeologists uncovered thirty-one graves – all of them disturbed. They also found some other features, including post-holes, as well as animal bones and charred grain, and evidence of ironworking. And there was a hint of a rectangular building – but nothing conclusively chapel-like.

Amongst the graves, only one had a stone grave-marker, (though there may well have been other gravestones, which had become lost in the shifting dunes). Katie Hemer, carrying out the osteological analysis on the human remains from the site, found that the marked grave contained an individual whose bones bore signs of a disease called diffuse idiopathic skeletal hyperostosis, or DISH. It's a long and convoluted name for a bone disease that we don't fully understand, but it does seem to be associated with certain conditions including obesity and type 2 diabetes. Katie also sampled the bones and teeth for isotope analysis. The oxygen isotope values for several individuals suggested that these people had grown up somewhere with a warm climate, such as the Mediterranean coast. The individual in the marked grave, with DISH, was one of these possible immigrants. It's tempting to suggest that this individual's high status, indicated by the grave marker and the possible signs of a particularly comfortable lifestyle in his bones, could have been linked to the person's origin. Could he have been an itinerant priest, an evangeliser? The evidence won't stretch far enough to let us answer that question. The Brownslade Barrow cemetery was in use for some seven centuries, with the earliest graves in it belonging to the early fifth century (the only other cemetery with such early dates is Croesgoch, in northern Pembrokeshire). The latest burials from Brownslade Barrow are eleventh-century. In total, the skeletal remains of fifty-two individuals were discovered in the cemetery: women and men, infants and children – some in simple, dug graves, others in stone-lined cists.

The cemetery at Angle Bay, near Milford Haven, was similar to St Ishmael's. Here it was not busy badgers, but storm surges that threatened the site. Human bones were eroding out of the sandy cliff and tumbling down to the beach below. Once again, old maps provide some clues. There's no chapel marked on them, but on an 1844 tithe map, the field containing the oval cemetery enclosure is labelled 'Church Field'. Historical records suggest a chapel dedicated to St Anthony existed in the area. A geophysical survey of the site revealed the traces of a rectangular building, possibly a chapel, within the oval boundary. But then there was also an outer, rectangular boundary – and inside that, evidence of a corn dryer or hearth. It looked like an earlier settlement had later been converted into a graveyard – in which there was a large number of infant burials. Of the adults buried at Angle Bay, some were found to have grown up elsewhere, just as at Brownslade Barrow. And once again, the cemetery had been in use over many generations – from the seventh to the twelfth centuries.

Whitesands Bay was similar in many ways – lots of infant

burials, lots of stone-lined cists. I visited the site while it was being excavated in July 2021, when the remains of a twelfth-century chapel were clear to see in the section, in the eastern side of the trench. But deep beneath the foundations of that chapel, there was a curious circular stone wall. In fact, a double stone wall. It looked like the foundations of some sort of round house. In its centre – directly under the floor of the later chapel – was a large, rectangular cist. The archaeologists had already removed the stone slabs which formed its sides – one had a cross carved into it – and dug down through the accumulated sediment inside it. But strangely, it was completely clear – no burial here. Had it been robbed out or the bones moved elsewhere in antiquity, I wondered. But archaeologist Ken Murphy, leading the dig, thought not. With no evidence of disturbance, it looked as though this cist or shrine had always been – quite mysteriously – empty. But there was no doubt it was special. Its size, its central position within this early circular enclosure, and the layer of quartz pebbles placed on top of the slabs that had once formed its lid, all marked it out. Ken judged these early features – the cist and the circular wall – to be eighth century in date. Later infant burials had been clustered tightly around the cist. Just as at Angle Bay, there was a high proportion of infant burials at Whitesands – and they seemed to occupy a central position in the cemetery. But there were graves of adults too, some of whom were buried in a prone position; some lay east–west, others north–south. Once again there seemed to be some evidence of industry, with a blackened, charcoal-rich layer. Pieces of characteristic, red-body, red-glazed Samian ware suggested that the site had been used in some way since late Roman times, at least.

But the association of a graveyard with a chapel in these

locations demands greater scrutiny. At Brownslade Barrow and Angle Bay, there are suggestions of a chapel – but nothing definite. At Whitesands, there is a very definite chapel – but it's late: twelfth century. Was the circular wall an earlier chapel? Or just an enclosure? The archaeologists thought it had perhaps always been a low wall, rather than what was left of a roofed building. But there was also that evidence of even earlier activity at the site – those smears of charcoal-rich sediment deep in the sand, even some waste from metalworking. And then it seems to have become a sacred place, with the building of the circular wall and cist, and a burial ground. The chapel itself came later. A similar pattern is seen at some early medieval Irish cemetery sites – which also possess evidence for metalworking and crop-processing – though it's rare for any chapels or churches to be associated with these cemeteries. Why the link between metalworking and cemeteries? To offer a mundane explanation, perhaps this is just expedience: locating dirty and dangerous smithing and disposal of the dead to somewhere near – though safely separate from – settlements. Or perhaps there is a more ritualistic connection: transformation of stone into metal, hot liquid ore into cold, hard bronze or iron; transformation of the living into the dead.

Place names in West Wales provide some clues to the whereabouts of early cemeteries – and perhaps even hint at that process where cemeteries preceded chapels. The prefix *llan* originally meant just 'an enclosed cemetery' and later came to mean 'a church within an enclosed cemetery'. Other ecclesiastical names, such as *eglwys* ('church') and *capel* ('chapel'), are less helpful as they came along in just the last five hundred years. There is another term that can be a useful clue, though, and that's *merthyr* – 'martyr' – indicating the grave of a victimised saint. On first inspection, there don't seem to be any instances of *merthyr* in Pembrokeshire, but it's there, in an anglicised version, in Mathry and Martletwy.

All of these early medieval cemeteries in west Wales fit into a pattern which is becoming clearer with each modern excavation. Around forty of these cist cemeteries are known, most of them on or very close to the coast, though Ken cautions that this may be because they are simply more visible – coming to light where you have bones falling out of cliffs. Perhaps more exist inland, but have yet to be discovered. But on the basis of available evidence, we do seem to be looking at a coastal phenomenon – and not just in west Wales; it's there in Scotland, Ireland, the Isle of Man and Cornwall too. Ken calls the stone-slabbed graves, containing bodies laid out in extended position, 'long cists' – to distinguish them from shorter, prehistoric cist graves, often containing crouched burials.

These long cists vary quite a bit. Some just have side-slabs, others have bases and lids or lintels. And there seem to have been no particular rules about who could be buried in a cist – men and women, young and old, are found interred in them. And alongside the cists in these cemeteries, there are simple, dug graves too. Extended inhumations became common during the late Roman period in Britain – and there's nothing especially Christian about them. The lack of grave goods suggests Christian burial, perhaps. But much more compelling, Christianity was literally written into the stones of the cists at Whitesands Bay, with several examples of cross-marked stones. Most were fairly crude and simple. One I saw from the side of the central cist had a slightly more elaborate cross, with crossed arms. (A slab with a hint of inscription on it had just turned up too, but it was incredibly faint – it looked like a name, perhaps.) And yet the Christian tradition doesn't mark a complete break with what went before; in some cases, the burials are very clearly associated with earlier monuments, just like the barrow at Brownslade. And perhaps that's true for Whitesands, too.

We may wonder who was buried in them. They could have been cemeteries for families from a few scattered local farms. Or there could have been as-yet-undiscovered larger settlements associated with them. That's certainly a possibility at Whitesands, which the histories tell us was once used as a harbour. Today, the Welsh name for Whitesands is Traeth Mawr, 'Great Beach', but it was once Porth Mawr – 'Great Gate' or 'Great Port'. In fact, there are hints of people living and working in many of these areas which became used as cemeteries. At Brownslade Barrow, there were broken quern stones and a piece of a bone comb. And there's a hillfort site just 600 metres away. The large rectangular enclosure and the corn dryer at Angle Bay also suggest settlement and agricultural activity. And just to the west is a coastal promontory fort – which may still have been occupied into the early medieval period. There's also a promontory fort close to Longoar Bay: Great Castle Head. Elsewhere, the circular churchyards at Jeffreyston and Llandysilio in Pembrokeshire, and at Eglwys Gymyn, Llangynog and Llanwinio in Carmarthenshire, may have started out as ditched Iron Age enclosures. There are many, many more – and they're not restricted to west Wales, or even to Wales. In the late 1980s, excavations on the Scottish island of Iona revealed the deep ditch or vallum forming the boundary of the famous monastery, founded by St Columba, to be Iron Age in date. The island was given to Columba either by the king of the Gaelic kingdom of Dál Riata (if you listen to the Irish annals) or by their enemies, the Picts (if you believe Bede). But whoever it was that handed over this gift, it seems that it may not have been a remote and uninhabited place for monks to hide themselves away on, but a settled island for many centuries.

Burial places close to settlements could also have been about staking a claim to land ownership. Brownslade Barrow represents the reuse of an even earlier, Bronze Age funerary monument – creating a link in the landscape with those ancestors. Perhaps that's part of the same territorial statement. And it's not a new idea that suddenly arises in the fifth century. That reuse of monuments happened during Roman times, right back into the Iron Age. And then there are plenty of early medieval examples from west Wales, where cross-carved stones and burials have been found associated with Bronze Age barrows, at Dyffryn Bern, Caerfarchell, Newport (Pembrokeshire) and Llandrudion. This reuse of monuments may be about connections with dead ancestors, but the living may have been just as important. Another theory suggests that these cemeteries are located at 'assembly sites' – traditionally important gathering places in the landscape.

The cemeteries fit into a wider story about burial and settlement that was playing out across northwest Europe. The extramural cemeteries of Roman times were being replaced with burial grounds which brought the living and the dead closer together. Archaeological investigations have revealed farms with cemeteries alongside appearing in the landscape around Winchester in the fifth and sixth centuries. By the end of the seventh century, there were also burial grounds inside the town. A very similar pattern is seen in France, Belgium and the Netherlands.

Writing about these sites, Ken Murphy is sure that the

early medieval cemeteries of Pembrokeshire were created by local communities — not by new arrivals in the area. Isotope analysis of skeletons from Brownslade Barrow and Whitesands lends support to this, with sulphur isotopes reflecting a coastal diet, and high strontium levels which suggest that these people were eating food grown in fields where seaweed was used as a fertiliser. But on the other hand, there are all those stories of connections across the sea, to Ireland in particular, and Brittany. And some of the stones in these long-cist cemeteries bear inscriptions, in fifth- to seventh-century Latin — and in ogham, the early medieval alphabet used for writing the early Irish language. But it's most likely that the occupants of those cross-marked stone cists were — in the main — local people from west Wales. Connections to Ireland and beyond were certainly shaping their ideas about life, and were reflected in the way they chose to bury their dead. There would have been some emigration, some immigration — of course; this had happened down the centuries. And that's how ideas travelled — including those powerful ideas that had first taken root far away in Judaea, then extended through the crumbling Empire — and kept spreading. Literary accounts from the early medieval period record these journeys and connections, with clerics and scholars travelling widely.

Conversion to Christianity in Wales started in the late Roman period, then gradually spread and gathered pace. The appearance of a new funerary practice might reflect this new religion taking root — but it could equally reflect more secular traditions. And in fact, the preceding Iron Age tradition in Wales is of inhumations close to settlement. We may be able to be reasonably sure about the religious nature of the burials in graves with cross-marked stones (with the caveat that some of these stones are clearly reused, and that it's always the living making these choices *for* the dead), but we should accept that both Christians and non-Christians may be buried in these cemeteries.

The emergence of that Levantine cult – one amongst so many – and its extraordinary success is one of the most enduring legacies of the Roman Empire. Adopted by Roman emperors, Christianity then became synonymous with Roman-ness, and it would enjoin its adherents into a Europe-wide political (and fiscal) system that was even more powerful and longer-lasting than the Empire itself. As the political Roman Empire contracted and crumbled, ambassadors for its religion kept reaching out – even to lands that lay beyond its original compass. Those ambassadors would be revered and remembered as saints.

The ruined medieval chapel at Whitesands Bay is tradition-ally attributed to St Patrick. We don't know if St Patrick ever did set foot on this beach in the fifth century, but the archae-ology shows us very clearly that at least some members of the community later buried there, close to the beach, thought of themselves as Christian. The early long-cist cemeteries of Pembrokeshire emphasise those enduring connections along and between the Atlantic coasts of Brittany, Britain and Ireland – connections which stretch back into prehistory. But they're also infused with religious ideas that started thousands of miles away, around the eastern Mediterranean, before washing up on these Welsh shores.

Around the eighth and ninth centuries, some of those long-cist cemeteries were abandoned, whereas others kept going, with churches or chapels built on them. Whitesands was one of these. St Ishmael's had its chapel close by. The burials came first; the chapel followed. But once the churches started to be linked with burial grounds, there was no going back. Christianity would continue to grow and extend its influence over matters of life – and death.

On the day I visited the excavation at St Patrick's Chapel on Whitesands Bay, a local rector turned up to lead a brief service at the edge of the trench. The small congregation sang a Victorian hymn, in English; and I wondered what the people buried in the cross-marked cists would have made of it all. I wondered if they would ever have expected their religion to last so long.

The singing died away, and all that was left was the scraping of the archaeologists' trowels and the murmur of waves gently breaking on the beach.

8.

BELONGING

A thousand years of history, a thousand years back. It feels like very ancient history until you connect with the personal stories, with the individuals buried in those graves: the man whose cremated remains were placed in the lead canister with the pipe so he could join in on feast days; the tiny victims of high rates of infant mortality, and perhaps a life sacrificed in an attempt to save a mother; the 'deviant' burials with their heads rearranged, potentially revealing a fear of the revenant enslaved; all those people with their buckets, perhaps laid low by the plague; the cunning woman of Scremby; the six in their shallow graves on Anglesey during a time of raiding and trading; the graves with cross-marked stones, from the Age of Saints, eroding out of the sandy cliffs of west Wales.

Running through all these stories are the tales of discovery, of the archaeologists and other scientists who draw those secrets out of the ground and give us these glimpses of forgotten lives, forgotten cultures. But these are also stories about identity. The identity of individuals, interred to be remembered, or buried to be forgotten. And cultural identities – in these islands that have never been insular. Those identities were forged through connections: to an Empire that crumbles but then resurrects itself as a religious realm, and across the sea in all directions: over the North Sea, across the English Channel and the Irish Sea, amongst the scattered archipelago that became the Kingdom of the Isles. Archaeology allows us to see ideas – about how to bury people, what style of brooches to wear, how to trade in hack silver – taking hold and spreading. But what we've never been able to do, until now, is to begin to plumb the social reality of the cultural transformations that we can read in the archaeological record. We can see patterns in the style of artefacts and burial practices. But what did that mean for the populations themselves? Are we seeing the movement of ideas, or of people? And then – of how many people, and who were they?

———

In the nineteenth century, an idea emerged in archaeology which became known as the 'culture-history' paradigm. It was essentially a concept that certain groups of people could be identified with and by their material culture: the metalwork they shaped, the tools they made, the clothes they wore – and the way they buried their dead. If you saw a new culture appearing in a landscape, that meant a new group of people had arrived there. In Britain, the culture-history paradigm led to a conceptualisation of history that saw wave after wave of colonisers or invaders sweeping in, one after another – wiping out what (and who) went before, replacing it. The way we divide up history – and certainly the way it's taught in primary school, at least – still harks back to this nineteenth-century concept. The Palaeolithic gives way to the Mesolithic gives way to the Neolithic gives way to the Bronze Age gives way to the Iron Age gives way to the Romans. Then the Anglo-Saxons sweep into England. And then the Vikings have a go, too, rampaging across northern England, Scotland, Ireland, the Isle of Man – and Anglesey. The Anglo-Saxon period ends when the Normans arrive (in the most memorable year in British history, 1066. I always imagine William assembling his troops in 1065, then having a think about it and deciding to leave it one more year, because the date would be so much more *historic*.)

What's the alternative, then? A stark antithesis is 'cultural diffusion'. Under this paradigm, we see each new culture arriving in Britain as being disseminated by just a few people – perhaps an influential, trend-setting elite. Most of the population isn't replaced; people just adopt new fashions, new technology, new languages.

This is the archaeological culture war: in one corner, culture-history, massive migrations and population replacement; in the other, cultural diffusion, a dissemination of ideas while the population stays put. Like any culture war, it's much too polarised and too clearly defined. History – *people* – are much messier than that. The answers are much more likely to lie somewhere in the middle. They sure as hell won't be simple – and each 'event' would also have been different and unique. And we're only just starting to get the data we need to understand these transitions.

Right now, ancient genomics is transforming archaeology – granting us an opportunity that's never existed before. It's the key to unlocking some of the most enduring questions about British history: precisely those questions about how new cultures arrived and spread across the landscape. We can now start to look at how people – and not just pots, or brooches, or buckets – were moving around in the past. By analysing genomes of people associated with a certain culture and comparing these with genomes of later people, with a different culture, we can see whether those two groups of people were very closely related and likely to represent genetic ancestors and descendants – or not.

In the nineteenth and twentieth centuries, archaeologists were often keen to track cultural changes through time, but were never really able to work out how those cultural transitions related to the movement of people themselves. This didn't stop them trying. By the 1960s, the culture-history paradigm, which lumped together ethnicity, material culture and language, was thrown out – it had come to be seen as suspicious and simplistic at best, dangerous at worst. The world had witnessed the terrifying potential for history and politics to be bound up in a package which had then been used as an argument for appalling atrocities, even genocide. Archaeologists could not condone their discipline ever being misused in such a way again. These concepts hold power, and used in the wrong way, they can be devastating. There were both scientific and sociological reasons for ditching the old obsession with serial population replacements – what Grahame Clark, at Cambridge University, had dubbed an 'invasion neurosis'.

The invasion models were largely replaced with theories which suggested much more continuity, with local evolution of culture. But in fact, starting out with any assumption that history *must* have happened in a certain way – either as a series of invasions on the one hand, or through relatively static populations adopting new cultural ideas over time on the other – means that we approach the evidence with prejudice, with a pre-formed idea of what that evidence will show. We lay a trap of confirmation bias for ourselves; quite simply, we're likely to find what we expect. A more objective approach might change the sort of evidence we collect, and certainly change how we interpret that evidence.

Our interpretations of archaeology can also be heavily influenced by history – by what we think we know about a period. And this is particularly pertinent when it comes to the arrival of the Anglo-Saxons in what would become England. And yet the job of archaeology is not merely to illustrate history. Archaeology is a discipline in its own right; it provides us with another way of examining the past – and then, with a means of interrogating the documentary evidence.

But firstly – what does the history really say?

The earliest mention of hordes of invading Saxons seems to come from the writings of a monk called Gildas, who apparently lived in south Wales in the sixth century. His *De Excidio Britanniae* – or 'The Ruin of Britain' – details the misfortunes befalling the British after they turn their backs on all things Roman: the Empire, standards in public life, and – of course – Christianity. Gildas described the Britons sending ambassadors to Rome in the fifth century, with letters asking for military support to help resist recurrent raids by Picts and Scots. The Britons were, they said, stuck between a rock and a hard place, or at least, between the barbarians and the sea. Rome's assistance was not forthcoming, and then a famine hit. But somehow, the Britons managed to regroup and drive back their enemies. But they did not, Gildas ominously declares, manage to drive out their own sins. In fact, once the Britons thought they were safe, they descended into utter hedonism and depravity. They became, Gildas tells us, notorious fornicators, liars and Satanists. There were some Christian priests around, apparently, but they were simply too drunk to lead anyone to salvation.

Even when they heard that their old, northern foes were on the warpath again, the Britons were so addicted to their vices that they didn't focus on defending themselves. By the time they realised they were in dire straits, it was really too late. And then the British council and the king, Gurthrigern (Vortigern), made a fateful mistake, sealing their own doom by asking for help from the 'fierce and impious Saxons, a race hateful to God and men'. Once the Saxons arrived in eastern England, Gildas says, they sank their claws into it. And then they were joined by even more 'bastard comrades'. (In case you're not sure, Gildas really hates the Saxons.)

And then there was a moment when the deal broke down. Invited over, the Saxons were initially given plentiful provisions. But they became too greedy, Gildas tells us. Seemingly frustrated at the inadequacy of their supplies, the Saxons went ballistic. They rampaged right across Britain, not stopping until the 'fire of vengeance . . . [dips] its red and savage tongue in the western ocean'. (Most historians doubt the battle ever reached as far as the Irish Sea.) Gildas, in full, Bible-thumping fire-and-brimstone style, leaves us in no doubt that these were Britain's just deserts. You don't get to be depraved, promiscuous and idolatrous without inviting God's divine wrath on your head, even if that comes at the hands of impious Saxons.

The straggling remnant of the traumatised British population clung on, Gildas says, up mountains, in forests and on rocky coasts. Eventually, the sole surviving Roman after all this bloodshed, a man by the name of Ambrosius Aurelianus, gave the Britons strength to rise up against the conquerors and seize victory, in a battle at Mount Badon (no-one is 100 per cent sure where this is – it might be a hill near Bath).

Another early mention of Saxons in Britain comes from a historian living quite some distance away – Zosimus, who lived in Constantinople in the late fifth into the early sixth century. He wrote a volume whose title was never going to stand the test of time for long, *Historia Nea*, or 'New History'. Rather like Gildas, he saw a civilisation rejecting religion and proceeding to collapse in on itself – except he was writing about the decline of the Roman Empire after it rejected traditional polytheism and jumped on the Christian bandwagon. There's a single decent manuscript of Zosimus's work surviving – in the Vatican Library, where it was kept firmly under wraps until the nineteenth century, perhaps not surprisingly, as Zosimus is very bad press for Christianity, being so unreservedly critical of Christian emperors.

In his *New History*, Zosimus refers to Britain a few times. He writes about the Roman military coup in Britain in 407, which saw an ambitious general, Flavius Claudius Constantinus, declared as emperor on British soil – before marching down to Italy with his army to seize Rome. He describes how, a couple of years later, 'the barbarians beyond the Rhine' were making incursions into the northern provinces; how Britain revolted against the Empire and was standing alone by this point; and how Britons 'freed their cities from the barbarians who besieged them'.

And then, of course, we have the redoubtable Venerable Bede. Writing in the eighth century, Bede fills in some of the gaps for us. Except – his principal source was Gildas, so he did some heavy-handed gap-filling. He is also – suddenly – very precise about dates. He tells us that it was in the year of our Lord 449 that Vortigern invited 'Angles or Saxons' over, to help fight the enemies in the north. But from the start, he says, their real intention was actually to conquer England. A larger army arrived, once again, ostensibly to provide auxiliary support, and the warriors were given lodgings and were also paid for their services. Bede also tells us that these newcomers hailed from several different areas on the continent – Angles and Saxons from northern Germany, together with Jutes from Jutland.

They came from three very powerful Germanic tribes [*de tribus Germaniae populis fortioribus*], the Saxons [*Saxonibus*], Angles [*Anglis*] and Jutes [*Iutis*]. The people of Kent and the inhabitants of the Isle of Wight are of Jutish origin and also those opposite the Isle of Wight, who are still called Jutes today. From the land of the Old Saxons came the East Saxons, South Saxons and West Saxons. And from the country of the Angles, the land known as Angulus,

between the Jute and Saxon provinces, are descended the
East Angles, the Middle Angles, the Mercians, and all the
Northumbrian stock (that is those people who dwell north
of the River Humber) as well as the other Anglian tribes.

In this paragraph he makes a leap from telling us where those
invited-in, auxiliary forces came from, to suggesting that they
settled and gave rise to recognisably distinct cultural groups
in England.

Like Gildas, Bede says that the incomers demanded more
supplies, and when these didn't appear, they broke their treaty
and laid waste to the island. Once again, this is described as
divine retribution on the Britons for their crimes. And again,
it was Ambrosius Aurelianus who would lead the Britons to
victory. But Bede clearly doesn't think that victory extended
to expelling the Saxons *et al.* because of the formative role he
grants them in contributing to the different English groups
that he recognises in his day. He also traces royal Anglo-Saxon
dynasties back to the first Anglian kings, Hengist and Horsa
('Stallion' and 'Horse'), who were themselves descendants of
the god Woden. Apparently.

The *Anglo-Saxon Chronicle,* created in the ninth century,
copies the story from Bede. And again, it's a piece of propaganda for the Anglo-Saxons, especially the kingdom of
Wessex. History is rewritten to create a myth of nationhood –
an identity with (apparently) deep roots that is also framed
in opposition to another set of newcomers in the north –
the Norse.

When we look carefully at these sources, we see that none
of them actually documents a mass invasion of Britain by
Saxons at all. Firstly, while referring to 'Britain' as a whole,

it's clear that these histories are focusing on events in southeast England. And then if we scrutinise the texts, trying to forget that idea of invading Saxons that we've been so sure about since primary school, the story is much more subtle – even when it forms the basis for a polemical (if extremely entertaining) sermon like Gildas's *Ruin of Britain*.

The Saxons described by Gildas and Bede didn't arrive as an invading force – they were mercenaries or auxiliaries, invited over to augment local garrisons to help fight against marauding Picts and Scots. These auxiliaries were probably billeted with civilians – which was standard practice in the late Roman period. But when the provisions and payment ran low – trouble ensued. You can even feel sorry for the Saxons. And although Zosimus apparently tells us that British cities were liberated from 'the barbarians who besieged them', which has often been taken to refer to invading Saxons, this could be read differently in a more literal translation, where the cities were reclaimed from outsiders who were 'pressing upon them'. Zosimus may just have been referring to the auxiliaries who'd been lodging in the towns: perhaps they were being booted out and sent home.

This could have been less of an invasion, then, and more of a rebellion by auxiliary forces, which is ultimately crushed. Almost as an afterthought, Gildas describes that other battle against the Saxons, at Mount Badon, forty-four years after the first landings. But he certainly doesn't describe widespread settlement by Saxons.

It's Bede who joins the dots and ties the threads together – giving us the phrase *Adventus Saxonum* (the arrival of the Saxons) and weaving the story of those Saxon auxiliaries, invited over in the early fifth century, into an origin myth of the English. He's trying to explain how different cultural groups in eighth-century England emerged. He can see similarities with cultures across the North Sea – so this narrative of tribes on the move in the fifth century fits the bill. He's presumably also writing this knowing that these populations in different parts of England *believe* their origins to lie abroad, across the North Sea.

So this myth of the English originating with those invading Saxons (and Angles and Jutes) does seem to be largely Bede's fault. We can see that it doesn't entirely stack up – that he's making connections and telling a story that's satisfyingly simple while being devastatingly misleading. But we can't reject it entirely because of what Bede's story seeks to explain, and also because of what it tells us about concepts of English identity in the eighth century.

While many archaeologists have been robustly challenging the traditional historical narrative of Anglo-Saxon mass migration into Britain in the fifth and sixth centuries, others have pushed back the other way, against the revisionist position that downplays the role of the movement of people in the cultural change that clearly took place. Christopher Scull is one such defender of the broad narrative provided by the histories. He argues that we should 'recognise a consistency in the fundamental narrative ... there were literate people in Britain, Gaul and Byzantium in the fifth and sixth centuries who believed – or were content to record – that parts of Britain had fallen under the control of Saxons in the fifth century and were ruled by Angles and Frisians in the sixth'. And he poses a challenge to the revisionists: 'If we seek to minimise the role of people from the Continent in the events of fifth-century Britain we also need to provide a convincing answer to the question: why does origin myth – if this is how we should view all "early history" – invoke a continental Germanic rather than an imperial Roman past?' And alongside that narrative, of course, lies the evidence of material culture, from archaeology, where – as Roman Britain comes to an end – we see Mediterranean styles certainly losing favour, and fashions from the Low Countries and Scandinavia definitely trending up.

It's hard to pin an exact date on that fifth-century Brexit. It was an unsettled time. The general Flavius Claudius Constantinus had risen to power during a violent military coup in Britain, where the troops declared him as the Western Roman Emperor in 407. (Rather awkwardly, there was already a Western Roman Emperor, Honorius. But he was to give in and accept Flavius Claudius Constantinus – or Constantine III – as his 'co-emperor' two years later.) Soon after he'd been proclaimed emperor in Britain, Constantine III left, with his army, for Gaul – to repel Germanic invaders there. Zosimus tells us how those barbarians-from-beyond-the-Rhine were generally causing trouble in Roman provinces – and also that this was a direct stimulus for Britain to revolt, 'freeing themselves from Roman law, to live as they pleased'. And this wasn't the case just in Britain: 'In a similar way, the whole of Armorica, and other provinces of Gaul, delivered themselves by the same means, expelling Roman officials and setting up their own governments.'

Freeing themselves from Roman bureaucracy and law in 409, the Britons would also relieve themselves of the not inconsiderable burden of Imperial taxation: they wouldn't be sending money to Europe any more. It seems as though the Britons decided they could defend themselves better than the Empire could – and in that case, there wasn't much point paying those taxes either.

The Romans would recapture Gaul – but Britain had escaped from the Empire for good. In the summer of 410, the emperor Honorius wrote to tell the British cities to defend themselves. We don't really know from whom. It could have been Saxons (and other Germanic tribes lumped in under the same label), but then Picts, Scots and Irish raiders had also been making incursions into Roman Britain during the fourth century. But anyway, Honorius's brush-off seems to be a fairly firm indication that Rome (or perhaps we should say Ravenna, as this is where the emperor was then siting his capital) now considered Britain independent, and on its own.

But why did Roman culture disappear so quickly in the former province? Britain (or at least most of the southern half of it) had been within the Empire for three and a half centuries, after all. The traditional story has it that it was all down to those marauding Saxon invaders, who effectively razed to the ground the last vestiges of Roman Britain then imposed their own culture on the country. Gildas paints that picture of the Saxon attacks in gory detail, with citizens being 'mown down, with swords flashing and flames crackling . . . and human body parts, covered with bright, clotted blood, looking as though they had been mangled in a press'. (Clotted blood is not at all bright, but Gildas is clearly more concerned with effect than forensic detail.)

As we've seen, though, Gildas's marauding Saxons actually seem to have been rebellious auxiliaries, not invaders and settlers. (Rampaging hordes are also a bit of a theme in his writing – rampaging Romans and Picts feature too, at various times; most historians think he was prone to just a bit of exaggeration.) But even if some Saxons did attack some east-coast English towns and cities, they did it decades after the Roman army had withdrawn and the remaining officials had been booted out, in 409. And over the early part of the fifth century, Roman culture was fading away right across England – not just in the east.

Archaeologist Miles Russell and historian Stuart Laycock have suggested that we – that Gildas, indeed – could have got things completely back to front. Could it be that an outbreak of violence was in fact the *result*, rather than the cause, of the collapse of Roman rule? Roman coins disappear from Britain in the early fifth century. In the absence of coinage, how could a government continue gathering taxes or paying its soldiers? It's a tempting hypothesis: that economic collapse was the trigger for more widespread political, social and cultural change. But then again, precisely the same economic factors were at play in Gaul – without that fallout. (Although there is a difference – in Gaul, the Romans were able to employ barbarian forces, in the form of the Visigoths, who were sympathetic to Rome, to crush uprisings.)

There are other possibilities – other potential destabilisers that could have made an impact. Disease is one – though there currently doesn't seem to be any evidence for a devastating epidemic in fifth-century Britain (though metagenomics research may well be about to change this story). Climate change is another distinct possibility. There was a climatic downturn in the fourth and fifth century, with the abandonment of some farmland. Although pollen records suggest that this was not particularly widespread or profound, there does seem to have been a shift away from arable farming and towards pastoralism around this time. But once again, Gaul was experiencing the same climatic conditions – without the comprehensive de-Romanisation that appears to have ensued in Britain.

None of these factors – economic collapse, disease or climate change – seems to provide an adequate explanation for the sheer speed of changing culture in fourth-century Britain. There must have been something different in Britain, compared with Gaul, that can explain the pattern.

Russell and Laycock believe they have the answer: that Roman Britain – was never in fact *that* Roman at all.

British resistance to Roman ideas and identity – to *Romanitas* – was detectable long before the army and the officials left – particularly when it came to religion. While the Church was strong in Gaul – and as much an instrument of the Roman Empire as the Church of England would be of the British Empire – it was weak in Britain. Although even ordinary people got hold of Roman pottery and coins, they were probably still quite un-Roman otherwise, in their way of life and in the language they used on a daily basis.

It's also important to remember that not all of Britain submitted passively to Imperial domination. Even in the lowlands of the south, there were rebellions – most famously, that led by Boudica. And large swathes of Britain remained determinedly unconquered – including most of Scotland. In those parts that were officially Roman Britannia, away from the Roman forts, cities and villas, the landscape was much as it had been in the Iron Age – scattered with farmsteads and small villages. This is not to suggest that Britons were hermetically sealed off from their Roman occupiers – they may have been treated as second-class citizens in law (indeed, not even citizens), but there's evidence of civilian towns growing up next to forts, British women marrying Roman men, and of Britons travelling abroad within the Empire, including soldiers and families. Nevertheless, British – particularly regional – identities appear to have stayed strong.

The political landscape of Britain seems to have been somewhat different under the Romans – and certainly after the Roman period – compared with the pattern seen elsewhere in western Europe and northern Africa. There, in the sixth century, large kingdoms formed – with the Visigoths (West Goths) in Spain and southern France, the Ostrogoths (East Goths) in Italy, and various Franks, Burgundians and Vandals gaining control of other territories. In Britain, the pattern was much more fragmented – and the shape, size and position of the fragments are important. They are recognisable – with some fusion and splitting – as the tribal territories of the preceding Iron Age.

Through the Roman period, these polities existed as administrative regions, each with its own regional capital, or *civitas*. Those territories then went on to form the basis for the British and Anglo-Saxon kingdoms. What I find even more remarkable is that this structure is still visible in many parts of England today – and still part of the political and administrative structure of the country. In some places, the names have hardly changed. The tribal territory of the Iron Age Dumnonii is now called Devon, with its county town of Exeter (the Roman *civitas* of Isca Dumnoniorum); the kingdom of the Durotriges, with its capital arguably focused on

Maiden Castle, is now the county of Dorset, with its capital at Dorchester (probably Durnovaria Castra in Roman times); the kingdom of the Cantiaci becomes Kent, with its capital at Canterbury; and many others. These territories may relate to very ancient land rights. The Romans were sensible; they made use of the existing administrative structures, sometimes even letting the local leaders stay in place – as long as they behaved themselves and signed up to being part of the Empire – at least, for a generation. But the old tribal identities persisted, and started to pull away from each other even before the province of Britannia was no more. (There seems so much contemporary resonance in this, in the UK, as we wrestle with just how much power should be vested in local government compared with central. Westminster may seem a long way from devolved nations like Wales and Scotland, but it also feels a long way from Devon and Cornwall – or Yorkshire and Lancashire. Interestingly, in Roman Britain, there doesn't seem to have been any political level existing above that of *civitates* – those Roman 'counties' were devolved entities.)

Regional differences may have been obscured to an extent by Roman culture – focused as it was in cities and elite social strata (and so archaeologically obvious and attention-grabbing as well – all those villas with mosaic floors we get excited about!). Hugh Willmott also believes that this overlay of Roman-ness might have obscured evidence of migration, too, which then becomes more obvious after the Roman period. 'Previously there were lots of continental connections through the Roman network,' he explained to me. 'The Romans operated a sort of Amazon Prime. If you lived in a villa in Yorkshire you could get pretty much anything you wanted, if you were willing to pay for it. When that economy starts to break down, you've either got what's available locally, or perhaps luxuries coming from elsewhere.'

And so, it's when Britain breaks away from the Empire that we start to see those regional differences re-emerging. In the east and the south, archaeology reveals how English identities were being forged with a sense of community with those neighbours across the North Sea – and perhaps even with a conscious opposition to *Romanitas* and *Christianitas*: the southern European identity that was both Roman and Christian. The idea that it was the ruling elites driving this change is compelling. There's much more evidence of continuity than has been previously assumed; it seems the old Romano-British elite in southern and eastern England may have been downplaying their Roman heritage and enthusiastically adopting new Anglo-Saxon styles – and perhaps a new political orientation too.

A proliferation of artefacts turning up from the fifth century – in burials but also as isolated metal-detected finds – allows us to see a much more complex picture than has been previously recognised. And while there are the new fashions which provide links with the North Sea coastal regions – across what is now Belgium and the Netherlands, northern Germany and Denmark – there are also some curious late-Roman-looking artefacts that persist into the early fifth century.

There's a wonderful example of such finds from a site very close to Dorchester-on-Thames. Sometimes mistaken for Dorchester, the county capital of Dorset, Dorchester-on-Thames is a rounded hundred miles away, in Oxfordshire, 8 miles southeast of Oxford itself. It's just a village today. But, somewhat surprisingly, a village with an abbey. In Anglo-Saxon times, it was a significant seat of power.

The common culture around Kent, and then in the areas around the Solent and the Isle of Wight itself, was most easily explained, as far as Bede was concerned, by a common origin for those people: they were all Jutes, originally from Jutland – the huge peninsula that forms the core of Denmark today. Instead, some historians are now viewing this cohesive culture as representing an economic alliance that effectively monopolised the trading routes to the emerging kingdom of Francia (in, unsurprisingly, what is now France), possessing two important, naturally safe harbours – in the Solent and the Isle of Thanet.

Control of trade along the Thames Valley, with the wealth and power that brought with it, would see another kingdom eventually emerging – that of the West Saxons or Gewisse, which would become known as Wessex. The original seat of power for that developing polity seems to have been Dorchester-on-Thames – which had been a settlement since the Neolithic, the site of a Roman fort-turned-town, and a place where important people were buried, with rare artefacts that may hold clues as to what was happening there, right at the end of the Roman period.

One of these artefacts is a broad belt, or rather, the metal fittings from a belt. I've had the privilege of seeing them up close, amongst a collection of artefacts that were excavated from a grave in the nineteenth century, and which now reside in the Ashmolean Museum. The bar-like bronze fittings and D-shaped buckle, ending with animal heads full of vicious teeth, together with four suspension rings, would have been attached to a wide leather belt or cingulum. This is an extremely rare find in Britain; belts like this are much more common in late-fourth- and early-fifth-century cemeteries, along what was once the frontier of the Roman Empire in France. Other artefacts from the same grave included a bronze strap-end and a bone disc decorated with double circles.

Alongside what's assumed to have been a soldier's burial was that of a woman, containing three bronze artefacts: a cruciform brooch, the bronze backplate of an applied brooch that would originally have had a decorated panel attached to the front of it, and a decorated buckle, again with two animal heads.

The story of the discovery of these two graves and these intriguing objects is an interesting one. They were uncovered during levelling of the southeastern end of an earthwork in the Dyke Hills, to the south of Dorchester-on-Thames, in 1874. A certain Mr A. H. Cocks of Yewden (yes, him again), who was an undergraduate at the time, helped to rescue the archaeological finds and to save the hill from further destruction. Bronze Age burials had been discovered in the Dyke Hills a few years earlier – the later graves seemed to be following that well-worn tradition of reusing Bronze Age barrows. The artefacts were given to Oxford's Department of Comparative Anatomy (the link between anatomy and archaeology goes way back) and later passed onto the Ashmolean Museum.

When the finds were finally analysed, in 1952, similarities were noticed between the Dyke Hills buckle and examples from Abbeville and Vermand in northern France. The bronze strap-end from the same grave was similar to ones from sites in Belgium and Germany, and to another English example, from

Milton Regis. The original interpretation of the various bronze fittings was that they had been mounted on an apron or some kind of sporran, but this has since been revised, and they are now thought to be parts from a wide belt of office, probably manufactured in an Imperial workshop in Gaul.

In the adjacent woman's grave, the cruciform brooch was pronounced at the time to be 'purely a north-Germanic type'. We now know it to be a very early type, known as a Nydam brooch – and the only example of this particular style ever found in Britain. Most come from the place they're named after: Nydam Mose or Nydam Bog in Danish Jutland. The buckle was of a style well known from late Roman Gaul.

Regretfully, the skeletons haven't survived, and we have the slightest of slight records of the excavation of the burials – but they do mention that the grave with (what we now know are) belt fittings contained a 'skeleton of enormous size', 'knees apparently bent' and buried in an approximately south-north orientation, with the head at the southern end. In the other grave, the notes record, was a 'skeleton of moderate size', determined to be female.

So who were these people? Their graves present us with a hybrid picture: we have distinctly Roman-looking objects like the belt fittings, combined with more Germanic artefacts like the woman's brooches. None are 'typical Anglo-Saxon cemetery material'. One explanation put forward in 1952 was that these were the graves of late Roman mercenaries – those *foederati* again – brought in to defend Britain as the legions were being withdrawn and posted elsewhere. As Roman power declined in the west, populations living close to the frontiers of the Empire were increasingly recruited into *foederati* troops, developing their own hybrid Romano-Germanic culture.

This theory was picked up and developed in the 1960s, explicity linking the early appearance of Germanic or 'Anglo-Saxon' brooches in Britain to the wives of mercenary soldiers. In this scenario, the decline of Roman authority and the rise of Germanic influence are not two separate phenomena; they're intrinsically linked. But evidence from this crucial period of transition remains rare – and as an osteologist with a keen interest in ancient genomics, I weep at the loss of the skeletons from those graves.

However, 2009 saw another discovery in the Dyke Hills – and it starts with the story of a dog lost down a rabbit-hole. A mechanical digger was brought in to excavate the warren in an attempt to rescue the dog – and turned up human bones. Simon Mays (yes, him again) inspected the skeletal material, and determined that it came from at least two people, one of whom was an adult male. Some of the bones had been stained green – which happens if copper alloy objects have been lying close to them in the grave. A sample from the right fibula was sent for radiocarbon dating and returned a date of 240–430 CE.

It felt like it was the right thing to do – to excavate the disturbed area with proper archaeological care, and this happened in September 2010. Several pieces of late Roman metalwork were recovered, including a bronze buckle with an elaborate pin; on it, two small animals whose tails curl around and turn into snakes' heads. It's of a similar general type to the 1874 Dyke Hills buckle, but the style matches up *exactly* with one from the Netherlands; it could even have been made in the same workshop. There were also pieces of belt strap-ends, and a fragment of a stiffening bar – and all these pieces are thought to have been parts of a single belt.

There were more bones too – around 60 per cent of an adult male skeleton, around thirty to forty years old when he died, and some fragments of the jaw and skull of a child. Mays carefully measured the skull of the adult, and used computer software called CRANID to compare these measurements with a database of thousands of archaeological human skulls from around the world. The closest match was found amongst skulls from Neolithic Denmark.

This was intriguing, but the analysis didn't stop there. A molar was taken for stable isotope analysis – and the oxygen isotope results meant that this adult man could not have come from Britain. Both the shape of his skull, which is an expression of ancestry, and his tooth enamel, which shows where he grew up, pointed to this man being an immigrant to Britain.

The style of the belt fittings suggests the man was buried no earlier than 400 CE. Combined with the radiocarbon results, this can be used to cautiously suggest a date of somewhere between 400 and 430. It seems quite likely that he came from the same military community as the two individuals whose graves were discovered in 1874.

The burial site, in the Dyke Hills earthwork, lay just 350 metres to the southwest of the walled Roman town at Dorchester-on-Thames, which had developed from a fort. Other cemeteries have been discovered just outside the town walls, to the south and north – in that classic Roman pattern of extramural burial. The Dyke Hills burials do seem to be about something different – with deliberate reuse of an ancient, Iron Age earthwork. Perhaps they were intentionally being associated with this ancestral feature in the landscape.

Within the walls of the old town, the gap closes between late Roman activity and early 'Anglo-Saxon' archaeology.

Recent excavations have turned up a hoard of more than fifty late Roman coins, of the House of Theodosius, together with very early Anglo-Saxon buildings. The evidence suggests a seamless flow from late Roman into Anglo-Saxon archaeology. Could the town have been a frontier post at the border between fragmenting Roman provinces? Rather than a shift involving new elites grabbing power as the waning might of the Western Empire left a political vacuum – the explanation that has so often been advanced for the 'arrival' of the Anglo-Saxons – Dorchester-on-Thames presents us with a picture of continuity. The belts from the graves are surely telling us that military power in the early fifth century – at least here – was still somehow linked to that traditional source of authority: the Roman Empire. So the Germanic influence doesn't arrive *after* Roman connections have disappeared – here, it's mixed up with that late Roman influence.

Those fifth-century graves from Dorchester-on-Thames, together with evidence of continued occupation in the town, suggest that the end of Roman Britain wasn't quite as abrupt as we might have assumed – in some places at least. Although Gildas says that cities had fallen to ruins in the fifth century, medieval archaeologist Susan Oosthuizen argues that it's clear that many aspects of society were still being run on a Roman model: judicial, ecclesiastical, military and administrative systems persisted, even while post-Roman Britannia evolved and fragmented (or re-formed itself) into separate kingdoms.

This sounds like a radical idea, and yet archaeology has been presenting us with this picture for quite some time. It's a picture that includes much more continuity than earlier proponents of a culture-history approach might have been predisposed to imagine, with farmers continuing to farm,

people continuing to live in villas and towns longer than previously recognised, and regional polities themselves persisting
through time.

The Church in Britain remained as perhaps the strongest
link with Rome (and a conduit for taxes, of course) – particularly in the west. Various religious missions to Britain can be
seen as attempts to maintain those connections; to stamp out
heresy and enhance 'brand awareness' – to prevent schisms
and drift which could have disrupted that lucrative arrangement; to cement new alliances with the aristocracy.

Two centuries after the Dyke Hills burials took place,
Dorchester-on-Thames's Roman heritage would see the
settlement gaining status. In 635, so Bede tells us, an Italian
missionary called Birinus arrived in Dorchester to baptise the
king of the West Saxons, Cynegils. (Remember him? The one
who fought and lost to Penda? Cynegils is another interesting
name for a Saxon. Once again, like Cerdic, it's not Germanic
at all, but British or Celtic; it means something like 'Grey
Dog'. There are several other 'Saxon' kings who seem to have
distinctly British, rather than Germanic, names.) Cynegils
rewarded Birinus by creating a new position for him, as Bishop
of Dorchester-on-Thames. It's an extraordinary moment.
Cynegils embraces Christianity – openly declaring his allegiance with southern European power structures. If you look
at it from a purely political point of view, you start to see the
early Church in Britain very differently – as a source of authority and power, and a system for controlling and channelling
wealth. It had grown out of the Roman Empire – and in many
ways, it was still that Empire.

We don't see Roman symbols of power and authority
persisting for long in the fifth century – but by the seventh

century, two hundred years later, it seems that an essentially Roman/Christian identity represented a potential source of strength and power again for British kings. It wasn't a coincidence that the capital of this episcopal see, this new bishop's territory, was Dorchester-on-Thames – which had been an important Roman town. In fact, that's *precisely* what Pope Gregory had instructed early missionaries to aim for, in the sixth century. He knew exactly what he was up to. He wanted people to make that link.

At Dorchester-on-Thames, then, we see what may be lingering traces of Roman military power in the fifth century, in those elite burials with Roman-looking artefacts, and then – later – the reaffirmation of an essentially 'Roman' identity with the installation of an Italian ambassador as a brand-new bishop in the mid-seventh century.

But in those fifth-century graves in the Dyke Hills, we're also seeing a clear Germanic signature. It's there in the recent discovery, in that man with a Roman-looking belt of office but a Danish-looking skull. And it's there in the female grave discovered in 1874 – in the form of a very typical Scandinavian-style brooch.

———

We get the impression of elites clinging onto power in the fifth century. And that may have been a bloody operation. It certainly doesn't look as though the old polities were especially friendly with their neighbours, judging by a series of huge, long earthworks or dykes that appeared, or were revamped, in various parts of the country around this time. There's the Wansdyke, on the border between Somerset and Wiltshire.

The impressive Bokerley Dyke stands on what would have been the old tribal boundary between the Durotriges and the Belgae – still part of the border between Dorset and Hampshire today. Fleam Dyke, in what is now Cambridgeshire, marked the border between the Iceni and the Catuvellauni, and the bounds of an administrative division, the Flendish Hundred, up to the nineteenth century. These dykes are still monumental features in the English landscape today, though now, they are great, grassy ridges, full of walkers and butterflies. Their creation, though, harks back to a time of deep unrest, of bitter disputes and bloody clashes – a real game of thrones, as emerging war leaders fought to become kings. Russell and Laycock draw a parallel with the political transformation of Libya after Gaddafi, when the country fragmented as militias scrabbled for power and territory.

Careful archaeological investigation, together with better dating, will allow us to understand the changing political landscape of the late fourth and early fifth centuries much better. It seems that Roman culture had largely disappeared by the time widespread Anglo-Saxon culture became evident – and yet the Dyke Hills burials show how Roman ideas, at least in a military-administrative context, may have lingered on in the minds of the elites.

The generally un-Roman nature of Britain may explain why de-Romanisation happened so quickly – though it doesn't explain why south and east England went on to become so thoroughly *Anglicised*. But once again, we could be seeing something which harks back to a time before the Romans set foot in Britain.

For southern and eastern England, connections across the North Sea had always been important, back into prehistory – and those links seem to rise to prominence again after the Romans leave. This could be linked to new elites coming in from north-west Europe, or it could be that emerging leaders stressed their links with allies over the water – perhaps claiming that their own origins lay abroad, or through new political allegiances. Intermarrying could have played a part too – a traditional way for elites to strengthen their networks of support. Elite families had held onto power under the Romans by accepting Imperial rule, adopting Roman fashion and marrying into Roman families; as the axis of power shifted, the elite could preserve their status by cementing alliances to the east. Perhaps this is what we're seeing at Dyke Hills.

The west of Britain and Ireland had always been connected across the Irish Sea, and across the Channel to Brittany, and it seems that these links also grew stronger in the fifth century, too. In fact, Gildas notes the link between Britain and Brittany and once more invokes a large-scale migration – Britons fleeing as Saxons rampaged across England – to explain that cultural connection, but again that might be a *post hoc* narrative.

The role of religion in creating these new alliances is fascinating. Southern and eastern Britain, as part of the late Roman Empire, would have been nominally Christian, though it's not at all clear how enthusiastically the state religion was embraced beyond the cities – and those areas then became even less Christian as part of the process of de-Romanisation. It's precisely the opposite in the west, though. With connections to Brittany and Gaul – where the Church had a very firm foothold – Ireland, Wales, western Scotland and southwest England would become *more* Roman. Latin inscriptions appear on tombstones, and Mediterranean pottery starts to turn up in archaeological sites.

The cemetery at Whitesands Bay with its cross-marked stones is one example of those westerly links. Another fantastic example has emerged from recent excavations at Tintagel – that iconic promontory on the north coast of Cornwall. Tintagel is steeped in myth and mystery; the King Arthur story starts here, with his conception – according to Geoffrey of Monmouth, at least. But perhaps there may be a kind of truth behind the legends. The summit of Tintagel Island is dotted with the ruins of over a hundred rectangular buildings, which were excavated back in the 1930s, and are thought to be part of a monastery which grew up here after the Roman period. But in 2016–17, an English Heritage-funded excavation, led by Jacky Novakowski and James Gossip, uncovered more substantial buildings, dating from the same period, on the southern slope of the Island. The buildings were well built and thick-walled, and together with a courtyard, form part of what looks like a much grander, terraced complex – possibly a palace. Amongst the ruins of the buildings, the archaeologists found some 1,500 sherds of pottery – many from imported vessels, coming in from France and from as far afield as Turkey. The vast majority were fragments of amphorae – large ceramic jars with handles – used to transport olive oil and wine. Whoever lived here was clearly wealthy – and powerful. And it's likely that the basis of that wealth would have been a precious local commodity that could be exported: tin. Going back as early as the fourth century BCE, the Greek explorer and geographer Pytheas said that the Britons were friendly to strangers, having many links with the outside world via the Cornish tin trade.

Nearing the end of their dig on Tintagel, the archaeologists found themselves lifting a large slab that had formed a window sill, only to discover that the underside bore inscriptions. Nothing like 'Arthur was here', unfortunately (and highly improbably, given it's likely that King Arthur didn't exist – sorry!), but what looked like a practice piece, perhaps for someone working up the courage to make a tombstone. There was a name on it, Budic, which seemed to be a local, Cornish name, but also what appeared to be more Latin-sounding names too: Titus and Viridius. The style of the 'A', with a V-shaped crossbar, was similar to that in ecclesiastical manuscripts. It seems this engraver must have been familiar with such documents. It's a small but important indication that Tintagel was linked into the literary, and literate, tradition of the early Church. It could be that Tintagel really was a seat of power in fifth- and sixth-century Cornwall. Arthur may not have been there, but perhaps there was a local ruler who inspired the myth.

The finds from Tintagel demonstrate how western Britain, in the centuries after the Roman period, during the so-called Dark Ages, was still part of a huge maritime trading network – maintaining and even strengthening its connections with Atlantic and Mediterranean Europe. But while the west was growing its cultural connections via an Atlantic network of trade and power, with Christianity very much part of that political system, the east was all about those links across the North Sea – and was distinctly non-Christian.

It's that non-Christian aspect that really got Gildas's goat, clearly. He gives us those lurid passages describing how the Saxons rampaged across England, attacking settlements and mowing down inhabitants, 'bishops, priests and people', right across England, from east to west. The story – one of genocide and ethnic cleansing – is repeated in the *Anglo-Saxon Chronicle* and, of course, in Bede.

Gildas, Bede and then the *Anglo-Saxon Chronicle* present this picture of a Roman, Christian culture destroyed by pagan, Saxon culture. But the archaeology seems to be showing a crucial temporal separation between those processes of de-Romanisation and the – later – Anglicisation of England. The archaeological signature of the Britons in the mid-fifth century, once Roman culture has ebbed away, and before Anglo-Saxon culture becomes widespread, is hard to see. Burials rarely include grave goods, but typically British (rather than Anglo-Saxon) artefacts such as penannular brooches and hanging bowls *do* turn up in fifth-century eastern England. There is some evidence of population decrease in the fourth and fifth centuries – but nothing abrupt, and agriculture appears to be largely uninterrupted. The way that Anglo-Saxon culture develops and spreads in the fifth and sixth centuries – as seen so strikingly with the cruciform brooches – is much more consistent with small groups of people arriving over time, and certain styles and fashions catching on – and not with a massive migration and replacement.

One problem with understanding this period has been the tendency to carve up history into segments, and for specialists to spend their time digging deep within their own periods, losing sight of what came before, and what followed. When the late Iron Age, Roman and Anglo-Saxon periods are considered together, incredible themes of continuity emerge, and cultural changes over time start to make more sense, from a political and anthropological perspective.

There's some evidence of increased raids across the North Sea from the third century onwards, possibly provoked by flooding and poor harvests linked to the climatic downturn. There's a near-contemporary Roman account of one very significant attack in the fourth century – called the Barbarian Conspiracy – where Picts and Scots conspired with Franks and Saxons to mount an attack on the Roman army. But the idea of Saxons persistently raiding and invading may have been overplayed. Third-century forts on the coasts of Britain and Gaul, once interpreted as defences against Germanic pirates, are now thought to have been well-defended customs depots.

Some Germanic troublemakers may also have been enlisted as mercenaries in tribal conflict within Britain – as *foederati*. This seems to have been a fairly standard practice in the late Roman period, across western Europe – striking deals with raiders, granting them land to settle, in return for military service. Perhaps that invitation to Saxon auxiliaries wasn't such a fleetingly temporary arrangement after all – there's archaeological evidence of very early culturally Anglo-Saxon settlements on the Kentish border. Miles Russell and Stuart Laycock have even suggested that different British tribes could have sought military assistance in this way from various regions across the North Sea. If the defence of Kent was to be bolstered with Anglian mercenaries, other tribes may have sought assistance from different allies – Saxons, Jutes and the rest. This seems like a much more credible hypothesis, explaining how the Anglo-Saxon kingdoms which emerged later came to respect the boundaries of the original Iron Age tribal states that had persisted as administrative regions through the Roman period. It's much more persuasive than the idea that different ethnic groups amongst these broadly Germanic settlers just happened to arrive, replacing the locals, but replicating their political geography. It starts with an invitation, rather than a hostile takeover.

Although there are no clear boundaries dividing up regional variation in culture, the archaeological evidence also points to a much wider zone of contact than with just Jutes, Angles and Saxons – with people and ideas also arriving from further north, from Scandinavia, and further south, from Frisia and Francia. (The Romans would have lumped all these together as Magna Germania – with *Germania* being a word of uncertain origins that they used for these northern lands beyond the fringes of the Empire.)

In fact, although the famous passage from Bede only refers to Angles, Saxons and Jutes, he does provide a more comprehensive list of immigrants to Britain towards the end of his *Ecclesiastical History of the English People*. The Angles and Saxons of Britain, he tells us, derive their origin from 'many different peoples in Germany' including Frisians, Rugians (from Pomerania), Danes, Huns, Old Saxons and Boructari (probably from Francia).

Despite Bede's afterthought (perhaps because of it), populations lying further north and south of the traditional Saxon homelands are often left out of the story. Even though there are no historical records of extensive contact with what's now Norway and Sweden, for example, the archaeology tells a different story. And Frisians, though often overlooked, are actually are mentioned in that later list of Bede's – so let's count them back in.

Frisia is certainly where you might expect a lot of traffic from the continent, being the region corresponding with modern-day Belgium and the Netherlands. And archaeologically, the culture of Frisia was very similar to that of neighbouring territories to the north – the lands of the Saxons, Jutes and Angles. But there's also a contemporary mention of Frisians in Britain. Writing in the sixth century, the Byzantine historian Procopius includes some notes on an island he's heard of, but they're a bit garbled – and include some serious mythologising. He wrote that the island of 'Brittia' lay in the northern ocean, not far from the coast – around 200 stades away – opposite the mouths of the Rhine, and between 'Britannia' and 'Thule'.

This starts to make some sense if 'Brittia' is in fact Britain, 'Britannia' is Brittany and 'Thule' is Norway. The distance from the Dutch coast near Rotterdam – at the 'mouths of the Rhine' – due west to Felixstowe on the Suffolk coast is 115 miles. The stade, a Greek unit of distance, is about 600 feet, and there are 5,280 feet in a mile. Converting that distance across the North Sea into stades gives us 1,012 stades. But the shortest distance between Britain and the continent – and that's surely the sense that Procopius is aiming for – is just 24 miles, between Dover and Calais. And that works out at 211 stades.

Another reason to think that Procopius's Brittia really is Britain is that he describes how ancient people built a long wall across the island. Here, he must surely have meant Hadrian's Wall. He describes how, up to the wall, the land is pleasant – warm in summer, cool in winter; people live there much as they do anywhere else; fruit trees and corn fields flourish. But beyond the wall, it's a whole other story. It's full of snakes and other wild beasts. It's impossible for anyone to even survive there for more than half an hour – in fact, if anyone crosses over the wall, they succumb quickly to the poisoned air. We can only presume Procopius never actually ventured as far as Scotland.

There are other peculiarities. Procopius tells us that people who come from Brittia are rubbish at riding horses, and this is because they've never even seen a horse: there are no horses in Britain, and there never have been. (At this juncture I should point out that, if there was ever any doubt, there's plenty of evidence of horses in Britain from the Neolithic onwards, and for Iron Age Britons being consummate charioteers, indeed.) But Procopius tells us something else – something potentially useful – about the inhabitants of Britain. He refers to three populous nations inhabiting the island: the Angles, the Frisians and the Britons, each ruled by a different king. And he doesn't mention anything about invasions. In the early twentieth century, a scholar trawling through place names and dialects would find another connection. Linguistic similarities exist between the Frisian languages and Middle English. And English place names also hint at possible Frisian settlement: from Frisby on the Wreake in Leicestershire to Frizinghall in West Yorkshire and Fressingfield in Suffolk.

And yet we've tended to reduce the story right down to Angles, Saxons and Jutes on the continent, and Angles and Saxons, or Anglo-Saxons, in Britain – until surprisingly recently. In 2017, the archaeologist John Hines reflected on the profound similarities between England and Frisia – language, culture, early laws – and wrote, 'It is genuinely surprising that this topic has not been more fully investigated before now.' Indeed, when the closest relative of Old English is sought, it turns out to be Old Frisian. It's closer than any other Germanic language.

But in fact it's the archaeology that's most persuasive. Perhaps not surprisingly – when historical sources are thin on the ground, what's under the ground becomes more important than ever. Frisia between the fourth and sixth centuries presents us with almost a mirror image of southern and eastern England. Pottery and brooches appear strikingly similar on both sides of the North Sea. Some styles – such as annular brooches – seem to originate in England and travel to the Netherlands. And there's one type of cruciform brooch that's almost exclusive to England and Frisia. By the late seventh century, it seems that England and Frisia also shared a common currency – the silver sceattas.

In 2016, an eighth-century cemetery at Great Ryburgh in Norfolk hit the headlines – the dead were buried in log coffins. It was so unusual – in England. But there was a very similar tradition in Frisia, from the sixth century onwards. History tells us that there was also religious influence in the other direction, in the eighth century: once the Anglo-Saxons had adopted Christianity as their new religion of choice (and power), the Church then flexed its muscles on the other side of the North Sea, encouraging the Frisians to join the club.

The Old English epic poem *Beowulf* relates how a Scandinavian king is killed on a raid into Frisia, and also records a battle amongst the Frisians themselves. Why would these events have even been relevant to the English, had they and the Frisians had no shared history? It seems more likely that this really is an Anglo-Frisian connection, being remembered as epic history, on its way to becoming the stuff of myth and legend.

Archaeology – and indeed, a more careful reading of the historical texts – is now presenting a much more nuanced version of events than the old idea of whole, discrete ethnic groups or tribes migrating across and bringing their distinct cultures with them. On the one hand, there's a much broader zone of contact, across the North Sea, and on the other, there's evidence of continuity that makes us very suspicious about any ideas of large-scale Anglo-Saxon invasions, genocide and massive population replacement. It seems prudent to accept that the culture change in fifth-century Britain involved *some* migration. In fact, it would be foolish to deny it, given that we have plenty of evidence for contact and travel across the North Sea, going way back into prehistory. But what was the scale of that migration? And how does it compare with the preceding Roman and Iron Age periods? In Europe, the fifth, sixth and seventh centuries have become known as the 'Age of Migrations' or the 'Migration Period' – but in fact, and quite remarkably, there is no concrete evidence for more migration at this time compared with any other time. Indeed, some archaeologists have argued for substantial settlement by culturally Germanic groups in Britain during the late Roman period, linked to the *foederati*, those auxiliary forces drawn from 'barbarian' tribes, as well as to trade. There must have been plenty of people arriving in Britain in the Roman period – not just army personnel, but officials, traders, envoys and other travellers, and raiders too. There would have been some people leaving Britain, too, of course. It's hard to know exactly how many people were coming and going, and how much that changed in the ensuing centuries after Roman rule, in the early medieval period – when history tells us the 'arrival' of the Anglo-Saxons took place.

Archaeologists have attempted to quantify the scale of the immigration into Britain during the fifth century and into the sixth, and have come up with an unsatisfyingly wide range of estimates ranging from just a handful of elite individuals to some 200,000 people rocking up in southern Britain. The models are divided between the traditional mass invasion and takeover on the one hand, and the immigration of just a few high-status individuals – the 'elite takeover' model – on the other. ('Takeover' is a tricky word, though – it suggests that the change was imposed rather than invited or embraced or even somewhat home-grown.) The truth probably lies somewhere in the middle (as usual) – with intermarrying between ruling families in Britain and across the North Sea, as well as some other migration. But we'll have a much better idea of the scale of the influx once we have more genomic data.

We're left wondering how this culture change took place. To begin with, the new Anglo-Saxon identity may only have been important in higher echelons of society, and largely irrelevant to poor farmers. Nevertheless, there may have been social reasons to aspire to Anglo-Saxon identity – and perhaps it wouldn't have felt too strange for 'the locals' to start adopting Anglo-Saxon fashions either. The cultural connections across the North Sea go way back. So although we see that Anglo-Saxon identity appearing as a 'new thing' in material culture, it could have felt much more familiar. Looking at the archaeology on its own terms, we can see a shared North Sea culture, connecting Britain to Scandinavia and the Low Countries. We've spent too long, perhaps, viewing the sea as a barrier rather than a corridor. Either side of the North Sea, societies may have had a shared religious outlook which was distinctly un-Christian and un-Roman. There were other aspects of shared culture too – simple timber houses, simple handmade pottery and burial rituals involving the reuse of existing monuments, such as Bronze Age barrows. And while the southern half of Britain, which had never been all that Roman anyway, was rapidly de-Romanising in the fifth century, northwest Europe was actually more 'Roman' than often assumed. Would people have even noticed this subtle cultural change?

Those cultural connections are clear when you look carefully at metal artefacts and some aspects of language. Early Anglo-Saxon metalwork is very similar indeed to late Roman military metalwork – with patterns chiselled into the surface in a technique called chip-carving, borrowed from woodworking. (Curiously, this chip-carved style in northwest Europe was once suggested to be evidence that Roman craftspeople had been kidnapped and bundled off, beyond the Rhine!) Even while fifth-century Britain was rejecting Roman culture in some ways, then, it would creep back in through the symbols of power – as it did with the Dyke Hills belts. The Empire had been so powerful, for so long, it still 'stood for' authority and military might. The iconic Anglo-Saxon cruciform brooches also evolved out of late Roman bow brooches.

And one of the Roman echoes in Anglo-Saxon culture resonates right down to the present day: Roman days of the week were based on the seven known celestial bodies, each associated with a deity; the Anglo-Saxons just swapped in their own equivalent gods:

Roman days	Anglo-Saxon days
dies Solis	Sunnandæg – Sun's day
dies Lunae	Monandæg – Moon's day
dies Martis	Tiwesdæg – Tiw's day
dies Mercurii	Wodnesdæg – Woden's day

Roman days	*Anglo-Saxon days*
dies Jovis	Đunresdæg – Thor's day
dies Veneris	Frigedæg – Freya's day
dies Saturni	Sæternesdæg – Saturn's day (looks like they couldn't come up with an equivalent here, so stuck with the Roman god)

But Anglo-Saxon material culture was also different once it took root in Britain, whatever its antecedents on the continent had been. Cruciform brooches were soon made locally and evolved their own distinctive British style. Wrist-clasps have Scandinavian roots, but there, they were worn by both sexes, while in Britain they're found almost exclusively in female burials. Some very common Anglo-Saxon brooch types, including flat annular brooches and disc brooches, seem to be completely home-grown styles, evolving out of Roman precursors. Even the styles which show clear connections with Germanic neighbours often include distinctly British elements – in both design and manufacture. Some brooches are enamelled – a technique used in Britain, but not on the continent. These objects tell us something really important: we're not seeing a material culture that's linked to a fixed ethnic group upping sticks and coming over; we're seeing a new culture – a new ethnicity – being forged.

But who's actually making and wearing these things? If we wonder whether it is newly arrived settlers, or locals influenced by high fashion brought over from the continent by elites, we're still mired in the myth. There won't be a simple answer to this question – but where these artefacts are included in graves – associated with an individual – this is something that we can look at using isotope studies to nail down origins, and genomes to explore kinship and ancestry.

Buildings are more difficult to read. Early Anglo-Saxon settlements often involve simple timber buildings, often close to old Roman towns and cities. We don't really know who is responsible, though – whether it's Britons who are building in an Anglo-Saxon style (which is really not that different to existing styles, away from Romanised towns and cities) or new settlers. The incomers may be easier to spot in death than in life – or at least in their cemeteries as opposed to their settlements.

Over on the continent, the predominant funerary rite was cremation. Early on, in the fifth century, large cremation cemeteries appear in England – like Spong Hill in Norfolk and Cleatham in Lincolnshire – looking like a direct import from northern Germany. The use of stamped cremation urns provides a very clear link – starting in Saxony and then turning up in Britain. But actually, inhumation seems to have been more common – just as it had been in late Roman Britain. In cemeteries like Sittingbourne and Scremby, then, people who *look* culturally Anglo-Saxon are being buried 'the British way'. And perhaps this is a clue that these are locals – people whose immediate ancestors came from Britain, but who were wearing new, Anglo-Saxon styles. Funerary rites tend to follow family tradition, though. As Hugh Willmott put it, 'It's deeply personal. You don't change your burial practice because some distant king, prince or thane tells you to. You're going to do it the way you feels honours your relative, or your gods.'

Sometimes it's been suggested that simpler burials in these

cemeteries, lacking grave goods, might represent Christian Britons – or at least, people whose ancestry was largely British rather than Germanic. But equally, those individuals could just have been poor. Conversely, we might jump to conclusions about burials containing artefacts as being 'pagan' – and yet there are examples of high-status Christian burials, with grave goods, on the continent. (Current funerary rites in Britain give us some perspective here – cremation was very much frowned on by the Church in the early twentieth century; now Christians are, like almost everyone else, more likely to be cremated than buried.)

It seems we can't rely on funerary rites to tell us whether someone was born in Britain or had lately arrived from north-west Europe. But then this is where those new archaeological sciences come to our aid: stable isotope studies and archaeogenomics. As people will have moved across the North Sea and the English Channel for centuries – for millennia, indeed – the question is not whether *anyone came* into Britain during the first millennium, and whether we can pick up genetic traces of that (of course they did, and so of course we should be able to, in principle) – but whether there was a much *greater* influx in the fifth and sixth centuries.

Geneticists have suggested – based on modern DNA, from living people – that the contribution from newcomers during this period could have amounted to around 10 per cent of the population. But this is really just a suggestion, with a high margin of error. It may be in the right ballpark – but it's a very large ballpark. At the moment, it's fair to say we don't have any evidence supporting a major population replacement in Britain in late antiquity – in the fifth through to the seventh century. But we should get a much clearer idea of the scale and tempo of migrations once a larger sample of ancient genomes has been sampled and sequenced.

We have a few glimpses already. In 2015, geneticist Stephan Schiffels and colleagues published the results of their analyses of ten genomes from three archaeological sites, in Hinxton, Linton and Oakington, all in Cambridgeshire. Three of the genomes were from people who had been alive in the late Iron Age, around 100 BCE; four were from the early Anglo-Saxon period, dated to the fifth or sixth century CE; and three were from the middle Anglo-Saxon period, covering the seventh to the ninth centuries. The researchers looked at the particular types, or haplogroups, of Y chromosomes and mitochondrial DNA amongst their samples. But these were all just what you'd expect for populations in northwest Europe so not particularly informative. They needed to look at less common features of the DNA to tease out connections between these people living in eastern England, and populations in continental Europe. They started by looking for rare variants in modern populations – from Finland, Denmark, the Netherlands, Spain and Italy. These particular genetic variants were so rare they only occurred in less than one in a hundred people. Then they trawled through their ancient genomes from Cambridgeshire to see if they could see any of those rare variants in them. They could – and the pattern was different in the Iron Age genomes compared with the later genomes. The three middle Anglo-Saxon individuals shared more rare variants with modern Dutch populations than with modern Spanish populations, whereas the Iron Age individuals shared about the same number of variants with each of those modern populations. It looked like there had been an injection of DNA from what's now the Netherlands between the Iron Age and the middle Anglo-Saxon period. The early Anglo-Saxon genomes were a mixed bag – two were similar to the later samples, one was more like the Iron Age genomes, one was in between.

Comparing the Anglo-Saxon genomes with modern British genomes – DNA from living people – Schiffels and his team could also work out how much of a genetic legacy those ancestors had left in the contemporary population. There was a large spread of 'Anglo-Saxon ancestry' across the country, ranging from around 25 per cent to 50 per cent: lower in Cornwall and Orkney, and (unsurprisingly) highest in Kent.

This study showed the power of whole-genome sequencing: it would have been impossible to map the rare variants which proved so informative using earlier, partial sequencing of genomes. But it also included a pitfall, which emerges into plain sight when you read the summary or abstract of this particular paper, and then compare the conclusions put forward there with the more detailed interpretation in the discussion section.

The abstract announced, 'By analysing shared rare variants with hundreds of modern samples from Britain and Europe, we estimate that on average the contemporary East English population derives 38 per cent of its ancestry from Anglo-Saxon migrations.' But the authors were more cautious in the discussion – because there's a large blind spot in their analysis: the four centuries between the end of the Iron Age and the beginning of the Anglo-Saxon period – when most of southern Britain was under Roman rule. They admitted, 'In the absence of a time series through the Romano-British period from the Iron Age to the Anglo-Saxon period, we should also consider the possibility that some of the genetic heterogeneity seen in the Oakington samples arose earlier due to immigration in Romano-British times.'

Somehow we do need to wrench ourselves away from the traditional story of Anglo-Saxon migrations and from the lure of Bede, and maintain a dispassionate, objective ambivalence – while the data is so thin on the ground. With the advent of large-scale, genome-wide studies such as the Thousand Ancient Genomes study underway in the Crick Institute in London, we'll have more data to draw on soon. The Schiffels paper ended with that sense of keen anticipation: 'Further ancient genomes . . . will enable us to resolve [migration and mixing] in more detail.' We need many more genomes, from Britain and from the facing continent, to plumb the depth of the Anglo-Saxon ignorance we're currently swimming in.

Isotope analyses have been carried out in a few fifth- and sixth-century cemeteries in England, where typical 'Anglo-Saxon' grave goods have been found. They've turned up very limited evidence of mobility, and much of that was within Britain, with only the odd incomer from continental Europe. More studies will add to the picture, but at the moment, there's nothing that supports a mass population replacement. Though there's an important caveat to bear in mind with isotope studies: with each result, you're only capturing data about mobility within a lifetime. Second- and third-generation immigrants will be isotopic locals.

What about the 'elite takeover' model? Well, at the moment, we can't see any evidence for that from isotope studies either (though again, it will be hard to spot). One study on a cemetery in Eastbourne, looking at nineteen individuals, found that nine had come from in elsewhere. But for eight of those, it's either probable or possible that this 'elsewhere' was still within Britain. Only one was definitely an immigrant from continental Europe, and that individual was buried in a fairly simple grave – so in this case, it was the locals who appeared wealthier.

I asked Hugh Willmott how important he thought migration was in this period. It was a particularly mean question at this stage of inquiry.

'That's a difficult one,' he acknowledged. 'We'll know more with these latest genome results, of course. But I think it's probably going to be somewhere in the middle.' He thought that current opinion may have swung too far towards the idea that populations were almost entirely indigenous and sedentary – and that people just started to wear different types of brooches. 'There has to be *some* movement of people,' he argued. 'But I wouldn't go back to that 1930s idea of mass migrations or invasions. I suspect it will turn out to be a lot messier.' Hugh also thought that the histories, while biased, contained some grain of truth. Bede may be too emphatic about Anglo-Saxon migrations and origins, but the early Welsh chroniclers and poets also saw the Anglo-Saxons as different. 'Whether that means there really was a significant migration, though – that's a different question. I suspect – when it all comes out – it will be a very mixed picture.'

Hugh was open-minded about the process which led to the appearance and spread of a recognisable Anglo-Saxon culture across England in the fifth and sixth centuries – and clearly very wary of swinging too far one way or the other. He wasn't simply sitting on the fence, but rather waiting until he could see which way the wind was blowing before nailing his colours to the mast. (And that, my friends, is an impressive if incongruent collection of three metaphors in one sentence.)

The isotope and genome studies remind us that the provenance or style of objects does not tell us where *people* came from. Culture and biology are not packaged up together like that. But with the coming of age of ancient genomics, together with more isotope studies, we'll be able to unravel those complex relationships between mobility, migrations and culture, without simply assuming that, when we see a new culture emerging, it must be because a wave of new people have swept in and brought it with them.

History dishes up a sequence of events – what else could it do? And it also tends to focus on the drama of high politics, kings and queens. Archaeology does something very different: it shows changing patterns, evolving styles, but also much evidence of continuity, and we can see gradual, long-term changes. We also see ordinary people doing ordinary things, laid out in their graves with their extraordinary-ordinary clothes and jewellery. Abrupt political disruptions and the shock of adverse weather events play out against a background of slower, longer changes as political power shifts and climate warms or cools. And whatever kings, war leaders and ambitious bishops get up to, there are always the people tilling the fields, sowing the crops, getting the harvests in. Those with political power depend on that agricultural productivity, that economic stability.

Despite the stories delivered to us by the likes of Gildas and Bede, there's no tangible evidence – so far – for an unusually high level of migration into southern Britain in the early medieval period. Of course there were incomers – there always are, there always have been. And ancient genomics will help to reveal the extent of the comings and goings in the first millennium. But there's also a continuity we've tended to miss, or at least pass over, in popular accounts – from prehistory into Roman times, into the early medieval period – and beyond. The story of the Anglo-Saxon migration and colonisation of what would become England has become so widely accepted – on so thin an evidence base, when we actually pause to scrutinise it. It fits into a much wider set of stories about the origins of modern Europe: the European Age of Migration is a compendium of similar myths that have all acquired 'historical' status.

And here we are at the dawn of this new age of archaeogenomics, and suddenly we have the tools available to start tackling some of these questions about population movement in the past, to look at how people travelling might have influenced the cultural changes that archaeologists have wondered about for so long.

And what we're not seeing – not yet, at least – is anything which looks as profound, dramatic or widespread as the later medieval histories might have suggested. The *Adventus Saxonum* looks more like evolution than revolution.

Another piece of the puzzle, and one which echoes down to us today, is language. The traditional story of the arrival of the Anglo-Saxons in Britain is not just about new people and new material culture. It's meant to explain the origin of the English language too. This is tricky. Given that one population clearly did not move off, while another took its place, how *did* the precursor of the English language become so widely adopted?

We're presented with a different story in what is now France and Spain. There, history tells us, hordes of assorted Germanic people – Goths and Franks – invaded the old provinces of the Roman Empire, creating new kingdoms; but in those places, the incomers apparently adopted local languages. The modern inhabitants of France and Spain speak Romance languages, not Germanic.

Could it really be true that Britons, across the country, were speaking various versions of Celtic languages – right through the Roman period too – and that when the Anglo-Saxons arrived, people in the south and east switched to an early form of English? It seems much more likely that people in eastern Britain would already have been able to communicate with their neighbours across the North Sea. This is considered a controversial suggestion – but that's only because it doesn't tally with received wisdom. But that 'wisdom' is really assumption. With virtually no inscriptions in any local language from the late Iron Age, or indeed the Roman period, we have to be honest with ourselves. From the survival of Celtic languages in the west and north, it's likely that these languages go back to Iron Age precursors, and may even originate earlier, in the Bronze Age. But we can't be sure what old languages were being spoken by people in most of England, alongside the Latin that came in with the new regime in the first century. And there are plenty of examples of written Latin – from inscriptions to graffiti to letters – showing that the language of Rome had gained much more than just a toehold in Britannia. Then there's a gap of a few centuries, until we find writing again – and this time, it's Old English. These documents tell us that the elite were conversant in this Germanic language, certainly – but is it what ordinary people were speaking?

Did the people of south and east Britain reject Latin just as they cast off the vestiges of Roman material culture in the fifth century? Did they eagerly adopt an early Old English – a language which, after all, they may have already known as a lingua franca from those long-standing links across the North Sea? Or – indeed – were they already conversant in some precursor of that language in late Roman times?

As the Roman hold on Britain loosened, the proximate sources of power were shifting. Perhaps alliances with federated power bases on the fringes of the old Empire now made more sense. And so the old bonds with those nearest neighbours across the North Sea, the bonds which stretched back millennia into the Stone Age, were being strengthened once again. And the languages you had in common, across that sea, were becoming more important than the old language of power and law and administration, which was suddenly unnecessary. Sailors and traders would surely have known those Germanic languages, as well as whatever version of British, or Brittonic, was spoken in different regions. And then, if you wanted to be anywhere near the top table as that axis of power shifted, it would be the Germanic languages, not the old Brittonic or Latin, that would help you strike the deals, gain trust, cement alliances. This seems to be a reasonable hypothesis. But how can we test it?

Place names provide some evidence, imperfect as it is. Cornwall is full of Celtic place names. Devon is not. Neither are Kent or Essex. The difficulty with place names, of course, is that they don't come with dates attached. Or – when they do – the date doesn't tell you when that name originated, simply when it was first written down. But, as archaeologist

Win Scutt once suggested to me, if people arrive in an already populated land, they don't tend to invent new names for natural features in the landscape; they ask the inhabitants what that hill, that river, that valley is called. Many rivers still retain their Brittonic names. And indeed, as we've seen, some of the Anglo-Saxon kingdoms simply took their names from those of existing British tribal states that had become Roman polities – Kent and Dorset for example. Plenty of towns and cities in the Anglo-Saxon kingdoms retained their Roman-period names – which themselves were often based on Iron Age names – eventually evolving into the modern names we're more familiar with: *Eboracum* becomes York; *Isca (Dumnoniorum)* becomes Exeter; *Londinium* becomes London. The suffix *saete* refers to people with a Romano-British identity, and links them to landscapes – we have Chilternsaete, Grantasaete and Summersaete, still familiar as Somerset.

Across Britain and through centuries, ordinary people carried on living off the land. The pattern of land rights and usage is – as archaeologist Susan Oosthuizen points out – the most consistent, conservative, continuous pattern we can see through both the archaeological and the historical lens. Emperors rise to power and fall, kings come and go. But farming families go on and on. And their collective land rights add up to create territories that emerge in prehistory, with those territorial names recorded by the Romans, and persisting – into late antiquity, the Middle Ages, even to the present day. Any incomers – however lowly or elite – had to fit into that system. There's a strong signal of this subsistence, land-rights-based continuity from prehistory to the dawn of the Industrial Age – when sources of energy, production and power shifted. (But that's another story.)

Quite a high proportion of the Roman names that we know

of have stayed on tongues, down through the centuries. Names that seem new to us in the Anglo-Saxon period may simply look that way because we have no record of what they were called in Roman times.

English itself also holds clues that it may be a language developed by Celtic-speaking people who were learning a Germanic language. While most words have Germanic roots, the grammar and sentence structure is quite un-Germanic. We get a peculiar idea that languages changed almost overnight, but the reality is that a single language was never replaced by another. Shifts in language happened in a context of bilingualism, even multilingualism.

It seems then that Britons may have embraced the Anglo-Saxon language – a tongue they were already familiar with – just as they embraced the material culture, adopting it and making it their own. And this tracks that reorientation of identity – rejecting the Roman, while reinforcing the links across the North Sea. It would have been a language of power, too, connecting the emerging elites of northwestern Europe. Just as powerful families had given their children Roman names, now they may have chosen Germanic names. (On the other hand, as we've seen, some of the early 'Anglo-Saxon' kings had distinctly British-sounding names, such as Cerdic, Cynric and Cynegils, all appearing in the *Anglo-Saxon Chronicle*.) 'Anglo-Saxon' seems to have been an identity you could adopt, or could be brought up in, regardless of whether your parents had been born in Britain, Frisia, Old Saxony, Jutland or Anglia (and probably much further afield). But still, we should be very careful not to equate language with ethnicity. People tend to speak the language that's most useful to them, wherever they are at a particular time.

Eventually, Old English would morph into English. The Anglo-Saxon kingdoms would battle it out and then unite and create an idea of 'Englishness' – one that's still hard to pin down today. All these centuries later, I wonder if English identities across the landscape are really just as disparate as they were in the Iron Age. We may have a better idea of the geographic abstraction that is 'England' – but the notion of Englishness (and indeed, Scottishness, Welshness, Irishness) seems to me to be much more discrete, more local. It is something different to be English in Somerset, I think, than it is in Yorkshire. People arriving in a particular county, either from elsewhere in Britain or from further afield, engage with culture as it is expressed locally. English as a language today varies from place to place, with many local accents and dialects that locate us in the landscape. The same is true of course for the other indigenous languages of Britain and Ireland. I have focused on England and the Anglo Saxons, in this final chapter, because the question of their 'arrival' exemplifies how archaeology can be used to challenge history, to tell a different story – and how archaeogenetics might contribute to our understanding of the past. We are trying to pick apart that puzzle of language, material culture, movement and migration – to find something much more complex and interesting than the old culture-history paradigm ever presented us with. And as we try to understand identity in the past, it sheds light on who we are today – the groups we belong to; the 'us' and 'them'.

Ethnic groups turn out to be illusory, or at the very least arbitrary – in the first millennium in Britain, and today. They have no clearly defined boundaries, and inclusion in an ethnic group is based on a range of different characteristics, principally geographic, with some biological and some cultural features thrown into the mix.

The idea of a significant migration into Britain after the Roman period has obviously played a role in the emergence of English identity. We can see that in the writings of Gildas and Bede, and in the way that Anglo-Saxon kings created those genealogies for themselves, so keen to emphasise their Germanic roots and connections. In those royal lineages, genetic connections (real or imagined) were important. In the wider community, Susan Oosthuizen argues that social identity – a sense of *belonging* to a certain group – was much more fluid and dynamic. Although Gildas, Bede and others refer to certain groups of people as what seem to be clearly identifiable and bounded ethnic units – those Jutes, Angles and Saxons – Oosthuizen presents an alternative view based on something much more real, physical and meaningful: landscape and subsistence. In this way, for example, the people who called themselves Haeslingas in what is now Cambridgeshire defined themselves by their rights to graze their animals in the fields flanking one of the Cam tributaries. The people of Somerset moved their herds onto the levels in the summer. And social identity could also be linked to following a particular political leader, which could include military service. If you lived somewhere that meant you ended up fighting for an English king, you'd probably think of yourself as: English. Identity for most was territorial, not genealogical.

Offshoring your origins could be problematic. Kings like Alfred the Great who stressed their (apparent) Germanic roots were tracing their origins and tracking their authority back to a distinctly non-Christian source. They had to perform a sleight of hand to explain how the barbarian hordes described by Gildas then did a U-turn and became fully signed up to the ideas of *Romanitas* and *Christianitas*. Or is that just our reading of it, drawing what we can from the literature of the time? Archaeology presents us with a somewhat different story – where local links were emphasised, ancient funerary monuments reused.

It seems very easy to reduce our ideas about the past – and indeed, the present – into dualities: indigenous versus immigrants, barbarians versus civilised, pagans versus Christians. By the seventh century, even Christianity in Britain had developed a dual identity: the English Church, presided over by the Archbishop of Canterbury, and the British Church. So religion fed into that emerging English identity within Britain too: English versus the rest. And in all these opposed ideas, there's an underlying sense of 'them and us' – and a sense in which 'us' is defined in opposition to 'them'.

We seem to have inherited this way of thinking about the world from the Romans themselves, who often wrote about the barbarians who lived beyond the borders of the Roman world, with some of them becoming absorbed into that Empire. We tend to write about and talk about indigenous Britons and invading Romans, for instance – in popular history, on television, on the radio and online. The word 'indigenous' might be used to describe people who lived in regions around the world before European colonisation in the last five hundred years, and to defend their rights. But when the term is applied in western Europe, it's often used in a way that further marginalises minority ethnic groups.

Boudica is sometimes used as a symbol of British courage and resilience – rising up, in the first century CE, against an oppressive regime in the form of the invading and occupying Romans. But then how do we feel about Roman Britain in the second, third and fourth centuries? Is that still a period of enemy occupation? Or is this a time when southern Britain enjoys the benefits of being part of a huge empire, and becomes civilised in a way that the far west and far north never quite manage?

It's important not to lump everyone together, and assume that similar attitudes and experiences existed across large geographic areas. Even across smaller areas, indeed. The attitude to becoming part of the Roman Empire may have been very different amongst wealthy traders and exporters of grain who were set to gain from the new political and economic situation. Boudica and her daughters should have inherited a kingdom, but were denied their inheritance, as well as being victims of violence, so you can understand why they were determinedly anti-Roman. But even within a village, opinions must have varied, just as they have varied more recently, with some British citizens keen to stay in the European Union, while others preferred the option of going it alone.

We can draw maps which show the limits of Roman control in Britain. Sometimes there are hard lines, when someone like Hadrian orders a wall to be built. In other places, there are blurry edges – how far did Roman rule extend into Wales and Cornwall? And even in those areas we know are firmly within the bounds of Britannia, reality was more complex and more nuanced. Roman culture is more obvious in cities and towns than it is in the countryside. We might find evidence of significant mobility and migration if we look at cemeteries associated with large settlements – but there may be much less mobility in rural areas. The same is true today, of course:

our large cities are much more cosmopolitan than small, rural hamlets tend to be.

These ideas about identity, about civilisation and barbarism, are also tied up with concepts of migration – and the values attached to that. In the far west of Europe, we might see the long history of Britain as a series of waves, starting in the east and spreading westwards, each bringing advances in technology and culture with it. In the Neolithic, the idea and practice of farming rippled out from the first fields in the Fertile Crescent in southwest Asia, until it broke on British shores, six thousand years ago. In the early Bronze Age, the arrival of metalworking technology, Beaker burials and possibly even Indo-European languages is linked to an expansion of a population starting in the great grassy steppeland, north of the Black Sea. Then the 'Celts' are meant to have arrived, perhaps from Germany, with some Iron Age culture (a migration for which there is very little genetic or archaeological evidence). Then the Romans, of course; here we have good contemporary documentary evidence for their invasion in 43 CE, and for various legions, officials and others coming over here. (And yet, we still don't know how significant that incoming population was compared to what we might tentatively call the indigenous Britons.) Then there are all the people who are meant to have arrived in boatloads from continental northwest Europe, somehow influencing the development of Anglo-Saxon culture and, eventually, English identity, not forgetting the Vikings. It goes on, of course – the Anglo-Saxon period officially ends in 1066, with the Norman invasion.

The idea of British culture (and the British population) being enriched by all these civilising influences – bringing farming, metalworking, Roman civilisation and the rest – is a colonialist construction: the incomers are a Good Thing. But this origin myth – the idea of civilising influences spreading from the east – is balanced against another in which indigenous culture evolves, with a home-grown hero like Boudica pitted against a tyrannical regime. The truth lies somewhere in the middle, surely. And still that 'truth' is generic. It doesn't encapsulate the experiences, hopes and fears of each and every person alive in Britain at the time.

Each phase of history is seen as ushering in a cultural change, and bringing in another group of migrants who may exist alongside the 'indigenous' population for a while, before merging with them. But the terms we use for the people here already and the incomers not only set up a duality but create an illusion of discrete groups – genetically and culturally – one existing inside Britain, one coming from outside, again and again. It also suggests a homogeneity in those groups which has never existed. There were genetic and cultural links between eastern Britain and the facing near continent before the Romans arrived, before the Anglo-Saxons (whoever they were) appeared. There were genetic and cultural connections between western Britain and Ireland and northern France going way back. Archaeologists have suggested that the use of the term 'indigenous', especially for Iron Age Britons, over-simplifies that complexity.

The complexity continues in the Roman period. 'The Romans' – if by that we mean people coming into Britain from elsewhere – were not a genetically (or indeed cultur-ally) homogeneous bunch. Analysis of ancient genomes from Roman burials in Southwark suggests ongoing migration, with some individuals' ancestry originating from north Africa and around the eastern Mediterranean. Isotope analysis of individuals from cemeteries associated with smaller towns shows less evidence of migration. There's a lack of evidence as you get out into more rural areas, where we might expect to find less immigration. And there's very little data on emigration out of Britain.

All the way through the first millennium, there would have been migration in and out of the country, as well as the exchange of stuff and ideas, and identities being moulded by all those connections – this is the complex, messy reality: there's always continuity *and* it's always dynamic. The pace and nature of changes vary from region to region; the picture is far from homogeneous across Britain.

The past is another country, but it bleeds and seeps into the places we inhabit today. We use history to help construct our own individual social identities – from family history to national and international history. It also underpins and flows through modern geopolitics – in how we construct ideas about nationhood, and how we think about borders, mobility and migration. History and archaeology do not exist in a bubble, sealed away from the present.

In 2016, the population of Britain was making its mind up about whether to stay in or leave the European Union. Some posts on social media likened the EU to the Roman Empire – in a bad way, with comments such as 'The last time that Britain faced imperial rule was in the days of the Roman Empire.' For those seeking to leave the EU, there was a perceived danger of British culture being subsumed into a homogenised amalgam, with an idea that this was precisely what had happened in the Roman period. There's some sort of grain of truth in that historical perspective – as Roman culture seems easy to identify, included the consumption of mass-produced goods, and opened up trading networks that demonstrably spread ideas and products more widely. But it's also incredibly narrow, and completely ignores the diversity that existed – especially away from military bases and large towns – as well as that whole idea of 'un-Roman Britain' so elegantly expounded by Miles Russell and Stuart Laycock. Essentially, it is trotting out a well-worn stereotype to bolster a political argument. But that is a criticism that can also be levelled at the 'Remain' contingent in the Brexit referendum. Over on that side, the Romans were evoked once again, but this time as a civilising influence, saving (half) an island full of barbarians, living in huts and eking out a meagre living, from their desultory existence.

The reduction of history to simple dualities – Romans versus indigenous Britons, civilisation versus barbarism – does no-one any favours. The past was more complicated than that, and the political choices we face in the present are, too. Missing from many of these oversimplified debates is any discussion of economics – as important in the Roman Empire as it is in modern Europe – and the distribution of power. The Roman administration brought benefits for some in Britain, threatened others, and for some, made very little difference at all. For certain people, in certain areas of Roman Britannia, at particular times, it may have felt like living under an oppressive regime enforced by a military occupation. Others may have seen their horizons, their lifestyles and their incomes expanding. For others again, it may have been almost an irrelevance in the context of daily life. And so often, we either forget or gloss over the reality that slavery was the fuel which kept the cogs of the Imperial machine turning – and indeed, powered Iron Age societies beyond the Empire. Of course, that didn't stop as we enter the medieval period, either. Moving onto the steamy heat of the industrial revolution, fossil fuels drove an economic boom for some nations, though slavery remained integral to the production of high-value foods and minerals. Longevity and quality of life have improved on average, around the world, in the last century and a half. Scientific and technological advances can be thanked for that improvement. But still, it's very unequal. I think all of us that write and read books know very well that there are people who, still, will never – can never – read our words.

If you can afford to buy a book, you probably have many other things that you have bought. Think about all the materials and components that constitute them, and all the people who have been involved in making them. Slavery still exists. If you were born into a particular society, in such a way that you have the potential to make choices for yourself and your children – you cannot ignore that advantage. In the same way, you cannot ignore the disadvantages that many people suffer, simply through chance. We think we're so civilised. And you'd have to be an extreme relativist and pessimist not to think that we have progressed, as a society, since the time of Roman Britain. When historians, archaeologists and anthropologists of the future look back on our civilisations, they will see reductions in infant mortality, improved longevity – but they will still detect deep inequalities. In so many ways, we are better off now. But there's still a lot of room for improvement.

Archaeology allows us to peer into the past and look at the lives of people who once inhabited landscapes that we are familiar with today. There's something extraordinary in that connection, through time. I love the physicality of archae-ology – looking at a brooch or bead in my hand that I know someone wore, centuries ago, and wondering what it meant to them; seeing the way that a body was arranged in a grave and thinking about who buried them, and how they made sense of that loss; looking at objects which have travelled immense distances to their final resting places, like that wonderful Byzantine bucket in a field in Hampshire.

New scientific and technological advances help to add details or answer questions that we might have once thought impossible to resolve. We're on the brink of some very excit-ing new discoveries as archaeogenomics joins the fray, and I look forward to seeing what revelations emerge from the Crick Institute as the Thousand Ancient Genomes project starts to grind out its results. Investigating the genetic landscape of England in the middle of the first millennium is a key focus for the project. But I'm also eagerly awaiting news on one set of samples in particular. Were those people buried at Breamore victims of the plague? We've tracked down those skeletons, they've been sampled – and Pooja Swali may know the answer very soon. Archaeology is a story that is constantly being revised and added to. It unearths new challenges to our old ideas about the past. It throws up challenges to our ideas about identity, past and present. It's part of who we are.

Our landscapes are full of the traces of ancient ancestors, heaped up in defensive dykes, piled up in tumuli, hidden in graves. They may not be direct relatives of yours, but they are people who once lived in the same place you do now. Some of them would have been from families who had lived in the same place for a long time, some would have been immigrants, and some – a mixture of both.

As we finally begin to be able to tackle the difficult questions about how migration has influenced culture over time, there's something important to remember, and it's that migration is part of all our family stories too. All those connections, back through time, that enrich us. Who we are, and where we feel we belong, aren't things that someone else decides for us. They're things we create, and that meaning may change throughout our lives.

The lessons from this archaeology, some gleaned from the analysis of old bones long buried, and the objects in their graves, are that people enjoy culture and represent their identities through the stuff they eat, use and wear on a daily basis and through the communities they engage with; elites are important influencers; the loss of a child was always traumatic, and people make sense of that in different ways that make sense to them; the poorest people are invariably written out of history (and rendered virtually invisible in our societies today) but rediscovered in cemetery excavations; the victims of raids are unceremoniously disposed of in a ditch, and as we brush the dirt from their bones, we give them back their personhood.

Although this is far from a comprehensive survey of all the funerary rites that existed across Britain in the first millennium, we still see a great range of different ideas about how the dead should be treated – from cremation to inhumation; from burial in domestic settings for infants to interment in large roadside cemeteries; burial outside and inside settlements; graveyards with and without churches; burials with and without grave goods; single and multiple graves; some burials exhibiting a distinct lack of respect for the dead body; others demonstrating the utmost care. Even if I were to attempt a comprehensive account of the archaeological evidence for burials across this time-frame, this book would be too heavy to lift, and I would still be missing so many of the dead. As burials became more common in the first and second centuries, particularly, there still must have been many people whose bodies were given other rites which are archaeologically invisible. As it is, the diversity we can see – even within these pages – is extraordinary, and reminds us that there is no standard funerary practice from which all others deviate: there is enormous variation, and that reflects a wider cultural diversity, across Britain and through time. Burial practices reflect political and religious shifts, but also local customs and personal choice.

Through studying these ancient burials, we also see clearly that Britain has never been an insular, self-contained island (or indeed, collection of islands), and what it means to be British (or indeed Northern Irish, Scottish, Welsh and English; Hebridean, Monian, East Anglian, Cornish) changes over time, and means different things to different people. If the early medieval English were English not because of their genes or their ancestry, but because they *lived in England*, the same goes for anyone here today. There was no *moment* when English identity arrived; there is no moment. The same goes for any part of what is – ephemerally – right now considered to be Britain. Or any other country.

Though these the stories in this book are distant, they speak to us. They do what all burials and bones do: they remind us of our own ephemerality, our own mortality. But they are also bound up with our own story. We imagine ourselves in relation to the ancestors who were here before us. Our landscapes are full of ghosts, full of traces of those who once walked over these hills, along these rivers, down to the sea; people who stood and watched the sun setting just as we do. Moments and moments, repeating themselves. We're the latest inheritors but each one of us will see a final sunset, too. The finite span of a human life is what creates its meaning; we have limited time here, and that prompts us to reflect on how best to use this precious time, and what legacies we'd like to leave. We might think about that in material terms. We might also consider how we'd like to be remembered. And that depends on the human connections that each of us forms during our lives – all those points of contact with other human beings: our close relatives, our friends and acquaintances, and with strangers, too. The last is the most challenging. Humans are naturally sociable, gregarious and altruistic. But we also have a deep tendency to tribalism. Today, we create tribes in many different ways – but at the heart of tribal identity is a feeling that there are some people we have more in common with, and then there are *others*. We each belong to many tribes. Some of our tribal identities play out on social media, where complex ideas and politics get so readily reduced to black and white, to polarised culture wars where the original focus may even be lost in the need to signal belonging to one side or the other. Other tribal identities may relate to gender, age-group, class, ethnicity, the religion or worldview we follow, the music we listen to, the clothes we wear, the place we live in, and the history in that place. On the one hand, we may turn to history and archaeology to deepen our appreciation of a landscape, and feel connected to it, through all those threads of past lives and past human experiences. But we need to be wary of our tribal tendency too; it can cut both ways, and we must take care that it doesn't turn us against each other.

We should rejoice in our differences, while celebrating our common humanity.

However much we might feel we can lump people together, each one of us ultimately resists being pushed into a category, a cipher, a stereotype. Just as you're an individual, with your own history, experiences, family, favourite things and idio-syncrasies, the people of the first millennium were too. And they're fascinating in all their diversity. Each one unique. And each one – part of the story of Britain.

POSTSCRIPT – A NOTE ON THE USE OF
THE TERM 'ANGLO-SAXON'

It's not just the idea of an Anglo-Saxon invasion or mass migration that's currently being hotly debated. It's the term 'Anglo-Saxon' itself. It enshrines that idea of Germanic origins, if not for a whole population, then certainly for its royal dynasties. But although later Anglo-Saxon kings were keen to stress their Germanic roots, there's plenty of archaeological evidence for much more widespread connections and influences – as with the Gallo-Roman-styled belts of office from the Dyke Hills of Dorchester, the Byzantine bucket at Breamore, and the Frankish and Byzantine vibes of the daintier cruciform brooch styles that developed in the late sixth century. The histories contain lots of oddities and contradictions too, like the *Anglo-Saxon Chronicle* telling us of Cerdic and Cynric coming over; but if they *did* come from somewhere else, we may ask, why did they have such distinctly British names? There's also a disparity between words and deeds in how the early medieval kings demonstrated their legitimacy. The royal genealogies drawn up by the likes of Bede demonstrate that Anglo-Saxon kings were descended from legendary Germanic forebears, including Hengist and Horsa, and all the way back to the god Woden (a tradition that stuck, even when the kings had turned Christian). But with those Germanic pedigrees on paper (or vellum), Anglo-Saxon royalty and elites were projecting different ancestral links with their burial practices – emphasising their connections with ancient British forebears, reusing prehistoric barrows, or making brand new ones which also harked back to those ancient practices and people.

Susan Oosthuizen points to an important image of Anglo-Saxon identity – presented to us on the 'Repton Stone', which is believed to be a representation of Æthelbald, the eighth-century Mercian king. The stone is just a fragment of the upright of a carved cross, and it shows a warrior on horseback, brandishing his sword and shield. His shirt and the seax at his waist are quite Germanic-looking. He has a moustache – very much a British or German fashion. But his hair and his pleated tunic look quite Roman or Byzantine in style. So Æthelbald – if it is him – displays Germanic fashions, without being overtly German, and Roman aspects, without being slavishly Roman. It's a hybrid identity – not a direct import from somewhere else, but something forged, actively created rather than passively received, coalescing into an idea of Englishness. Would he have seen himself – in the eighth century – as an 'Anglo-Saxon'? Probably not. We must remember that so many of the labels we use for particular groups of people in the past, however convenient we may find them, were never used by those people or their contemporaries. The term 'Celt' is quite similar in this respect. It's often used now to refer to people living in Britain and Ireland during the Iron Age, and yet – quite remarkably – there's a not a single mention of 'Celts' in these islands in the contemporary Greek or Roman literature, and it was only in the eighteenth century that the Gaelic, Irish, Welsh, Cornish and Breton languages came to be described as 'Celtic'.

The first mention of the term 'Anglo-Saxon' comes along in the late eighth century; not from Britain, but from Italy, when the historian Paulus Diaconus, Paul the Deacon, referred to the *Anglisaxones* in England. It seems to have been used as a way of differentiating the Saxons in England – in Wessex, Sussex, Middlesex and Essex – from the continental Saxons. So the Angles would not have been described as Anglo-Saxons at that time. And indeed, while people on the continent may have used the term *Anglisaxones*, it seems that the people in question were already using a simpler name for themselves, *Anglici* – 'English', even in the southern kingdoms where people also called themselves Saxons.

One of the most excellent and almost undoubtedly apocryphal puns in history depends on this simpler name. In the sixth century, Bede tells us, Pope Gregory sees some beautiful, white-bodied boys with unusual hairstyles being sold as slaves in a Roman market, and asks where they come from. Being told that the boys are from Britain, he asks if the island is Christian or still mired in paganism. When he's told that they're pagan, he sighs deeply and says it's a shame that such bright-faced men are trapped in darkness – lacking internal grace while looking graceful on the outside. Gregory goes on to ask what race, what *gens*, the boys are – and he's told they're *Angli*. 'Good,' he says, 'for they have the faces of angels, and should be heirs alongside the angels in heaven.'

The passage is usually read as providing a motive for Gregory sending Augustine to Britain to save the wretched, heathen Angles by converting them to Christianity. But it has – since the sixteenth century – also been interpreted in a more salacious way, Gregory's eye being drawn to those beautiful, blond boys. (This interpretation, from a time of rising Protestantism, seems to be, quite simply, an anti-Catholic slur.)

In the way that wit often improves with the telling, Gregory's words have also been sharpened up a bit in some accounts, so that when he's told the boys are Angles, he replies, *'Non Angli, sed angeli'* – 'Not Angles, but angels'.

Regardless of the truth of the story, or just how witty Pope Gregory ever really was, Bede – writing in the early eighth century about something that may or may not have happened in the sixth century – suggests that the generic name for people living in southern Britain may have been *Angli*, English. But there's a further complication – which is that Bede may have been using *Angli* in a broad sense, commensurate with 'English', in that Pope Gregory story – but then he also uses it in a much more discrete sense to describe Anglian groups or tribes in Britain, whose ancestors, he believed, hailed from Angulus in northern Germany.

But by the ninth century, the rulers of Wessex were using the term 'Anglo-Saxon', describing themselves as kings of the *Angli Saxones*. Perhaps these were Saxon kings trying to smooth things over with the Angles, who'd now become subsumed into their kingdom. Or it could have been an ethnic term with a geographic adjective, the 'English Saxons' or the 'Saxons of England'. By the late tenth century, kings tended to describe themselves simply as *rex Anglorum*, reigning over the *Angli*, the English – though Edward the Confessor, in the eleventh century, still used the duplex 'Anglo-Saxon'. By this time, certainly, it seems to have been broadly synonymous with 'English'.

Back in 1985, the medieval historian Susan Reynolds wrote a paper whose title was a question: What do we mean by 'Anglo-Saxon' and 'Anglo-Saxons'? The answer is complicated, as the term has clearly meant different things at different times. The way we use it now, in an archaeological and historical sense, is much more broad than it ever was in the first millennium – reaching right back into the seventh, sixth, fifth centuries – to cover a time period in southern Britain from 410 up to 1066. It's sometimes used to refer to the language which is also known as Old English. And it's used to describe a certain material culture – including brooches, seaxes and moustaches – and the people who made and wore that culture.

These different uses of the term, and the way its meaning has grown beyond its original medieval application, may not be too problematic, as long as they don't narrow our perspectives or constrain our research too much. We have to use *something* to refer to groups of people in the past, after all, and 'Anglo-Saxon' serves as a useful linguistic shortcut. We have very similar issues when it comes to 'Celts', 'Romans' and 'Picts'. None of these terms is perfect, but they're better than nothing. Just like the word 'migration', though, we need to be aware and explicit about how we're defining them.

But there is a major difference in the way that such terms were used by medieval scholars compared with modern researchers. And it's that writers like Bede were not just using these terms in a cultural or geographic sense – but in a racial sense. Pope Gregory didn't ask what country those enslaved boys were from; he asked what *race* they were. And Bede of course explains the origin of different Anglo-Saxon groups – each from a different Germanic tribe migrating into Britain, each with its own ancestry.

There's something very simple and superficially appealing about that explanation of different regional identities, each with a different origin and common genetic ancestry. But most anthropologists and geneticists now reject the whole idea of race as 'biologically meaningless' – and many avoid using the term at all. (This doesn't mean that we should abandon using any sort of categories in genetics or biological anthropology – but we must recognise the essentially arbitrary nature of the groups we put people in, which will change depending on which characteristics we're focusing on. Any prior ideas about categories also affect the data we collect. And we must absolutely recognise the political implications of what we do, and the potential for *any* idea of human groups to be misused.) Race and ethnicity – as social constructs – are powerful concepts; so are the myths that underpin them. The origin myth of the Anglo-Saxons is a very persistent one. It's also a myth that implicitly accepts the concept of a 'natural' division of human populations into racial or ethnic groups, and the replacement of one with another. We seem to have accepted Bede's origin story with only the very slightest pinch of salt imaginable. It's a myth that has become history, rather than the other way round. But the Anglo-Saxons cannot be thought of as a racial group, genetically distinct from everyone else in Britain, and from the people who lived in Roman Britain (not least because the idea of such racial groupings is a fallacy in itself). Defining them as an ethnic group – with a common identity – is also problematic; firstly, as we're imposing that category on them, and secondly, because ethnicity can carry (erroneous) connotations of common ancestry. Ditching any idea of a biological basis for the group, Susan Reynolds saw the Anglo-Saxons as defined primarily by culture – and particularly by military allegiance. 'Anyone who lived in an area dominated by an English king and who therefore owed allegiance to him', she wrote, 'was likely to come to consider himself and to be considered English.' The English Church would create another point for identity to coalesce around. And then various Scandinavians, in the form of Vikings, would deliver another impetus. After all, there's nothing better to bring people together than a common enemy to fight against.

This means we can use 'Anglo-Saxon' to mean: a group of people living in a certain part of Britain at a particular time; the culture and language associated with those people; a polity. We should not use it to imply an ethnicity – if we're assuming that would imply a common (and exclusive) ancestry for those people.

How did the inhabitants of what is now England see *themselves* from the fifth to the tenth centuries? As an increasingly unified group, with a common culture, as both 'English' and 'Anglo-Saxon' might suggest; or as a more loosely bound confederacy of individual kingdoms, who all happened to speak a similar language? (We may indeed ask ourselves whether the latter is more true of the English counties today.) Whatever the nature of that wider identity, Reynolds also argued that medieval and modern ideas about what constituted a political unit – and why – were very different.

Modern sensibilities suggest that a group of people with a common culture and language *ought* to be united in a single political entity – as a pragmatic, workable solution to government. The medieval concept of a kingdom was different – and it enshrined ideas of race and the 'natural order': the political unit mapped onto, or naturally emerged from, a racial or ethnic group. That's just how the world *was*. Medieval kingdoms reflected the natural order – with the stratified nature of society and the authority of kings as part of that. Interestingly, this didn't stop kingdoms trying to conquer or absorb each other – far from it; the medieval concept seems to have been conveniently flexible enough to demand fealty without limiting expansionist ambitions. One kingdom in England would eventually swallow up the others: in 886, King Alfred of Wessex, having wrested London back from the Danes, declared himself king of (all) the Anglo-Saxons. In 927, the southern part of Northumbria was added to the territory, and Æthelstan became king of the English.

So there does seem to be some concept of 'Englishness' – with political, linguistic and cultural dimensions – that emerges in the latter half of the first millennium in southern Britain. It may have started as a rejection of some Roman ways, with the widespread adoption of a new language, reinvigorated political allegiances and cultural links across the North Sea; later, it would be framed partly in opposition to Scandinavian influences as well, and coalesce around an expanding kingdom that would become England. It may have been driven by elites – even if those elites were not all Germanic.

But why do we persist in using the term 'Anglo-Saxon' rather than plain 'English'? Bede seems to have been using 'English' as a generic term in the eighth century, the epithet 'Anglo-Saxon' was quickly dropped by the English kings, and by the time William the Conqueror arrived, he was invading a kingdom of the English.

Susan Reynolds finished her essay musing on this question. She thought the term had introduced some confusion, and that 'even if we must continue to use a name that has become well established in tradition, we might do well to remember that the early medieval English did not call themselves Anglo-Saxons. If we want to call them that, we ought to think hard about what we mean, and what others may think we mean, by the name that we have chosen to use'.

Throughout this book, I have used the term 'Anglo-Saxon' while acknowledging that it drags a considerable weight of historical and cultural emotional baggage along with it. The debate over invasion versus diffusion, migration versus continuity might seem esoteric and highly academic, but when we begin to look at more recent transitions, the darker side of the culture-history paradigm raises its ugly head. And never so menacingly as with the advent – and invention – of the Anglo-Saxons. We've seen just how difficult it is to pin them down, and how the simple term fails to capture the complexity of what was happening in the part of early medieval Britain which would eventually become England.

But a much more grievous problem has emerged through a more modern application of 'Anglo-Saxon'. In the eighteenth and nineteenth centuries, 'Anglo-Saxon' became a term broadly applied to the descendants of northern European colonisers of North America – linked with an origin myth of *those* people – and tied up with abhorrent ideas of nationalism, imperialism, racial purity, superiority and white supremacy. In the twentieth and twenty-first centuries, modern racists like to imagine themselves as the inheritors of a romantic, medieval idea of nationhood, birthed in a glorious Anglo-Saxon Golden Age, and generating a 'pure', white ethnic group that must not become polluted by mixing with others. Twenty-first-century racists are just as obsessed with nationalist origin myths as their predecessors in the nineteenth century were. The twentieth century provided several lessons in how evil ethno-nationalism could become. And the rest of us cannot afford to stand idly by while such ideas gain popularity again.

In 2019, Dr Mary Rambaran-Olm, the vice president of the International Society of Anglo-Saxonists – an organisation dedicated to the study of early medieval history and culture – resigned from her position. Her resignation was tendered in protest at various criticisms of bigotry, including the reluctance of the International Society to consider changing its name. Rambaran-Olm argued that the use of the term was no longer tenable, because of its modern, racist connotations.

As the English historian Michael Wood has written, the debate has come as 'quite a shock to those who, for decades, have seen "Anglo-Saxon" and "Anglo-Saxons" as "neutral" and "purposeful" terms'. In the UK, the term is still used for the time period, and for the people living in the area that would eventually become known as England, in the way that I have used it in this book – and this is the way it's taught in our schools as well. The context of contemporary Anglo-Saxon historical and archaeological research is important too: the current focus of Anglo-Saxon archaeology is very much about exploring ethnic and cultural diversity in the past.

If we can restrict the use of the term 'Anglo-Saxon' to early medieval contexts, perhaps it can be reclaimed and retained. We can't ignore Alfred's title or Paul the Deacon's *Anglisaxones*. But we should keep the term more tightly contained in its historical context, and resist it sprawling out. And we certainly shouldn't ignore the debate happening in the US. I've defended the use of the term 'Anglo-Saxon' in reference to the fifth to eleventh centuries in southern Britain – because it seems historically reasonable. It makes the subject matter more accessible. But I'm constantly questioning my use of such terms, and trying to listen to a wide range of perspectives and not be blinkered about how powerful, and powerfully damaging, words can be. Most archaeologists and anthropologists are continually appraising their use of language in the same way.

Those keen to eliminate the term 'Anglo-Saxon' from academic discourse suggest replacing it with 'early medieval English' or 'early English'. This might feel like it's solving the issue – but it just replaces one ethnically, politically loaded term with another. If anything, it's even worse as it implies more of a direct link between English people alive today and those inhabitants of England in the latter half of the first millennium. At a population level – yes, there are links, just as there are genetic links between the population in the fifth century and that in the Roman period, the Iron Age, back into the Bronze Age. But what we're completely missing is any appreciation of migration and mixing – the dynamic nature of human populations through time. Although we don't fully understand the scale, nature and tempo of migration that occurred in the post-Roman and early medieval period in what would eventually be England, it seems not to have been the wholesale population replacement that it was once imagined to be; connections across the North Sea had always been important to Britain.

There's no reason why words shouldn't change over time. Language evolves. Terms are discarded when they become awkward, obsolete, lacking in relevance or derogatory. There may be a moral and political reason for dropping one term and replacing it with another, especially if it has developed negative connotations, morphing into slurs or insults.

If it's possible to retain 'Anglo-Saxon' in the historical sense, then it must be constrained to describing a polity, a particular period in English history, and even a particular culture – and explicitly *not used* as an ethnic definition. In this way, the term is much more about an era and political allegiances, as Susan Reynolds suggested – similar to the Elizabethans, the Georgians, the Edwardians. That means that we can talk about Anglo-Saxons in the past, where they belong – but cannot talk about them existing in the present. There are no living Anglo-Saxons, in the same way that there are no living Elizabethans.

There are good reasons for holding onto 'Anglo-Saxon', as well as very valid reasons to want to get rid of it. Anyone working in the field or writing about it should certainly be aware of the controversy, and anyone who chooses to continue using the term must do so advisedly and responsibly. But it's also important to have these conversations – and to keep re-examining the language we use, and not simply to hang onto words for the sake of tradition. Academic research doesn't exist in a bubble, away from current political and social realities.

ACKNOWLEDGEMENTS

A book like this draws on the work of many people. I am grateful to many kind and generous-hearted colleagues and friends who have helped me with sources of information, shared their insights and interpretations with me, and reviewed chapters. The book is much better for their attention and input, and any errors that remain are, of course, mine alone.

Thank you very much to all these wonderful friends and colleagues who have helped with this book in so many ways: Jonathan Musgrave, my wonderful mentor and friend at Bristol University, who taught me how to analyse cremations; Julie Reynolds (formerly curator at the National Roman Legion Museum, Caerleon); Richard Brewer, National Museum Wales; Jill Eyers, Chiltern Archaeology; Rebecca Redfern, Museum of London; Kate Robson-Brown (who also helped to divert me from a career in surgery), University of Bristol; Simon Mays, Historic England; Grace Campbell, James Rolfe and Rachael Abraham, Suffolk County Council Archaeological Service; Kerrie Bull, Andy Peachey and Lindsay Lloyd-Smith, Wardell Armstrong (formerly Archaeological Solutions); Sally

Worrell, Institute of Archaeology; Phil Harding, Wessex Archaeology; Dana and Damian Goodburn-Brown; Hugh Wilmott, University of Sheffield; Mark Redknap, National Museum Wales; Katie Hemer, UCL; Ken Murphy, Dyfed Archaeological Trust; Adam Rutherford, UCL; Miles Russell, Bournemouth University; Pontus Skoglund, Thomas Booth and Pooja Swali, The Francis Crick Institute; Henry Taylor, University of Birmingham; Win Scutt, English Heritage. There are many more. Thank you all so much.

Thank you to all the producers and crew who have worked on *Digging for Britain* and helped to bring archaeology to a wide audience through the medium of television over the years. And especially John Farren, the original creator of *Digging for Britain*. I feel privileged to have seen so much and learned so much in the process of making these television programmes, and I am endlessly grateful to all those archaeological colleagues who share their discoveries and expertise so generously.

I'm grateful as always to my brilliant literary agent, Luigi Bonomi, and to my fantastic editor, Holly Harris at Simon & Schuster. And huge thanks to project editor Kaiya Shang and my very patient copy-editor, Jonathan Wadman.

I must thank my family. They put up with me hiding away to write and then emerging to test my ideas out on them. I depend on my husband's culinary skills to keep me nourished throughout, and my children for suggesting that a dog-walk, ice-skate or bike-ride might make a nice break from writing.

I mentioned the 'trowelblazing' Tess Wheeler in Chapter One. For more of her story, and those of other pioneering women in archaeology, visit trowelblazers.com.

Finally, and very sadly, one of the people I really wanted

to thank is no longer with us: Kate Edwards, who first roped me in to *Time Team*, sadly passed away at the end of 2021. I hope her family can accept my thanks on her behalf, and my sympathy.

THE CHAPTER ILLUSTRATIONS

REFERENCES

Prologue: A Blessing and a Curse

Hurst, H. (2016) The textual and archaeological evidence. In Millett, M., Revell, L., Moore, A. (eds) *The Oxford Handbook of Roman Britain*. Oxford University Press, Oxford, 95–116.

Wallace, L. (2016) The early Roman horizon. In Millett, M., Revell, L., Moore, A. (eds) *The Oxford Handbook of Roman Britain*. Oxford University Press, Oxford, 117–33.

1. Water and Wine

Barrett, A. A. (1979) The career of Tiberius Claudius Cogidubnus. *Britannia* 10: 227–42.

Bouchard, M. (2004) Graveyards: Russian ritual and belief pertaining to the dead. *Religion* 34: 345–62.

Dio Cassius. *Roman History*. Translated by Earnest Cary, Herbert B. Foster. Loeb Classical Library 32. Cambridge, MA: Harvard University Press, 1914–1927.

Greiner, M. *et al.* (2019) Bone incineration: an experimental study on mineral structure, colour and crystalline state. *Journal of Archaeological Science: Reports* 25: 507–18.

Lucan. *The Civil War (Pharsalia).* Translated by J. D. Duff. Loeb Classical Library 220. Book VIII. Cambridge, MA: Harvard University Press, 1928.

McKinley, J. (2000) The analysis of cremated bone. In Cox, M., Mays, S. (eds) *Human Osteology in Archaeology and Forensic Science.* Greenwich Medical Media, London, 403–21.

Noy, D. (2000) 'Half-burnt on an emergency pyre': Roman cremations which went wrong. *Greece & Rome* 47: 186–96.

Panourgiá, N. (1995) *Fragments of Death, Fables of Identity: An Athenian Anthopography.* University of Wisconsin Press, Madison.

Ward, C. (1990) The Romano-British cremation cemetery at Frog Farm, Otford, Kent, in the context of contemporary funerary practices in South-East England. Available at Kent Archaeological Society website, https://www.kentarchaeology.org.uk/Research/02/ODAG/01/00.htm (accessed 17 November 2021).

Wheeler, R. E. M. (1929) A Roman pipe-burial from Caerleon, Monmouthshire. *Antiquaries Journal* 9: 1–7.

2. Bones in the Villa

Bennett, H. (1923) The exposure of infants in ancient Rome. *Classical Journal* 18: 341–51.

Brookman, F., Nolan, J. (2006) The dark figure of infanticide in England and Wales: complexities of diagnosis. *Journal of Interpersonal Violence* 21: 869–89.

Carroll, M. (2011) Infant death and burial in Roman Italy. *Journal of Roman Archaeology* 24: 99–120.

Dunn, P. M. (1995) Soranus of Ephesus (circa AD 98–138) and perinatal care in Roman times. *Archives of Disease in Childhood: Fetal and Neonatal Edition* 73: F51–F52.

Fittock, M. G. (2017) Fragile gods: ceramic figurines in Roman Britain. PhD thesis, University of Reading.

Gowland, R., Chamberlain, A., Redfern, R. (2014) On the brink of being: re-evaluating infanticide and infant burial in Roman Britain. *Journal of Roman Archaeology* S96: 69–88.

Hanlon, G. (2016) Routine infanticide in the West 1500–1800. *History Compass* 14: 535–48.

Laes, C. (2008) Learning from silence: disabled children in Roman antiquity. *Arctos* 42: 85–122.

Mays, S. (1993) Infanticide in Roman Britain. *Antiquity* 67: 883–8.

Mays, S. *et al.* (2014) An infant femur bearing cut marks from Roman Hambleden, England. *International Journal of Osteoarchaeology* 24: 111–15.

Smith, P., Kahila, G. (1992) Identification of infanticide in archaeological sites: a case study from the Late Roman–Early Byzantine periods at Ashkelon, Israel. *Journal of Archaeological Science* 19: 667–75.

Toynbee, J. M. C. ([1971] 1996) *Death and Burial in the Roman World*. Johns Hopkins University Press, Baltimore.

Woods, R. (2007) Ancient and early modern mortality: experience and understanding. *Economic History Review* 60: 373–99.

3. Off with Their Heads

Alterauge, A. *et al.* (2020) Between belief and fear: reinterpreting prone burials during the Middle Ages and early modern period in German-speaking Europe. *PLOS One* 15(8): e0238439.

Armit, I. (2012) *Headhunting and the Body in Iron Age Europe.* Cambridge University Press, Cambridge.

Caffell, A., Holst, M. (2012) *Osteological Analysis, 3 and 6 Driffield Terrace, York, North Yorkshire.* York Osteoarchaeology Ltd for York Archaeological Trust, York.

Crerar, B. (2014) Contextualising deviancy: a regional approach to decapitated inhumation in late Roman Britain. PhD thesis, University of Cambridge, doi.org/10.17863/CAM.16547.

Crowder, K. D. *et al.* (2020) Romans, barbarians and foederati: new biomolecular data and a possible region of origin for 'Headless Romans' and other burials from Britain. *Journal of Archaeological Science: Reports* 30: 102180.

Diodorus Siculus. *Library of History*, Volume IX: Book 19:115. Translated by Russel M. Geer. Loeb Classical Library 377. Cambridge, MA: Harvard University Press, 1947.

Lethbridge, T. C. (1936) Further excavations in the Early Iron Age and Romano-British cemetery at Guilden Morden. *Proceedings of the Cambridge Antiquarian Society* 36: 109–20.

Livy. *History of Rome*, Volume VI: Books 23-25. Translated by Frank Gardner Moore. Loeb Classical Library 355. Cambridge, MA: Harvard University Press, 1940.

Gordon, S. (2015) Monstrous words, monstrous bodies: irony and the walking dead in Walter Map's *De Nugis Curialum*. *English Studies* 96: 379–402.

Maraschi, A. (2019) There is more than meets the eye: undead, ghosts and spirits in the *Decretum* of Burchard of Worms. *Thanatos* 8(1): 29–61.

Mays, S. (2016) The ghostly child in medieval north-west Europe. *Childhood in the Past* 9: 109–19.

Milella, M. *et al.* (2015) Patterns of irregular burials in western Europe (1st–5th century AD). *PLOS One* 10(6): e0130616.

Monument record WLG 038 – land north of Fenton's Farm, Great Whelnetham. Suffolk Heritage Explorer, https://heritage.suffolk.gov.uk/Monument/MSF37189 (accessed 17 November 2021)

Polybius. *The Histories*, Volume III: Books 5-8. Translated by W. R. Paton. Revised by F. W. Walbank, Christian Habicht. Loeb Classical Library 138. Cambridge, MA: Harvard University Press, 2011.

Redfern, R. C. (2018) Blind to chains? The potential of bioarchaeology for identifying the enslaved of Roman Britain. *Britannia* 49: 251–82.

Strabo IV.4.5.

Tucker, K. (2012) 'Whence this severance of the head?' The osteology and archaeology of human decapitation in Britain. PhD thesis, University of Winchester.

Tucker, K. (2013) The osteology of decapitation burials from Roman Britain: a post-mortem burial rite? In Knüsel C., Smith M. (eds) *The Routledge Handbook of the Bioarchaeology of Human Conflict*. Routledge, Abingdon and New York, 213–36.

4. The Beautiful Buckets of Breamore

Hines, J. H. (2010) Units of account in gold and silver in seventh-century England: *scillingas*, *sceattas* and *pæningas*. *Antiquaries Journal* 90: 153–73.

Hinton D. A., Worrell, S. (2017) An early Anglo-Saxon cemetery and archaeological survey at Breamore, Hampshire, 1999–2006. *Archaeological Journal* 174: 68–145.

Hughes, S. S. *et al.* (2018) Isotopic analysis of burials from the early Anglo-Saxon cemetery at Eastbourne, Sussex, UK. *Journal of Archaeological Science: Reports* 19: 513–25.

Keller, M. *et al.* (2019) Ancient *Yersinia pestis* genomes from across Western Europe reveal early diversification during the First Pandemic (541–750). *PNAS* 116: 12363–72.

Mango, M. M. *et al.* (1989) A 6th-century Mediterranean bucket from Bromeswell Parish, Suffolk. *Antiquity* 63: 295–311.

Schiffels S. *et al.* (2016) Iron Age and Anglo-Saxon genomes from East England reveal British migration history. *Nature Communications* 7: 10408.

5. The Meaning of Bling

The Anglo-Saxon Chronicle ([1996] 1998) tr. and ed. Swanton, M. Routledge, New York.

Booth, P. (2014) A late Roman military burial from the Dyke Hills, Dorchester on Thames, Oxfordshire. *Britannia* 45: 243–73.

Buonasera, T. *et al.* (2020) A comparison of proteomic, genomic, and osteological methods of archaeological sex estimation. *Scientific Reports* 10: 11897.

Davidson, H. E. ([1962] 1998) *The Sword in Anglo-Saxon England: Its Archaeology and Literature*. Boydell Press, Woodbridge.

Doggett, N. (1986) The Anglo-Saxon see and cathedral of Dorchester-on-Thames: the evidence reconsidered. *Oxoniensia* 51: 49–61.

Goodburn-Brown, D., Price, V. (2013) CSI: Sittingbourne: conservation science investigations in a town center shopping mall. In Rogerio-Candelera, M. A, Lazzari, M., Cano, E. (eds) *Science and Technology for the Conservation of Cultural Heritage*. CRC Press/Balkema, Leiden, 393–6.

Härke, H. (1990) 'Warrior graves'? The background of the Anglo-Saxon weapon burial rite. *Past and Present* 126: 22–43.

Harland, J. M. (2019) Memories of migration? The 'Anglo-Saxon' burial costume of the fifth century AD. *Antiquity* 93: 954–69.

Higham, N. J, Ryan, M. J. (eds) (2011) *Place-Names, Language and the Anglo-Saxon Landscape*. Boydell Press, Woodbridge.

Hines, J. (2017) The Anglo-Frisian question. In Hines, J., IJssennagger, N. (eds) *Frisians and Their North Sea Neighbours: From the Fifth Century to the Viking Age*. Boydell Press, Woodbridge, 25–42.

Kirk, J. R, Leeds, E. T. (1952–3) Three early Saxon graves from Dorchester, Oxon. *Oxoniensia* 17–18: 63–76.

Lyons, J. M. (1918) Frisian place-names in England. *PMLA* 33: 644–55.

Oosthuizen, S. (2019) *The Emergence of the English*. Arc Humanities Press, Leeds.

Richardson, A. (2009). A prehistoric and Anglo-Saxon cemetery at the Meads, Sittingbourne. *KAS Newsletter* 79: 1–3.

Russell, M., Laycock, S. (2011) *UnRoman Britain: Exposing the Great Myth of Britannia*. History Press, Stroud.

Thompson, E. A. (1980) Procopius on Brittia and Britannia. *Classical Quarterly* 30: 498–507.

Yorke, B. (2018) Competition for the Solent and 7th century politics. In Jervis, B. (ed.) *The Middle Ages Revisited: Studies in the Archaeology and History of Medieval Southern England*. Archaeopress, Oxford, 35–43.

6. The Vikings in the Ditch

Fellows-Jensen, G. (1985) *Scandinavians in Dumfriesshire and Galloway: The Place-Name Evidence*. Copenhagen, 65–82.

Hemer, K. A. (2010) In the realm of saints: a reconstruction of life and death in early medieval Wales and the Isle of Man. PhD thesis, University of Sheffield.

Jennings, A., Kruse, A. (2009) From Dál Riata to the Gall-Gháidheil. *Viking and Medieval Scandinavia* 5: 123–49.

Kruse, A. (2005) Explorers, raiders and settlers: the Norse impact upon Hebridean place-names. In Gammeltoft, P., Hough, C., Waugh, D. (eds) *Cultural Contacts in the North Atlantic Region: The Evidence of Names*. Scottish Place-Name Society, Lerwick, 155–72.

Redknap, M. (2016) Defining identities in Viking Age north Wales: new data from Llanbedrgoch. In Turner, V. E., Owen, O. A., Waugh, D. J. (eds) *Shetland and the Viking World: Papers from the Proceedings of the Seventeenth Viking Congress, Lerwick*. Shetland Heritage Publications, Lerwick, 159–66.

Roberts, A. (2001) Report on the human remains from Glyn Llanbedrgoch.

Roberts, A. (2012) Osteological report on the human skeletal remains from Glyn Llanbedrgoch (GL98: 654 (B1); GL99: B2–5; GL01: 1120; GL00: 2704).

Stewart, T. W. (2004) Lexical imposition: Old Norse vocabulary in Scottish Gaelic. *Diachronica* 21: 393–420.

7. The Birth of Churchyards

Costambeys, M. (2001) Burial topography and the power of the Church in fifth- and sixth-century Rome. *Papers of the British School at Rome* 69: 169–89.

Groom, P. *et al.* (2011) Two early medieval cemeteries in Pembrokeshire: Brownslade Barrow and West Angle Bay. *Archaeologia Cambrensis* 160: 133–203.

Liber Landavensis, Llyfr Teilo; or, The Ancient Register of the Cathedral Church of Llandaff (1840) translated by Rees, W. J. William Rees, Llandovery, 351–2, 370.

Ludlow, N. (2009) Identifying early medieval ecclesiastical sites in south-west Wales. In Edwards, N. (ed.) *The Archaeology of the Early Medieval Celtic Churches*. Maney, Leeds, 61–84.

McCormick, F. *et al.* (1993) Excavations at Iona, 1988. *Ulster Journal of Archaeology* 56: 78–108.

Shiner, M. R. (2021) Burial in early medieval Wales: identifying multifunctional cemeteries. *Oxford Journal of Archaeology* 40: 268–85.

8. Belonging

Booth, T. J. (2019) A stranger in a strange land: a perspective on archaeological responses to the palaeogenetic revolution from an archaeologist working amongst palaeogeneticists. *World Archaeology* 51: 586–601.

Cobb, H. L. (2012) Digging diversity? A preliminary

examination of disciplinary diversity in UK archaeology. *Journal of Archaeological Method and Theory.*

Harris, S. J. (2002) Bede and Gregory's allusive angles. *Criticism* 44: 271–89.

Hines, J. et al. (2020) The responsible use of the term 'Anglo-Saxon'. Available at http://www.fmass.eu/uploads/pdf/responsible_use_of%20the%20term%20_AngloSaxon.pdf (accessed 17 November 2021).

Hingley, R., Bonacchi, C., Sharpe, K. (2018) 'Are you local?' Indigenous Iron Age and mobile Roman and post-Roman populations: then, now and in-between. *Britannia* 49: 283–302.

Oosthuizen, S. (2019) *The Emergence of the English.* Arc Humanities Press, Leeds.

Rambaran-Olm, M. (2019) Misnaming the medieval: rejecting 'Anglo-Saxon' studies. History Workshop website, 4 November, https://www.historyworkshop.org.uk/misnaming-the-medieval-rejecting-anglo-saxon-studies/ (accessed 17 November 2021).

Reynolds, S. (1985) What do we mean by 'Anglo-Saxon' and 'Anglo-Saxons'? *Journal of British Studies* 24: 395–414.

Williams, H. (2020) The fight for 'Anglo-Saxon'. *Aeon,* 29 May, https://aeon.co/essays/why-we-should-keep-the-term-anglo-saxon-in-archaeology (accessed 17 November 2021).

Wood, M. (2019) As a racism row rumbles on, is it time to retire the term 'Anglo-Saxon'? *BBC History Magazine,* December.

INDEX